ORIEN

MAGIC

This important research text is described by Professor Louis Marin, Director of the Ecole d'Anthropologie, as "A serious contribution to the knowledge of magic". Following its original publication in 1956, it was translated and achieved a wide general sale as well as being regarded as a classic by students of the history and diffusion of ideas.

The literary weekly *Time and Tide*: "a rich source of data for psychologists, anthropologists and psychical research workers."

The scientific journal *Nature*: "a point of view of which too little has been heard in the past."

The religious review *Hibbert Journal*: "illuminating... helpful... stimulating."

This edition contains the entire text of the original work.

Books by Idries Shah

Sufi Studies and Middle Eastern Literature

The Sufis

Caravan of Dreams

The Way of the Sufi

Tales of the Dervishes: *Teaching-stories Over a Thousand Years*

Sufi Thought and Action

Traditional Psychology, Teaching Encounters and Narratives

Thinkers of the East: *Studies in Experientialism*

Wisdom of the Idiots

The Dermis Probe

Learning How to Learn: *Psychology and Spirituality in the Sufi Way*

Knowing How to Know

The Magic Monastery: *Analogical and Action Philosophy*

Seeker After Truth

Observations

Evenings with Idries Shah

The Commanding Self

University Lectures

A Perfumed Scorpion (Institute for the Study of Human Knowledge and California University)

Special Problems in the Study of Sufi Ideas (Sussex University)

The Elephant in the Dark: *Christianity, Islam and the Sufis* (Geneva University)

Neglected Aspects of Sufi Study: *Beginning to Begin* (The New School for Social Research)

Letters and Lectures of Idries Shah

Current and Traditional Ideas
Reflections
The Book of the Book
A Veiled Gazelle: *Seeing How to See*
Special Illumination: *The Sufi Use of Humor*

The Mulla Nasrudin Corpus
The Pleasantries of the Incredible Mulla Nasrudin
The Subtleties of the Inimitable Mulla Nasrudin
The Exploits of the Incomparable Mulla Nasrudin
The World of Nasrudin

Travel and Exploration
Destination Mecca

Studies in Minority Beliefs
The Secret Lore of Magic
Oriental Magic

Selected Folktales and Their Background
World Tales

A Novel
Kara Kush

Sociological Works
Darkest England
The Natives Are Restless
The Englishman's Handbook

Translated by Idries Shah
The Hundred Tales of Wisdom (Aflaki's *Munaqib*)

This house-decoration in Northern Sudan is an unusual example of the blending of magical symbolism. The star-and-crescent (Islamic and Byzantine) motif is supported by ancient Egyptian and African magical designs.

ORIENTAL MAGIC

Idries Shah

Foreword by Dr Louis Marin
Member of the Institut de France, Director of the Ecole d'Anthropologie de Paris, Deputy-President of the International Institute of Anthropology

ISF PUBLISHING

ISBN 978-1-78479-042-4

First Published 1956
Entire original text: 1968
Published in this edition 2016

Requests for permission to reprint, reproduce etc., to:
The Permissions Department
ISF Publishing
The Idries Shah Foundation
P. O. Box 71911
London NW2 9QA
United Kingdom
permissions@isf-publishing.org

In association with The Idries Shah Foundation

Additional research, verification and unpublished materials by
Richard Drobutt, John Grant, Ibrahim Yusuf Musa,
Morag Murray, Amina Ali-Shah

Line illustrations:
Pauline O'Donovan, Idries Shah
(Author's collection and photographed from manuscripts)

Contents

List of Illustrations

Foreword

By Dr Louis Marin
Member of the Institut de France
Director of the Ecole d'Anthropologie de Paris
Deputy-President of the International Institute of Anthropology

THE ORGANISATION OF the academic disciplines which we in France associate with Descartes has, in the course of the centuries, so developed that today the scientific method permeates every aspect of humane studies.

No longer does the scholar faced with some new, strange and hitherto unexplained phenomenon turn away from its study. In our time, he takes full account of it, keeping it under observation, in the hope of finding a way of explaining it.

Magic is a subject which was long considered to be outside the ambit of academic study. Yet it is of importance in the discipline of anthropology. Curiously enough, magic has greatly intrigued ethnographers on account of the strangeness of its practices in all parts of the world, while at the same time it has been frowned upon by them as being hardly susceptible to scientific study and as repugnant to religion and the social order. Yet witchcraft used to be widespread in the western world, and even at the Court of Louis XIV and in the age of Voltaire; it has not died out even today.

There used to be some confusion of religion and magic, it being thought that the latter was simply a primitive form of religion. We know better now, and can distinguish between religion, which is submission to an almighty Creator to whom we raise our prayers, and magic which consists of rites intended to compel supernatural forces, whatever they may be, to do the sorcerer's bidding.

We must admit that almost all the religious ideas of primitive peoples are comprised in magic. This raises another great difficulty for the scholar, for it requires an effort of the imagination to enter into the mentality of primitive peoples who in their ignorance of the workings of nature feel compelled to construct for their own protection a system of magical observances.

One must try to discover what primitive peoples are really thinking by observing them directly, without allowing one's fancy to run away with itself. However backward the particular people whose magic is under description may seem to be, it will often be noticed that their practices are survivals, sometimes of so distant an origin that the practitioner himself can no longer understand the words he speaks or explain the gestures he performs.

A further complication is created by the fact that most magical rites are enshrouded by the reticence of the initiates. The arcana present a particularly difficult obstacle to the researcher when, as is nearly always the case, the magic formulae are in the possession of a hereditary caste of magicians who regard the secrets as their special heritage. This leads to the magicians as a body deliberately encouraging the ignorance of their followers, who, in their turn, fear the anger of the initiates if they should reveal anything.

The fact that magical rites resemble each other in all parts of the world leads to the difficult question as to whether they came into existence first in any one place, and if so, by what means, whether by cultural borrowings, by migrations or invasions, they were carried to such distant regions?

These are the lines of enquiry which Idries Shah has followed in dealing with oriental magic. Of Afghan origin, he spent five years studying his subject in the Middle and Far East.

His book is a serious contribution to knowledge and deserves to find a wide audience of educated readers.

Preface

THE DIFFUSION OF MAGIC

It is only as recently as Victorian times that archaeological science has established the remarkable fact that magical origins in High Asia have influenced communities halfway across the world. There is a fascinating story, too, in the westward sweep of the prehistoric Accadians, the Turanian people who brought Asian ways to the Mediterranean, founding the civilisations of Assyria and Babylonia. Very many of the frightening thaumaturgic rites of the magicians during the development of the pre-Semitic[1*] age here are preserved in the *Maqlu* ("Burning") Tablets, and the vast library of King Assur-bani-Pal.[2]

The type of "witch-doctoring" (shamanism) practised by allied Turanian tribes took root in the East, in China and Japan. These rituals include psychic phenomena familiar to Western mediums – and they are duplicated, again through Turanian-Mongolian inspiration,[3] among the Finns, Lapps and even the American Indians of North and South America. Naturally there is no documentary evidence of the westward drift of these peoples. Painstaking deduction carried out within the confines of a host of sciences has established that there is every likelihood that such migrations did in fact take place.

It is not, however, only the people of Turanian origins who practised the magical arts of their forebears. As Dr Schütte

[*] The references will be found on pages 291 to 297.

and others have shown, in some of the most intriguing of scientific deduction,[4] the prehistoric Scandinavians, for example, inherited a considerable lore from these peoples. Another important factor is the discovery that prehistoric communication between peoples was far closer than is generally assumed. It is common to imagine that early societies were more or less independent and developed apart from each other: some in remote mountains, deserts and plains, others in towns and villages. It is not commonly known that in addition to trading, both intellectual and social intercourse between peoples widely separated by culture, speech and distance, was considerable. The difference between this contact and the relationship between peoples familiar in our day was simply that geographical factors made communication slower. The same considerations probably accounted for greater sympathy between peoples, as there seems to have been less "inevitable" hostility between different groups.

For centuries, perhaps thousands of years, magic flowed slowly but powerfully through the human race. In its most ritualistic form, the flow was distinctly from east to west.

At a date allegedly during Old Testament times, after the supposed Turanian migrations, Celtic legend has it that Aryan migrations from Central Asia passed through the present Middle East area and Egypt, certainly imbibing mythology and magic on the way.[5]

The early Greeks and Romans, too, played their part in adopting Semitic and Egyptian magical lore, and transmitting it to Europe. Later Latin and Greek magic was a mixture of formulae and incantations which can often be traced to these roots.

The interrelation of the magic of Egypt and the surrounding countries is less clear. It is thought, however (as pointed out later in this book), that Africa and later Southern Arabia influenced the miracle-makers of the valley of the Nile.

With the rise of such comparatively recent systems of thought as Buddhism, Christianity and Islam, the religio-magical beliefs of earlier cults underwent a now familiar relegation: their deities became inferior spirits – even their priesthoods took on a more markedly magical and secretive character:

> Religion may succeed religion, but the change only multiplies the methods by which man seeks to supplement his impotence by obtaining control over supernatural powers, and to guard his weakness by lifting the veil of the future. The secret rites of the superseded faith become the forbidden magic of its successor. Its gods become evil spirits, as the Devas or deities of the Beda become the Daevas or demons of the Avesta, as the bull worship of the early Hebrews became idolatry under the prophets, as the gods of Greece and Rome were malignant devils to the Christian Fathers.[6]

In some cases, superseded processes lingered on as purely magical rites: tolerated and even adapted to newer cults. Was this because, as some believe, there were secrets known to the older systems which really *did* produce some strange evidence of supernatural power, which could be harnessed by humanity for its own use? Or, as the alternative contention holds, was it because magic had become so superstitiously rooted in man's mind, that the only way to control it was to divert it into "legalised" channels?

Organised religions tended to absorb spells and charms, belief in which was very deeply entrenched. Among the southern Sudanese and other Africans I have myself seen that Christianity has been adopted side by side with traditional magic: only in rare cases has it supplanted the demons and powers of the supernatural. Often, again, miracles related of earlier native sorcerers have been simply brought forward in time and added to the new beliefs. Evidence of this psychology is abundant and has been exhaustively studied elsewhere.

Whether we like it or not, magic and religion, all over the world, are linked as are few other human phenomena. If you believe that, say, cures can be effected by touch, then you are believing in magic by its widest definitions – and in some forms of religion. On the other hand, there is a striking development in occultist thinking which can just be discerned today, at its inception. This is the third possibility. Magic is a field where intensive and creative study may show that many so-called supernatural powers are in fact reflections of hitherto little-understood forces, which may very possibly be harnessed to individual and collective advantage. This is a part of the basis of this book.

If there were in reality certain truths known to those nebulously referred to as the "ancients", there is only one way to rediscover them: the scientific method. And the scientific method demands the sifting of every fact, every hint, every clue, back along the chain of transmission. In the magical context this means that we must have at our disposal the actual materials from which Western occultism springs. Hence a rite which is found in, say, a Latin version of the *Key of Solomon*[7] may prove to be merely a transcription of some spell designed to combat, perhaps, a flood in Assyria. Further investigation may show that the spell was based upon some entirely irrelevant thing such as invoking the name of a supposed genie whose initials by some happy chance spelt the word for "drought". And so the search must go on anew. Whether you are, therefore, a general reader, an anthropologist, or just interested in the occult – here are some of the materials. They are not generally available in any other book.

IDRIES SHAH

CHAPTER 1

Magic Is International

"If a man has laid a charge of witchcraft upon another man and has not justified it, he upon whom the witchcraft is laid shall go to the holy river, and if the holy river overcome him, he who accused him shall take to himself his house."

—Code of Hammurabi, *circa 2000 BC.*[8]

THE DEEPER ONE goes into the study of the supernatural and its devotees, the clearer it is that similar trends of thought have made men's minds work alike among communities so diverse that they might belong to different worlds.

According to the occultist this strange identity of magical rituals and beliefs means that there is one single arcane science, revealed to its adepts, and handed down to every people. Advocates of the culture-drift theory will have it that occultism is just one of those things whose spread followed with the natural social intercourse of peoples.

Whatever the truth may be, the study of miracle-workers in many countries is one of the most fascinating occupations. Near Chitral, in Pakistan, there lived some years ago a holy man, believed to possess mystic powers. None cared to pass his cave lest he cast an evil spell over them for trespassing – the general belief being that he was a familiar of Satan himself.

Sometimes frontier brigands, whose depredations took them near his home, saw him. To these he became one whose good opinion they sought, to ensure their success in thieving.

The strength of his name became such – he was variously termed the Spirit of the Mountains or Spirit of the Air – that when he died the cave became a shrine. That hermit's nest was shown to me when I passed that way. In common with his Western counterparts, he had collected stocks of dried serpents and a pile of wax figures pierced with pins littered one corner of the cave. Even today hopeful devotees say a prayer or utter a wish over a piece of rag, which is then tied to a solitary tree outside the saint's abode. Buried face downwards, in order that any evil that might be in him would pass right through the earth, his body lies, as is the custom from China to Morocco, interred where it was found.

About the same time, on the Indo-Chinese border, a noted witch who might have come straight out of *Macbeth* flourished as a spell-dealer and general wonder-worker. She took violent and unaccountable dislikes to people. It was said that she knew everything about people's private lives – which may or may not have accounted for her predilections. Her chief delight, however, was to punish those who caused unhappiness to others, and for that reason she was venerated by many as a saint. This Sita claimed to be over a hundred and fifty years old: a conclusion that was said to have been independently reached also by the oldest inhabitant of the nearest village. The centenarian told how the earliest among her recollections included memories of Sita as a very decrepit and shrivelled sight: exactly as she appeared a hundred years later.

The method of summoning the witch was as follows: people in trouble, henpecked husbands, wives whose husbands were cruel, the sick and needy, went to the roof of their house, and called the name of Sita three times. The local owls, acting as her familiar spirits, swiftly carried the message to her. By the next morning the offender would be taken ill with severe pains in the head. Alternatively, some stroke of good luck would come the way of the invocant.

> When I reached her brushwood lean-to hut, provided with the fruit cake which seemed to be her consuming passion, she seemed very little different from any ordinary old woman of that part of the world. Most of the time she talked, freely enough, of the valuable work she was always doing, in warning young women about the true characters of their menfolk. Though she appeared to be of a great age, her eyes were strangely clear. Instead of the sunken shoulders and hollow cheeks of the classical witch, she stood well over medium height, and moved with surprising agility. Some of her frank monologue, however, seemed to be confused; and when I asked her about the way in which supernatural effects were obtained, she looked at me like a naughty child, and said that I could not possibly understand.
>
> There seemed to be no doubt that Sita, in common with many magicians, really believed in her powers. She denied that her successes could be attributed to autosuggestion on the part of clients, while agreeing that this was a well-known phenomenon. She also claimed to have been taught all her knowledge by her mother, and repudiated occult books and all formal religion as fraudulent deception. I cannot say that her personality was magnetic, or compelling, or had any of the strange features usually felt by mere ordinary mortals in the presence of hidden power. The only thing that really impressed me about her was the fact that she described things which would happen to me: and these things did subsequently occur.[9]

That there may well be a continuity of transmitted occult lore amongst the Mongolian peoples has been accepted by more than one authority. The shamanistic practices of the Chinese, Japanese and other Far Eastern magicians have clear parallels with the rites of the Eskimos and some mongoloid Amerindian tribes: a notable example of this is to be seen in the mediumistic trance state leading to prophecy and clairvoyance which is common to all. India, Mexico and ancient Egypt all have their snake-cults. The snake, in fact, is one of the most important shared symbols of the higher esoteric lore of the Old and New worlds – which has been used as an argument to support the Atlantis theory.

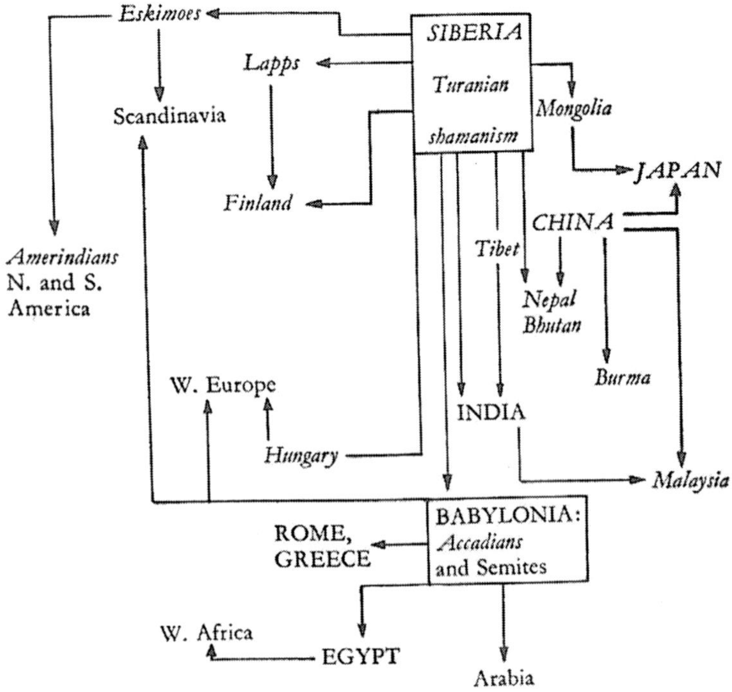

Schematic diagram illustrating the supposed geographical diffusion of Turanian magic

1. *Areas of Mongol-Turanian population (italics)*
2. *Centres of magical synthesis and rediffusion (capitals)*
3. *Turanian-Mongol centres of magical development and rediffusion (italic capitals)*
   Pre-Islamic period: (up to VIIth century AD.)

The Mexican snake-god demanded not only the sacrifice of human life, but the drinking of the victims' blood as well. When a young, wild snake was caught, it did not become a deity until six human sacrifices had been celebrated in its name and presence. The actual blood from the sacrifice had also to be drunk by the snake, thus "potentialising" it as a magical power. In India today, snake-worship is rife – snake-charmers only represent the popularised facet of this important cult. Snakes bring good fortune, guard souls and hidden treasures, form the outlet for occult utterances. Both in Uruguay – very far south of Mexico – and in Konia, which is a long way from India, I found distinct traces of snake-cults. Like the Mexican sorcerers, the snake-shamans of Asiatic Turkey have to undergo a rigid training before they reach the stage where they can manipulate and commune with snakes. Both in Mexico and Turkey the same criteria are accepted for testing when a person is sufficiently developed to become a master of the snake ritual: the eyes must be wide open, the pupils contracted to pinpoints. It is quite possible that this reptile cult has drifted with human migration from India and Africa to South America. One can still find Guarani (Amerindian) peons in the River Plate area who place great importance upon the carving of a snake, painted red. The symbolism of blood and the sacrificial note descending from the Mexican inspiration is too obvious to escape attention.

In Mexico the snake rites had their own distinguishing peculiarities. So great was the competition for the honour of becoming a serpent sacrifice, that it was only with the greatest difficulty that daughters could be prevented from caressing the sacrificial snakes to induce bites.

The priests certainly had no lack of victims. In many cases families which had thus lost more than one daughter were sold anti-snake charms by the sorcerers themselves. Like the Indian snake-worshippers, Mexican followers of the rite used to make a stew of this reptile's flesh, and eat it. In both communities this eating of the holy flesh was supposed to confer all manner of blessings and especially occult powers.

Tabu and propitiation rites may be the origin of many superstitions which are with us – in the East and West – even today. In ancient Egyptian and Greek temples there was always a spot which it was forbidden to touch, or to walk upon. It was dedicated to the gods – and especially evil ones – in return for their implicit agreement not to stray into provinces where they might molest mankind. The same idea obtained in parts of Scotland. Uncultivated pieces of land were left fallow, and termed the "guid man's croft" – following a Celtic custom of naming those who were feared "*good*". Folklorists have dealt at length with the theory that the fairies (or "good people") were, in fact, very much the reverse, being merely propitiated evil spirits.

Greek amulet against enemies: IVth–Vth centuries. Similarities with Hebrew, Arabic and Chinese magical notations are striking *[See pp. 34 and 225]*

At the instigation of the Church many such places were ploughed up in Scotland, Ireland and Wales. Tradition had it that storms and ill-luck would follow such disturbance, and it is reported that ploughing had to be stopped through frightful storms and blizzards which overcame the ploughmen. As a result these places are known today as the "devil's own" land.

The international fraternity – or conspiracy – of magic is perhaps as significant in its general principles as in specific rites. While, for example, it is generally conceded that magic in one form or another may be practised by most people, yet there have always been those whose particular province it was. Forming a kind of initiated priesthood, secrecy is the general rule. A modern occultist cult sums up this almost primordial urge for secrecy in one of its dicta: "Knowledge is Power; Knowledge shared is Power lost." Following the principles of secrecy and initiation, other important common features are magical words and special ceremonial dress. Rituals, with few exceptions, involve some form of sacrifice, actual or implied, and the use of symbolism, Magical words – words of power – are uttered; mystical movements are made; special apparatus, in the form of weapons and talismans, are extensively employed. Next in significance comes the preparation of spells and charms, generally with animal, vegetable and mineral contents, in that order of prominence.

While a belief in supernatural beings is very general in all forms of magic, nevertheless many maintain that the actual names and rites, the very paraphernalia of magic in action, carry special powers, capable of producing supernatural results. The Wand, for instance, is potent because of its consecration: not necessarily because it conjures up a spirit to perform an action.

The objects of magic are known to most people: certainly to those who have studied the subject to any extent.

Rituals, too, are contained in many works, written by "adepts" or commented upon by their opponents. I have already mentioned the possible historical and ethnological importance of a study of the roots of occult practices. There will still remain a number of people who are not interested in culture-drift but want to know "Is there anything in magic?" The answer to this is that there very possibly is a good deal "in magic". What it is, however, and where it might lead, is for researchers to show.

What was there "in" alchemy? For one thing, there was modern chemistry; though what is left in it is not for me to say. Hypnosis, now not only an accepted fact but a very valuable technique, comes direct from magic. As to what there is "in" modern spiritualism, the descendant of Mongolian shamanism, again, I cannot say. One thing, however, is certain: that magic as it stands, in the mere repetition of the rituals which are available to general readers, is of very little value to anyone. According to Hindu occultists, as is described in these pages, many forms of magic, and hence certain well-documented so-called miracles, are accounted for by the existence of an undiscovered force (*akasa*), which seems to have some connection with magnetism. Arab-Islamic writers, too (who gave the world modern science), suspected the presence of this force. If it is there, it is up to experimenters to find it.

Man is a "symbol-inventing animal". This fact has led anthropologists to conclude that the strange similarity between arcane rites in communities without apparent mutual social intercourse is coincidental. Man, they argue, is limited in his very definition. His range of experiences, his hopes and fears, desires and hates, are very little varied, wherever you may go. Does this not mean that he should come to similar conclusions about supernatural subjects, independently of what is called inspiration or occult communication?

The scope of this work is not to seek to prove that all magic has its root in some single, original revelation. It is doubtful, indeed, whether such a contention could ever be proved. But, buried in Eastern folklore, in untranslated manuscripts and legend, in magical books by Eastern writers, there is a vast amount of information which sheds considerable light on the origins of much of the magic which flourished in Europe up to the beginning of the nineteenth century.[10]

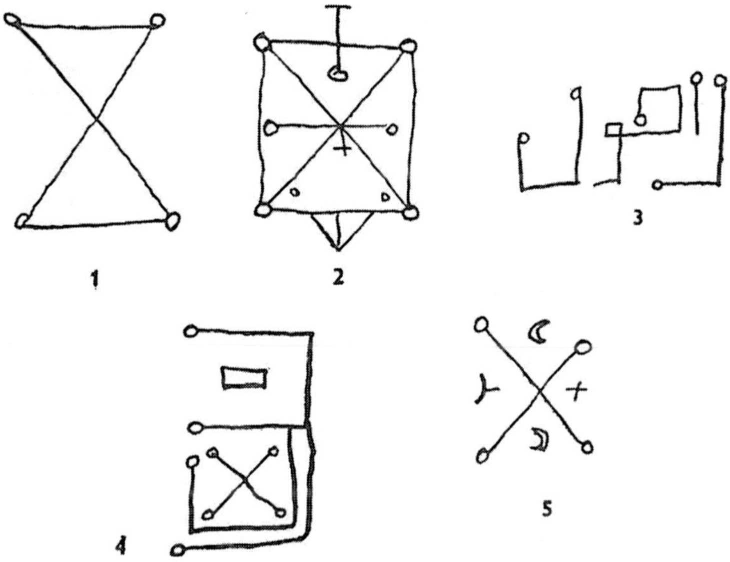

Diffusion of cross and circle symbol in magical usage: (1) Character from the Seal of Solomon. (2) Seal of the Spirit Ose, according to the Grand Grimoire. (3) Arabic exorcism formula ("La Hawl"). (4) Chinese character with constellations, from "felicity" talisman. (5) "Seal of Decarabia", from the Grand Grimoire [See pp. 33–4]

The actual practice of magic is still carried on, in Europe and Asia alike. How widespread this is, it is not my object to investigate. At the same time, it is very widely conceded that the study of magic is of considerable historical, cultural and ethnological interest.

Magic is a part of human history. It has sometimes played a decisive part, as in the case of Moses at the court of Pharaoh. More often it has been of less, though still great, importance. In either case it cannot be ignored.

Very many characteristics of magic as contained in Western grimoires have been traced by such authorities as Sir Wallis Budge to Eastern, and particularly Mediterranean, sources. The magical circle, from which refuge the magician may summon spirits, has been traced to Assyria, and is important in nearly every ritualistic operation of this nature in the Far East. Knowing the names of spirits, and the possession of magic words, familiar even to juvenile readers of fairy tales, is equally, if not more, widespread and highly regarded. The "Words of Power"[11] by which the Jinn were summoned by Solomon, formed an important part of ancient Egyptian teaching.

The diffusion of the wax-image type of curse is as wide as almost any other spell. It is still in use today; as I have myself seen. An early instance is preserved in an incantation from Assurbanipal's bilingual tablet, originating in the Accadian, and probably derived from the rites of Mongoloid tribes from Central Asia. This tablet, from the royal palace at Nineveh, contains twenty-eight spells, and even in 700 BC was considered to perpetuate extremely ancient rites. Part of it runs as follows:

He who forges images, he who bewitches,
The malevolent aspect, the evil eye,
The malevolent mouth, the evil tongue,
The malevolent lip, the finest sorcery,

Spirits of the heavens, conjure it!
Spirit of the earth, conjure it!

All these interdicted items are still standard constituents of magical processes.

Magic shares with religion more characteristics than most people have cared to discuss. The inevitable clash, based on the supposition that like repels like, is most marked in the organised campaigns against sorcery carried out by such bodies as the Inquisitional tribunals of Spain. Either due to this, or because the Church insisted that magicians were servants of the Devil, magic in Europe took on a characteristic of evil which is not so marked elsewhere. Christian theologians took the stand that propitiation of any spirit meant an automatic reduction in the belief that should be reserved for God alone. From this thesis, and certain Biblical references, it was taken for granted that magic meant devil-worship. In this general attitude, Catholicism followed Rabbinical precedent in relation to the growth of magical activities among the Jews.

The second great instrument which – consciously or otherwise – stimulated the study of magic in the West was the Catholic Church. Compelled, by references in the Old and New Testaments, to acknowledge the reality of supernatural phenomena, including the power of witches and sorcerers, Roman Catholic theologians took up a stand against witchcraft ("Thou shalt not suffer a witch to live", Ex. xxii, 18) which caused the subject to be considered as one worthy of investigation, if not study. This attitude towards occult sciences continues in that Church in a form very little altered from that which obtained at the time of the Spanish Inquisition. According to the *Catholic Encyclopaedia*,[12] witchcraft definitely exists, the fact being proved by the Bible.

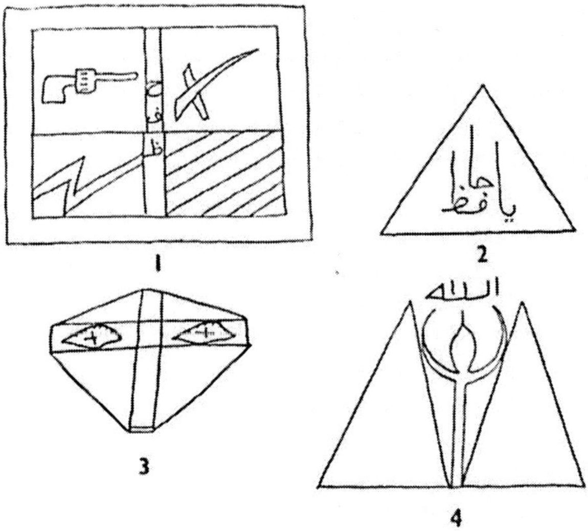

Oriental talismans from the author's collection: (1) Modern amulet for protection (Pathan). (2) Arabic amulet for protection (Turkey). (3) Christian Arab woman's charm against the Evil Eye (Lebanon). (4) Mahdi victory talisman (Sudan)

Many of the codices of Jewish and Solomonic magic which are preserved today in Latin and French examples bear distinct traces of Christian interpolation. Many of the rites of the *Key of Solomon*, for example, have been "Christianised" – almost certainly by priestly hands – to give the impression that thaumaturgical results can be achieved through them, with the Christian additions.

Among the Muslims and other great religions of the East, a compromise brought about the theory of the division of magic into "Permitted" and "Forbidden" – roughly parallel to the Black and White magic distinction in the West.

Magic none the less remained, and still remains, something which organised religion has neither effectively absorbed nor destroyed. Like religion, it has a supernatural basis: the appeal to a force greater than man. From a belief in this force stems the desire for protection, followed by the positive demand for greater power over other men, over the elements, over "fate" itself.

Shared with religions are the paraphernalia of magic: the instruments of the art, the robes and vestments, the fumigations and the repetitions of words, phrases and prayers. Following a belief in the reality of supernatural power comes the desire to enter into contractual relations with that power; hence the "Pact". There is a contract between man and God, between man and spirit. Theologians of the Middle Ages and later were fond of complaining that magical books aped the rites of the Church; that they sought to make compacts with the Devil, just as God made compacts with men. More recent research has shown[13] that the "contract" element of magic is at least as old as magic itself: and hence antedates many of the great organised religions that survive today. Even to the consecrated place of working, magic and religion operate in parallel.

CHAPTER 2

Jewish Magic

"There shall not be found among you... an observer of the times, or an enchanter or a witch, or a charmer, or a consulter with familiar spirits, or a wizard, or a necromancer."

—Deuteronomy xviii, 10

IN ARAB TRADITION the Jews were the greatest magicians of all times. In the Middle Ages of Europe, too, both the Jewish rank-and-file and the Christians among whom they lived more often than not looked up to some reputed sorcerer of Hebrew origin as a miracle-worker. The Jews, on their part, frequently described Jesus as a magician:[14] but that is neither here nor there.

As to whether Hebraic magic is an original product of this Semitic people, it would be almost impossible to decide – without knowing what part of their magical heritage was of foreign origin. There can be no doubt that magic has been very widely practised among the Jews.[15] Justly or unjustly, literally thousands of codices attribute their roots to Hebrew originals: and Moses himself was a magician in one sense of the word.

According to the Samaritans, all magical teaching stems from one book: the *Book of Signs*, which Adam brought with him from Paradise, to enable him to have power over the elements and invisible things. As the *Book of Raziel*, this work is still extant, if, indeed, it is the same one.

Raziel, "meaning Secret of God", is supposed to be the real transmitter of secrets. His *Book* claims to have come from Adam. In another place the reader is informed that it was entrusted to Noah, just before he entered the Ark. Like many other magical texts it traces its history to Solomon, son of David, giant among miracle-workers. Bibliographical research has so far been able to do little in tracing the history of the *Book of Raziel.* Containing a very large number of magical figures, signs and instructions for making talismans, it claims originally to have been engraved upon a tablet of sapphire, though only recent copies are available for study.

The apocryphal *Book of Enoch*[16] is another work claiming intellectual descent from Solomon and Moses. As in other fields of historical research, there seems little doubt that some of the books which are thought to be typical of Jewish magical texts are at best badly interpolated. In other cases substitution may have taken place. Many scholars believe that much of the Jewish magical ritual contained in ancient manuscripts has been lost. For not only was Rabbinical hostility to be faced by Hebraic sorcerers,[17] but sometimes the fury of the people of the country in which they lived, often as a minority of their race. Their aid may have been invoked time and time again as rainmakers by the Moors or the Poles: but should anything go wrong they were generally blamed. Then the law of transmission, whereby only very few could be initiated into the mysteries, may have prevented the writing down of much magical lore.

The *Book of Enoch*[18] has the following legend in explanation of how magic came to the Jews:

Two angels (Uzza and Azael – one of them adopted later by the pagan Arabs as a god, and the other as an angel) were sent by God to tempt mortals, as a test of human frailty. Being themselves unfortunately overcome by love for a woman, they were condemned to divine punishment.

The one hangs from the heavens, head downwards; the other lies chained beyond the Dark Mountains: he it was, incidentally, who taught women to paint their faces!

The *Books of Hermes*[19] – said by some to be forty-two in number – were the attributed work of the Egyptian god Thoth; and they were certainly used by Jewish magicians, as a multitude of references amply show. Thoth is called Theuth by Plato, who states that he was a *man* of great wisdom who lived in Egypt. It is upon his works, we are told, that the ancient Egyptians based their religion and widespread magical practices.

Who was Thoth or Theuth, and what were his magical discoveries? Cicero takes up the tale and tells us that he was indeed a man of Thebes, a "lawgiver". The teachings of the books of Hermes that are extant (out of a reputed forty-two to 36,525 volumes, according to your source) seem at first sight to be confused, mystical, contradictory and magical. Are they Egyptian? This has been very seriously doubted. It is likely that the works of Thoth were, as used to be the practice, transcribed, edited and passed on in a more or less altered form. That they now contain traces of Christian, Muslim and Gnostic thinking seems to be obvious. I have, however, met active supporters of the thesis that these are prophetic writings, and some maintain that their real meaning is clothed in esoteric symbolism. If this be the case, it would surely need more than a lifetime to unravel it without some sort of initiation. So Thoth remains an almost closed book.

The *Zohar*[20] is another important work of Jewish magic. Full of demons and spirits, hells and devils, it gained wide currency in Europe in the fourteenth century. Perhaps it is this work, and the cabbalistic school which it stimulated, which may be regarded as the greatest single force in giving the Jews their fame as magicians in the West.

It is through Jewish sources, or from texts claiming Jewish inspiration, that most of the sacrificial and propitiatory rites of what we now call High Magic are to be traced. The fumigation and incense, candles and knives, the pentacles – even most of the words used in the ceremonies – parallel Hebrew religious procedures in a manner not dissimilar to the parodying of the Christian Mass by Black Magicians.

The *Book of Sacred Magic of Abramelin the Mage* is one of many borderline works.[21] With a reputed authorship of one Abraham, son of Simon, first produced about the year 1458, it may be the work of a Christian. Yet it clearly owes much to Hebrew magical tradition. It is probably, in fact, a mixture: the work of a Christian initiate in oriental magical art. Short of introducing a complete translation here it would be hard to give precise details about the nature and scope of this remarkable black book. It claims that its original was in Hebrew, and that it is – as the title would lead us to believe – "Sacred" and not "Profane" magic. In accordance with the belief of High Magic, the author states that angels and demons may be used by means of this book, for good or evil: for is it not the same book that was given to Moses, Solomon and others? Its processes are similar to those found in most grimoires – grammars of the sorcerers. Details are given for casting spells, for conjuring up spirits, for the recovery of lost objects, to produce love or hate. Small wonder that tradition made it binding upon every initiate of this type of magic to communicate no part of it to anyone unless he was himself convinced that the recipient was "ready to receive it".[22]

To Solomon is also ascribed the much-coveted *Grimorium Verum*, which contains material from the Key of Solomon,[23] which will be examined in due course. Not only does this small tome contain the "true and authentic secrets of Solomon the

King", but it was actually discovered in his tomb! By means of it the sorcerer may prepare himself for the difficult exercise of the Art, can make the various instruments which are essential to the difficult art of raising spirits, and can evoke and dismiss a large number of powerful beings. Although the title-page says that it was collected and published by "Alibeck the Egyptian" in 1517 (at Memphis), it is more likely to date from the eighteenth century, and was probably printed from a much older manuscript. No collated version of the *True Grimoire* is known, though parts which are missing in this edition are apparently available in the more modern Italian texts.

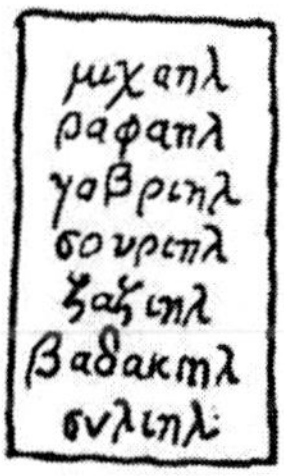

Greek talisman from a papyrus, containing Hebrew names of seven archangels, viz.: Michael, Raphael, Gabriel, Souriel, Zaziel, Badakiel, Suliel

Another important work which was to be found among the prized treasures of every medieval sorcerer was *True Black Magic*. This, again, was reputed to be taken from Hebrew sources. It is, in fact, derived from *Solomon's Key*. Noted for its concentration on death spells and works of hatred, it may have been copied from a parallel manuscript to that from which all the more recent versions of the *Key* spring. Only one edition of this book is known – and that most rarely: the edition of 1750. Like all grimoires, copies can be bought only from collectors, or seen at a few libraries. Until these textbooks of sorcery are made more generally available, it will not be easy for students of occultism to compare the interrelation of culture and myth which resulted in magical practices in both Europe and the East.

Two main forces were responsible for the spread of occult study of eastern magic in the West, apart from professional magic-workers themselves. In the first place, Arab researchers, obeying literally the Prophet's injunction "Seek knowledge, even as far as China", studied and translated whole libraries of Hebrew books, making them available in Arabic, Latin and Greek through their famed universities in Spain. Western scholars brought this learning to Northern Europe, where occult studies as well as more mundane sciences took root.

Quite apart from accounts of magic and magicians, buried in little-read works on Hebrew life and customs, there is another source from which a mass of data may be obtained: the Bible. During Biblical times Jewish magic recognised several types of operators: Diviners, who saw visions, by scrying and gazing (Gen. xliv, 5); people who took counsel from images, livers and so on – another kind of diviner, as in Ezek xxi, 21 – Minianites (Num. xxii, 7); and diviners among the Philistines, as we see in I Sam. vi, 2.

All these had their counterparts among other oriental nations; quite a large part of their magical heritage seems to come from the Turanian Mongols who preceded the Assyrians in that area. A wizard, according to Rabbi Akiba, is a person who decides upon lucky and unlucky days for journeys, sowing, and the like. Several Jewish authorities hold that magic arts were learned during the Egyptian captivity, and these seem to be the type of sorcerers mentioned in Lev. xix, 31, and Deut. xviii, 11. There is, however, a reference to soothsayers, and probably astrologers, in Isa. ii, 6, xlvii, 13 and elsewhere, which shows that they were a subdivision of the main body of sorcerers. The "engravers" were people who specialised in the making of talismans, with which Europe became familiar in later days. Large sections of some Western *Grimoires* were devoted to these talismans and their making.

Spells, counter-spells, possession by demons, and supernatural contests: these are the ingredients of the magical world of the Semites. Most people will recognise such practices as the attempted reading of the "writing on the wall", the interpretation of signs as evidences of occultist activity. Perhaps less obvious is the background of the famous magical battle between Moses and Aaron and the Egyptian priest-magicians.[24] It was a well-known trick of the magicians of the day (and still exists in contemporary Egypt) seemingly to convert rods into serpents. What actually happens is this: the viper is put into a state of cataleptic rigidity by pressing its head. It then resembles a staff. When it is thrown down on the ground, the shock rouses it, and breaks the hypnotic state. This was what the Egyptians did. As this book is not concerned with apologetics, it is not proposed to discuss the question of whether Aaron's rod (which may have been a similar snake) actually did or did not devour the opponents' staffs. Further reference on this interesting point can be made to such writers as Maury, Lane and Thompson.[25]

Jewish demonology, armed with the accumulated devils and evil spirits of all the civilisations that Israel was heir to, makes impressive reading. Rabbi Menachen knew that devils are so numerous that if they were visible to the naked eye it would be impossible for man to exist. Not everyone is equally subjected to their attacks, however: it is rabbis that they seek out to torment. The main reason for the wearing of rabbinical cloaks is to ward off elementals. It is possible that the robes which all sorcerers adopt may have this protective aspect and origin.

The worst time for contact with spirits is the night, when Igereth flies in company with hundreds of thousands of excited lesser demons, all primed to do evil, and see that it is done.

At night, continues this authority, none should sleep alone, lest Lilith work her evil. Lilith, of course, is the Biblical Succubus, who seduces men. There is a very large literature in rabbinical legend about how this spirit took female shape and deceived Adam. She is a devil of Accadian (Far Asian) origin – Gelal, or Kiel-Gelal – and her name in Hebrew and English is derived from the Assyrian Lil or Lilit.

One belief among Jewish cabbalists was that the elusive Most Great Name, the puissant Word of Power, was SCHEMHAMPHORAS. With its aid, anything magical could be performed. But it could only be used, like the Book of Thoth, by initiates, on pain of awful supernatural punishment. Later Hebrew writers even claim that it was this very same Name which was used by Jesus to work miracles.

Where demons were implicitly believed to abound, witches and wizards were constantly at work. That many of the reputed witches were in fact mere eccentrics seems possible. At this distance it is hard to know where to start in order to separate one from the other. Take for example in the twenty-second chapter of Exodus the famous line *Thou shalt not suffer a witch to live*. What type of witch is this lady of verse eighteen? Some say that the Hebrew word *Chasaf* used here means simply "poisoner" – which changes the entire meaning. It is similar to the word *veneficus*, by which it is rendered in the Latin version of the Septuagint. The truth probably lies somewhere in between: that a witch was considered a poisoner, either in a symbolic sense or in actual fact. Many cases are reported in the sixteenth century of witches who were said to have resorted to poisoning a victim when magical means failed. One such case was the murder of Sir Thomas Overbury.

As we have already seen, witchcraft was distinctly disfavoured by the established authority of the Hebrew Semites. But like many another forbidden thing, it nevertheless permeated human life of the period. Those who did not subscribe to the scriptures provided recruits for the cult. Even among believers, history shows that times of stress and doubt would cause otherwise devout people to dabble in witchcraft. Theologians recognise this link between a reduction of faith and a turning towards "dark" (i.e. magical) arts. And of course, Job's virtue was tested by a succession of disasters.

Deuteronomy xviii, 10, says: "There shall not be found among you any one that maketh his son or his daughter to pass through the fire, or that useth divination, or an observer of the times, or an enchanter, or a witch, or a charmer, or a consulter with familiar spirits, or a wizard, or a necromancer."

Manasses, according to II Kings xxi, caused his son to pass through fire. The Arabs of today sometimes pass over a flame, in order to discourage any evil spirit that may be following. The same king of Judah "observed times, and used enchantments, and dealt with familiar spirits and wizards"; altogether a type of magician-king.

Saul, King of Israel, discouraged at the trend of affairs, and disappointed in his subjects, had given up hope of receiving replies from God, and was driven to consult the Witch of En-Dor. In his own trouble, he forgot that he had himself often sought out witches and killed them.

He was told by the witch that she saw an old man, wearing a mantle (no actual materialisation here, it seems) whose description was recognised by the King. Sinking upon his knees, Saul listened to what seems to have been the voice of Samuel – which he heard but could not see anything – telling of his own defeat and death. This return to the traditional practice of kings to consult – even to maintain – magicians and sorcerers may have been most reprehensible by monotheistic standards. It could not equally be said to be unprecedented. Magicians, like the practitioners of other arts, have from time immemorial basked in the benign patronage of monarchs. One comes across indications which show not only the power wielded by wonder-workers, but the fact that the rewards could be great indeed. Perhaps one of the largest sums paid to a seer was when Benhadad, King of Damascus, gave forty camel-loads of wealth to Elijah, in return for discovering whether his illness would prove fatal.

The great stream of Jewish magic stretches, in its modern form, far from the eastern Mediterranean shores. A worthy descendant of those Biblical seers was the amazing Nostradamus, who remains an enigma even today. So little disbelieved are his strange prophecies that a film was recently made to illustrate some that had come true.

Born at the beginning of the sixteenth century, in Provence, he claimed descent on his maternal side from a physician-seer to King René. From his early years he had shown an aptitude for magic: "at the age of ten he was giving lessons in hidden things to people of twice his age"... in spite of the fact that his father disapproved, and wanted him to take up a medical career.

Be that as it may, Nostradamus[26] grew into a handsome, bearded man, and in the year 1525 – when he was but twenty-two – plague followed famine, and the district was swept with both. Doctors were few, and he set out with a cure which he had developed. The result was a succession of spectacular recoveries. He would not – or could not – explain the basis of the remedy to doctors who knew only that he had a secret powder: and that it worked. He was therefore given an honorary doctorate in medicine, and continued his studies in the occult.

The next strange thing about him was that he seemed to develop a power of prescience. There is no indication as to how the power worked. Naturally he was suspected of being in league with Satan – and another plague burst upon the people in the midst of the accusations, to which he would not deign to reply. This scourge was attributed to Nostradamus himself. But he overcame the disease, carrying his powder into places whence all recognised physicians had fled. A pension was pressed upon him by grateful townspeople.

After he had combated another plague in Lyons, again been accused of sorcery, and made a number of further predictions, Nostradamus was called to King Henry's court, and appointed the royal physician. The only clue to the possible background of his studies is the recorded drawing of the horoscope of the king, and the assertion that his studies were mainly in cabbalism, that esoteric philosophy of the Jews.

Cabbalism was studied, and its results practised in secret. Its literature, like that of the Sufis and other philosophers in the realms of the so-called "High Tradition", was plentifully adorned with symbolism. Next to alchemy, there is probably no subject which is more difficult of understanding to the uninitiated, even in its terminology.

Power, it was held, hid itself from publicity. It was to be obtained only in secrecy, and through secrecy. Similarly, its use was to be secret. Even the teachings themselves were actually weakened by being told to incredulous people: "knowledge is power... knowledge shared is power lost". Silence, discretion, faithfulness, these were the hallmarks of the cabbalistic student.

All good emanated from one point – which is called God in cabbalism. Equally, all good power was reached and exercised only through this point. The power and characteristics of God were divided into ten categories, the *Sephiroth*.

These esoteric secrets were matched, and at times equated, with other systems, Jewish and non-Semite, both during the Eastern and Western heydays of occult practice. The Gnostics used gems and ciphers to conceal what they believed to be great truths; some groups of "masters" taught their disciples that the symbolism of their rites was divinely revealed in dreams, others that they were merely receptacles for the quintessence of wisdom, crystallised by aeons of study and illumination. With the Jews, as with other peoples, angels were known in multitudes, good and bad ones: dreams and portents all had their proper and improper places.

The Platonists believed in the "angels that failed" – there being as many in the inferior as the superior world. These are prototypes for apparitions and familiar spirits. There is the revenge of the wicked and the godless; evil and wicked spirits willing and anxious to hurt and affright. Four mischievous kings rule over them: they inhabit places near the earth, yet within the earth itself.

Others divide these evil spirits into nine degrees: the first are false gods who succeed in being worshipped and require sacrifice. Such, they said, was the one who spoke to Jesus, showing him all the kingdoms of the world. And a similar tale is told of Muhammad and the evil spirit who tried to pervert his mission. In the second place are the spirits of lies, such as went from the mouth of Ahab. The third are the vessels of iniquity: we are told in Genesis how Jacob said, "Vessels of iniquity are in their habitations, into their council let not my soul come."

Fourthly, in later Jewish-Christian thought, there follow the revengers of evil, who imitate miracles, and serve witches and sorcerers: such it was said spoke to Eve. Their prince is Satan, who "seduces the whole world, doing great signs, and causing fire to descend from heaven in the sight of men". Sixthly are those that join themselves with thunder and lightning, corrupting the air and causing pestilence and other evils: the spirits that were thought to aid Nostradamus. They have power over the land and sea, controlling the four winds.

Their prince is Meririm, a raging, boiling devil – called the "prince of the power of the air".

Francis Barrett – the last of the great self-confessed wizards – wrote in the early nineteenth century about these powers, and about their revelation of themselves to man in diverse ways; of prophecies, symbols and signs – and the whole gamut of the magic of the West, almost all inherited from Jewish sources:

"The soul," says the *Magus*,[27] "can receive true oracles and undoubtedly, in dreams, yields true prophecies: wherein unknown places and unknown men appear, both alive and dead. Things to come are foretold. Yet there are those whose intellect being overwhelmed with too much commerce of the flesh is indeed asleep or its imagination is too dull that it cannot receive the species and representation which flow from superior intellect, which means, I say, this man is altogether unfit to receive dreams and prophesying by them."

Dreams, then, are regarded by this adept, as by his predecessors and confrères throughout the world, as valuable avenues for the transmission of occult knowledge. Some of the more modern psychological anthropologists even suggest that it is to the dream that we must look for the very inception of a human belief in the supernatural. Dreams may well have been the first thing which caused man to suspect that there might be other worlds and beings worth communicating with. Several processes are recorded in Jewish and other magical writings "for the procuring of dreams", and they have always played their part in occultism.

CHAPTER 3

Solomon: King and Magician

> *"Verily, Solomon was the greatest of the magicians. He had power over the birds and beasts, and over men, from the highest to the lowest. Call, then, spirits and the Jinn in his name, and with his Seal: and you shall triumph, if it be the Will of Allah!"*
>
> —Miftah el-Qulub *(Key of the Hearts), Persian MS. of the 1000th Year of the Flight*

IF THERE IS any bridge between the magical arts of Egypt, Israel and the West, that bridge is the collection of works, processes and traditions ascribed to Solomon, son of David, third King of Israel.

Both the Bible and the Qur'an contain references to the wonder-working king: his life has been embroidered upon in the *Arabian Nights* and countless other works of fiction and fancy. In more recent European grimoires his name is used by the magical practitioner to raise and subjugate Lucifuge, and compel that spirit to disgorge treasures. Out of the mass of legend and pseudo-history, dating from the ninth century before Christ, how much can we establish about the real life and activities of this man? It would need an entire volume to assess the magical life of Solomon alone – but certain common ground can be discerned. It will be necessary to remember throughout that some of the magical documents supposedly derived from writings left by King Solomon may in actual fact be the work of rabbis or others with the same name. It is by no means easy, either, to prove that many of the codices are not forgeries.

The Arabian chroniclers, above all others, excel in the minute attention paid to the occult side of this extraordinary man.

According to most of them, he not only travelled through the air, but did so with his entire Court, on the original Flying Carpet. Made of a sort of green silk, this carpet was capable of carrying hundreds at a time, and was always escorted by flights of birds. In a Jewish tradition it is claimed that the carpet was sixty miles square and its green silk interwoven with gold.

Solomon's powers over all spirits and elements, and especially the *Ján* (genii), are supposed to have been gained through the possession of a magical ring, set with the jewels of the angels presiding over the four elements. It is also said that the ring had within it a portion of a wondrous root. Instructions for the making of similar rings are contained in grimoires published under Solomon's name, which circulate even today. The Qur'an takes up the story, in Sura xxi, 81, 82:

"And to Solomon we taught the use of blowing winds which moved with his command towards the land on which we had placed our blessings... and we subjugated to him some of the evil ones who dived for him and did other things besides." One of his wives was a daughter of Pharaoh, king of the Land of Magic, and commentators have held that it was through her that secrets were disclosed to the King of Israel.

Secret Seal of Solomon, from the Lemegeton

The lapwing or hoopoe is also much mentioned as a bird used by Solomon as a messenger; and contemporary Arabian manuscripts carry instructions for the use of this bird's bones and "nest-stone" identical with those found in grimoires published in the Middle Ages, in Solomon's name.

I have come across an old reference to an obscure passage in the Bible, which may link with the hoopoe.

In I Kings 11, 22, we are told that "Hadad" urged Pharaoh to send him away, that "I might go to mine own country". Arab commentators urge that this Hadad is the same as the magical *bird* Hudud, referred to in the Qur'an as being a messenger of Solomon (not a man at all), who brought news of the Queen of Sheba.[28]

However that may be, there are several references to the magical powers of Solomon in the Qur'an. "And most surely we gave David and Solomon knowledge... and Solomon became David's heir and said 'O ye men! We have been taught the expression of the birds and we have been given of all things. Most surely this is a clear distinction.' And the armies of the Jinns and the civilised ones and birds were assembled for Solomon, and they were paraded. Until they came to the valley of the Ants. Said one of the ants: 'O ye of the Ants! Go into your dwellings, and let not Solomon crush you unknowingly.'"[29]

This passage, read in the original Arabic, shows that Solomon is credited with knowing the language of birds, which is another widely held idea. The verse goes on to say that Solomon heard what the ant referred to above said, and laughed, thus showing his ability to hear and understand what ants were supposed to be saying.

Solomonic magic links also with certain very important aspects of ritual observance common to almost every magical system. Most people are familiar with the Seal of Solomon – the figure with which he was able to attract, bind and seal spirits. It was by means of this seal that the Genie in the *Arabian Nights* story was confined to a bottle for tens of thousands of years. There has been some confusion of the five-pointed Star (seal) of Solomon with the six-pointed Star or Shield of David – also considered to be a powerful talisman against evil, and used in much the same way as the Cross was later employed for protection. Both forms of the Star are used in various magical rituals of Arab and Jewish origin.

The ancient Egyptian theory of the "Most Great Name of God" – a Word of Power – which is so potent that it cannot be spoken or even thought – is found in Solomonic magic. In fact, some writers claim that a great part of the king's powers were derived from a ring inscribed with the Most Great Name. Both Arab and Jewish writers concur in this, the former adding that the ring was made of brass and iron, joined together.

The *Testament of Solomon*,[30] ascribed to him, but impossible of proof as to its authorship, tells that he appealed to the angel Michael for help to overcome demons. The angel presented him with a magical ring, engraved with a seal. Thus armed, he could conjure all evil spirits, and obtain from them valuable information. This was accomplished by "binding" the demon with magical spells and compelling it to summon another, who brought a fellow – and so on – until the whole infernal multitude was present. Solomon was then able to ask each demon individually his or her name, sign and the name in which it was to be summoned. This information forms the bulk of the *Key of Solomon*, ascribed to him: a work which has appeared and reappeared in many languages, throughout the centuries. It is perhaps the best known grimoire.

This *Key* is called in Hebrew the *Mafteah Shelomoh*, while Latin versions are generally entitled *Claviculae Salomonis*. The work is divided into two parts, and embraces invocation, incantation and the making and use of various kinds of pentacles.

An Arabic work on magic, entitled *Kitab al-'Uhud*, is probably the same as the *Book of Asmodeus*, which is mentioned in the Jewish cabbalistic *Zohar* as having been given to King Solomon by the spirit Asmodeus, and contained formulae for the subordination of demons.[31] It forms a link with the *Key of Solomon*, and has had a considerable influence upon magical treatises of the Middle East.

A very large number of writings claimed to be by Solomon are either extant or mentioned in other magical works. Important among these is *The Divine Work*, said to have been dictated by angels, a book of medicine and alchemy, which greatly influenced Arab studies of the Hermetic art. Other treatises, which have been lost, dealt with various more philosophical subjects. Another, which gave rise to the title *Almadel*, used in several magical books, is the Hebrew *Sefer ha-Almadil*, about the magic circle, that indispensable figure within which all magicians must take refuge against the malice of spirits. The making of the circle, its location, and the signs to be written within its concentric rings, form a significant part of Solomonic magic, and, indeed, of most of the world's sorcery and witchcraft rites. It is thought that the name of the book may derive from the Arabic *Al Mandal* – "The Circle". It is interesting to note that some of the signs which are used in Solomonic magic – whether in circles or seals – bear a more than superficial resemblance to similar signs used in Chinese magic and astrology. One of the most striking samples of this similarity is to be seen in the symbolism used in marking constellations and stars in both the Jewish and Chinese systems. I am not aware that this fact has been observed or pointed out before.

CHAPTER 4

The Occult in Babylonia

"Fallen, fallen is Babylon the great, and is become a habitation of devils, and a hold of every unclean spirit, and a hold of every unclean and hateful bird."

—Revelation XVIII, 2

DEVILS, DEMONS AND supernatural powers described by the various peoples of Assyria and Babylonia form the archetype of much of the demonology which the West – and parts of the East itself – have inherited. As has been mentioned in an earlier part of this book, many of these spirits were brought by the Accadians (who really established the Babylonian culture) from the far steppes of High Asia. Thus we find that many of the rituals and spells carried westwards by the Aryans, the Greeks and Romans, the Arabs and the Jews were derived from supernatural activities which originated in what is now Asiatic Russia. The same rites and beliefs, in some measure, linger on in their primitive state among communities of arrested cultural development throughout the world: principally Siberian, Eskimo and other Mongoloid peoples. Other civilisations (like the Chinese and Japanese, the Assyrians and Egyptians) adopted and adapted the cults to their own brand of thinking. This is one of the answers to the vexed question as to whether all magic has a parent root, somewhere. It is not, however, the complete answer.

The pure Accadian (Mongoloid) forms of this magic are still preserved in the bilingual tablets of such collections as Assur-bani-Pal's Library; while other tablets show the fusion of Semitic and other beliefs with those of the highland conquerors.

The raising of the hand was to the Babylonians a sign of the commencement of a magical or religious rite – a concept which is retained in signals of benediction and blessings in general, and which has been fully described by Ernest Crawley. Although Assur-bani-Pal's tablets were not collected until the seventh century BC,[32] they date back almost to the earliest days of the Turanian (Mongoloid) arrival in the Eastern Mediterranean.

The tablets are a treasure of magical lore: for the King seemed to have a mania for book-collecting. Everything that was written – and this was mostly books on magic and occult matters – had to be copied and brought to him. There are even letters (also tablets) extant, asking that anything of any interest at all should be copied on to clay and sent to him forthwith, from every quarter of the kingdom.

Early in the series the tone is set: Assur-bani-Pal himself curses anyone who effaces his name from a tablet: "May Assur and Bilit cast him down in wrath and anger and destroy his name and those of his posterity."[33]

Some of the tablets, it is true, have prayers and incantations directed towards only one god; but most contain the names of a multitude of individual spirit-gods who are the forefathers of our evil spirits, as known to the Church, and so sedulously hunted by ecclesiastics.

Many of the tablets refer to evil influences abroad, and prayers and supplications were made to avert them. Magical rites were undertaken, and specific mention is made of the implements of the art: not forgetting incense and the special kinds of wood used in the kindling. Offerings of honey, dates and grain form an important part of the ritual, and it is here that we find the earliest form of the magical circle, which is used the world over to safeguard the magician and his assistants.

Some of the tablets advise certain invocations, incantations and offerings for the healing of the sick. As with Arabic magic and other Semitic rites, a knot is tied in a cord and then loosened, that the sick man may be well again.

Babylonians were fortunate in being able to consult such processes to defeat eclipses: otherwise the shadow would remain for ever: to effect this the priests repeated the following:

> O Sibziana. In the Heavens, they bow down before thee; Ramman the prince of Heaven and earth; at thy command mankind was named. Give thou the word, and with thee let the great god stand! Give thou my judgement, make my decisions. I, thy servant Assur-bani-Pal, the son of his god; whose God is Assur, whose goddess is Assuritu. In the evil of the eclipse which has taken place. In the evil of the powers, of the portents, evil, not good; which are in my palace and my land. Because of the evil spectre which is bound to me, I have petitioned and glorified thee! The raising of my hand, accept! Harken to my prayer free from my bewitchment! Loosen my sin! Let there be turned aside whatever evil may come to cut off my life. May the favourable Sidu be ever at my head and at thy command let me live![34]

There has been a good deal of painstaking research into the origins and functions of gods and spirits in Mesopotamia, the cradle of civilisation. But it is interesting to note that the functions of gods as aids to magicians have been largely passed over by occultists. The Babylonian system, all the same, was based upon the magical and supernatural character of gods and the human relation with them.

Each victory over an enemy was recorded, together with the spirit-god with whose help it had been achieved. Gods often possessed human form coupled with superhuman faculties and wisdom. Moreover they had lived in the world, had loved and died like ordinary men. They were married, and represented stars and elements, like the demons and spirits of true sorcery.

When they died their powers became absolute. When a disciple prayed to them, they could utter magical Words of Power and weave spells of strange mystery. Storms, floods, earthquakes and pestilence were the work of angered gods: when these upheavals made themselves felt the gods had to be appeased. There was no other way to safety and rescue.

Enlil, the god of the Earth, was worshipped at Nippur; Ea was god of the deep. Uru-ki was the moon god, Udu the god of the sun. Marduk, the god of Babylon itself, had the greatest possible reverence paid to him. Among other important spirit-deities was Eshidam, in the city of Cuthah – the god of those killed in battle.

Of the goddesses we hear less. Their children became gods through their fathers. The most important goddess of all was Ishtar, the Semitic goddess of battle, and the local deity of the city at Sippar. In other places she was known as the deity of love. She it was who later became Aphrodite with the Greeks, and Venus to the Romans. I visited her shrine in Cyprus: once the greatest place of pilgrimage of the ancient world. Here, even today, there are many magical superstitions concerning the immense ruined place among the local Greek population.

The centre of the earth was believed to be the place of the dead: the cavern called Arallu. This place (which was a sort of hell, where all humanity went whether good or evil) was surrounded by high walls, watched over by demons. There was little belief in reincarnation, for the name of the place was *Mát lá tári* – the "place of no return". The dead lived in utter darkness, eating dust. And to this destination everyone went; there was neither reward nor punishment for deeds of this world in the Babylonian hereafter.

The demons were horrific creatures, part human, part animal, and probably were the prototypes of Western demonology. It is interesting that many of the demons sculpted in the Far East resemble these Near Eastern devils, and probably sprang from similar origins, in the imagination of the nomad tribes of Central Asia. These Nedu (gatekeepers) had lists of those who were to be taken to hell, their "teeth long as fangs, their eyes glaring and large balls, their claws long and sharp". As soon as a person died, the demons of the *Mát lá tári* presented themselves and took charge of the body after burial, escorting it to the abode of the goddess Allatu – the Al-Lát of the Arabs, and one of the images smashed in Mecca by Muhammad himself. Allatu bore the frightening appearance of having a lion's head, and grasped a serpent in each hand. Great care had to be taken with the burial of the dead, lest the ghost (*eskimmer*) be caught by a sorcerer and used to bewitch the living relatives of the corpse.

This background of the atmosphere of Babylonian life is essential to those who seek to understand the often very complicated rites and incantations which were considered essential to humanity of those times.

EXORCISM RITES

Where there were demons, and as they were expected to attack men (and women) at any time, there was clearly grave need for methods by which such possession could be combated. When a man asked Jesus to cast the evil out of a possessed person into a herd of swine, he was asking for the repetition of one of the standard methods of Semitic exorcism. The nineteenth formula from one of Assur-bani-Pal's protection rites (now in the British Museum, in fragment form) gives the words of this rite:

"May the wicked demon depart! May they [*sic*] seize one another! The propitious demon, the propitious giant, may they penetrate his body! Spirit of the heavens, conjure it! Spirit of the earth, conjure it!"

The great Chaldean system of magic from the Nineveh excavations is contained in the three important magical works of the Turanian Accadians. The first was entitled *Wicked Spirits*, and dealt exclusively with magical operations for repelling demons and spectres when they attacked, and, of course, to safeguard people against their approach.

The second book, of which not much has been recovered, is a work of occult medicine. The third contained invocations and hymns addressed to various gods.

As has been pointed out before, it is likely that these were three separate rites: one book for each class of sages: the astrologers and divines, the magicians proper, the physicians and philosophers. These are catalogued as such in Daniel. As with most occult writings, the originals, in the then dead Accadian language, were believed to be the most potent. The actual spells and hymns were evidently recited in Accadian: for each is accompanied by a translation in Assyrian, which was the living tongue at the time of their copying.

ACCADIAN-ASSYRIAN GOD-SPIRITS

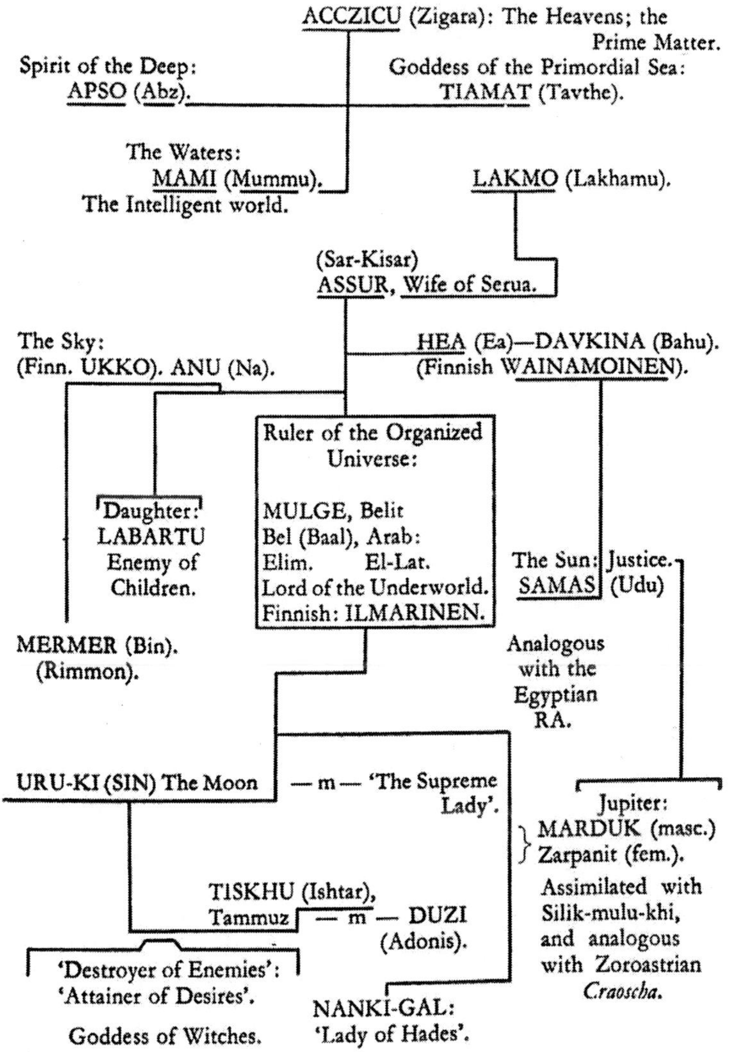

The organisation or plan of a spell was simple, though the endless repetition of its words were wearying. From an examination of the wording it is clear that the actual Words of Power – the "Abracadabra" – were the phrases "Spirit of the

Heavens, conjure! Spirit of the Earth, conjure!", which were always added, as was the word *Amanu* – Amen, translated from the Accadian *Kakama*, which had the same meaning of "truth" or "so it be". Sometimes the "Words of Power" formula itself was extended, making an appeal to several spirits. The actual content of the spell did not seem to have been so important. Thus we have, in the case of a person wishing to be secure against witchcraft, an appeal that evil-doing should be banished, with the ending:

Spirit of the Heavens, conjure it! Spirit of the Earth, conjure it!
Spirit of Mul-gelal, lord of the countries, conjure it!
Spirit of Nin-ge-lal, lady of the countries, conjure it!
Spirit of Nin-dara, powerful warrior of Mul-gelal, conjure it!
Spirit of Nusku, sublime messenger of Mul-gelal, conjure it!
Spirit of Eni-zena, eldest son of Mul-gelal, conjure it!
Spirit of Tiskhu, lady of the armies, conjure it!
Spirit of Mermer, king whose voice is beneficent, conjure it!
Spirit of Utu, king of justice, conjure it!
Spirits, Archangels, great gods, conjure it![34]

Where does the Babylonian pantheon "fit in" with oriental magic as a whole? This is the point at which the much-contested question, the lingering tradition, of an esoteric, supreme priesthood of magic seems to take shadowy shape. For not only are the gods and goddesses of the Turanian (ancient Babylonian) system connected, by adoption and abstraction, with powers venerated in the Finnish, Aryan and Semitic systems:[†] but in very many cases the magical rites of these and other nations depend upon the powers of those gods, as the multitude of spirits which are associated with

† And, of course, China and Japan.

them. Here, too, we come across the *mana-akasa* theory: the belief that there is a supernatural force which permeates the atmosphere and which is personified as a power within all men. Towards the concentration of that elusive power, and its aid in influencing spirits and gods, the activities of magicians are directed.

There have been attempts at linking the pantheons of the Greeks, Egyptians, Babylonians and Hindus: some more plausible than others. Such is not the intention of this book. At the same time this subject does touch our investigation at a number of points. Reference to the schematic representation of Assyrian-Accadian deities and their spheres of power given here will show this link-up more clearly than words alone.

Thought-concentration among the Finns, for example, was attained in a manner familiar to the Indians or even the men of the Sudan, where I watched their preliminary rites of "frenzy-induction":

> "According to the Finnish creed, every man bore within him from his birth a divine spirit who was his inseparable companion for life. This spirit became more closely united to its subject, in proportion as the latter tore himself from earthly things to retire into the sanctuary of his soul. This was an important source of the magician's power."[35]
>
> Here we have a close parallel with many mystical systems, including those of the Gurus of India and the Arab-Islamic Sufi principle.
>
> "He aspired to a transcendental ecstasy, TULLA INTOON, to a great state of excitement of the soul, TULLA HALIORHIN, in which he became like the spirit dwelling in him, and entirely identified with it."[36]

> Again the spiritualist (spiritist) and again the frenzy and identification principle of the dervishes and fakirs....
>
> "He used artificial means, intoxicating drugs for instance [compare Western witch-cults], in order to attain to this state of excitement, for it was only then that he succeeded, so to speak, in deifying himself, and received the homage of the genii and spirits of nature... this doctrine... prevailed also in the Accadian [Babylonian] magic books. This furnishes an affinity of conceptions and beliefs *which is of great importance, since it is not one of those natural ideas which arise independently* amongst widely differing nations." (My italics.)[37]

Whence, ultimately, came this power of magic? Who taught it, or initiated it? What, in fact, is the fountain of mana-akasa: Life-Force? This is where an understanding of the demonology and theology of prehistoric nations is vital.

Magicians, among the Finns, concentrated their invocations round the spirit of all life: Wainamoinen. It was he who taught magic to me; he who was the foundation of all life, lord of the waters: spirit of fire. In these respects he was almost certainly identical with the Accadian *Hea*, Lord of Life. Like Thoth of the Egyptians, he not only created magic but gave the knowledge of the Words of Power to men. He is thought to have been similar in conception to the Egyptian Ra – and he shares with Ra even the relatively minor function of distributing power and beneficence through the sweat from his body.

The powers which the Scandinavian magicians acquired by this dedication to the Earth Spirit are not unlike the traditional thaumaturgy of sorcerers everywhere:[38]

> Lemminkainen went into the house which was full of people who talked among themselves. Some, wearing long robes, sat upon the seats, singers outside, reciters below the portals, with musical instruments all around the walls. Sorcerers sat near the hearth, at the place of honour. Then he began to weave spells. As soon as he started to sing, even the best singers found that they could utter only discordant notes. Even their hands were as if held in gloves of stone, on their heads was stone, their necks were bound with collars of stone... the men were flung into a sledge pulled by a strange-coloured cat... which carried them off into the World of Evil Spirits... and when he again recited, they threw themselves into Lapland's Gulf, the waters which are the drink of the thirsting sorcerers.... And then he sang yet again: and the people were tossed into the turbulent gulf, which devours.... Then Lemminkainen showed that he thought that the middle-aged and the young were fools, by means of his magical rites...

The comparison of the magical and religious rituals of other nations has brought to light quite a number of correspondences between the secret powers formerly believed to have been unique to, or at least invented by, one or the other community. In the Accadian-Assyrian myth and legend, as well as in their spells and incantations, references to the histories and powers of the gods have enabled commentators to compile a partial list showing their relationship with one another. These facts have produced some interesting conclusions.

The trinity formed by the Sky, Earth and Underworld are seen to have been fundamental in the Finnish and Chaldean systems as the elements to be propitiated and cultivated as sources of power. Samas (the Sun, and in some ways an aspect of the Earth) was connected with the Egyptian Ra. Even more interesting is the connection, in the Semitic and other systems, of the Accadian god Mulge. This spirit, very widely appealed to for magical purposes, is both the heart of Accadian sorcery and a central figure in several systems of the supernatural. As Bel, it was known as Baal in the Bible – and as Set in Egypt. To the Semitic Babylonians, Mulge was Belit, Lord (sometimes as the female Lady)[39] of the Underworld: the Finnish *Ilmarinen.* This was the ancient Semite god of love and war, the Phoenician Black Stone, the Al-Lat of Arabia, who married her own son, Saturn. She was worshipped and invoked as Ishtar, sometimes called the demon Astaroth, beloved of the sorcerers. Called by the Greeks Aphrodite, this god of many aliases was also known as Tiskhu or Tammuz: "Destroyer of Enemies, Attainer of Desires" – Venus to the Romans, who carried her cult as far as Britain, the bride of Adonis, the ancient god Duzi, and sister of none other than the Accadian Nanki-Gal, "Lady of Hades". Here we are at the very root of the demon-spirit-god system whence springs so much of oriental – and Western – magic as we know it today. For her titles "Destroyer... Attainer" are a perfect summary of the desires of magicians.

In addition to the gods, Babylonian magic took cognisance of a vast array of spirits, generally connected with the invisible world, and linking that world with mankind. That the gods and demons were closely allied is shown, for example, by the fact that the daughter of the Accadian Anu (God of the Sky) had a demon-daughter, Labartu, the Enemy of Children. All these elements, gods, spirits and planets, were linked in a system which gave birth to astrology, and probably to the Jewish Cabbala, the science of numerological philosophy which affected many other systems, including the Gnostics: all of which profoundly influenced Western magic.

The genii or spirits included the following, who have Semitic and other parallels: the ALU, destroyers, whose province was the chest of man; the EKIM, who worked in the bowels, and who had a Secret Number (so far undeciphered) of forty-sixtieths; the TELAL, or warriors, who were connected in some way with the hand, and whose mystical number is still unknown;[40] the *Maskim*, "Layers of Ambushes", with the fraction of fifty-sixtieths; the *Utuq*, formerly evil demons in general. In addition to this there were the ARDAT, or nightmares; the Succubus (Lilith, *Elit*), the *Uruku*, hobgoblins, giants, known as *lamma*. The latter were similar in some ways, it seems, to the good and bad genii of the Arabs. Many forms of genii were good or evil, according to how they were used. This form of thinking seems to continue from here into Western magic, with processes for the evocation of spirits, "which will do whatever you wish". The spectres, phantoms and vampires belong to the class of Labartu, daughter of the god Anu, the Sky.

CHAPTER 5

Egyptian Magic

"Get thee back, for thou art cut asunder, thy soul is shrivelled up, thy cursed name is buried in oblivion, and silence is upon it, and it hath fallen..."

—From the Ptolemaic Book of Overthrowing Apep.

THAT THERE WAS a connection between Jewish and Egyptian magical practices is abundantly proved by the many references to this fact in works of literature and religion. In addition to this testimony, we also know that the Semites – like the Greeks, Romans and others of the ancient world – were firmly convinced of the superiority of Egyptian magic over the thaumaturgy of other lands.

Moses, as we learn from the Bible and the Qur'an,[41] was one of Egypt's greatest foreign disciples in the practice of the Art. Like the Egyptians, he used a magical staff or wand; like them, he caused the waters to be divided. He even knew some of the mystic "words of power" of the Pharaonic priesthood.

When Moses fought his famous magical duel with the sorcerers of the Nile, magic was already a flourishing and integral part of Egyptian religion. Royalty, the priesthood and the people were bound inextricably by magic. Was it not the magician son of Rameses II himself who pitted his arts against Moses in 1300 BC?[42] Two hundred years earlier, the Westcar Papyrus tells us, a miracle identical with the reputed "parting of the waters" by Moses was performed by the Chief Priest of the day.

So flourishing was the practice of magic in the Egypt of about 3000 BC, that the very name of the land has passed into our language as a synonym for it. Just as the ancient Semitic word *imga* produced the English term Magic, so one of the oldest names for Egypt (*kemt* – dark, black) came to be translated Black, in place of Egyptian, Magic. Egypt, of course, was called "The Black" not because of the diabolism of its magic, but from the colour of its earth when flooded by Nile water.[43] A second term alchemy (Arabic *al-kimiyya*) also stems from this same name. In other words, both the phrases "Alchemy" and "Black Art" are to be traced to an original meaning of "Art of Egypt".

With the possible exception of the controversy about Atlantis, there surely has been no country about whose ancient history and occult activities so much has been written, from so many points of view. Garbled versions of rituals performed in the Valley of the Kings were taken back to the desert by Arabian bedouins, and embroidered upon until, all over the Near East, Egypt was implicitly believed to be peopled by a race of sorcerers. Throughout the Dark Ages this idea, stimulated by Biblical quotations and Semitic magicians, gained a firm grasp on men's minds. Even during the period of the scientific investigation of the Pyramids and other Pharaonic monuments, Western occultists have vied with one another to deduce mysteries from everything Egyptian. Naturally, this produced a reaction. A group of observers – many of them with perhaps less real knowledge than the empiricist school – denounced Egyptian magic as something which had no true reality. The only "magic" that the Egyptians had, they held, was their religion.

The amulet of the Soul

The truth, as usual, lies somewhere in between. We know that ancient Egyptian magic and religion were strongly bound up together. We know, too, for that matter, that most forms of magic have an affinity with religious systems. Papyri and tomb-inscriptions give us many indications that rites which are familiar to students of the occult were known, and even probably originated, in ancient Egypt. And this leaves unsaid the testimony of the vast volume of secondary sources – the Greek, Arabic and Hebrew records – which contain processes which very possibly include some of those practised by the priesthood of Isis.

Were the Egyptian priests miracle-workers? Did they in fact have knowledge which is still hidden to us? Those who want to believe these things will say yes. Those who take the Jewish, Christian and Muslim scriptures as true will unhesitatingly say that there is no doubt. Others will just have to examine the evidence and try to satisfy themselves.

Generally speaking, the religio-magical rites of these people were concerned with the maintenance of prosperity, and the security of the spirit in a future life. It is against the historical background of Egyptian life, therefore, that their rites are to be examined. Works involving power and success, like those of the destruction of an enemy, form a slightly different class. These latter were, it seems, originally part of the secrets held by the initiated priesthood as a sort of political magic. Naturally, it was one of the aims of royalty to ensure that the most powerful magic was of its own group. Later, however, as the finding of tens of thousands of scarabs and other amulets testifies, magic took on a popular aspect. This remains the position, though there are a few *official* royal magicians in practice.

It is necessary to have some idea of Egypt in order to attempt to put oneself in the place of its people. The climate and geography – which governed so many aspects of ancient Egyptian life – have altered little in the past five thousand years. Dominating all else is, of course, the Nile. That fact alone is one of the central thoughts in the religion of Egypt, as in its magic, art and literature. For all practical purposes the country consists of a long strip of cultivable land. For nearly twelve hundred miles this strip is bracketed by mountain chains. Beyond these there is little else than desert. In the centre flows the powerful current of the Nile itself, depositing the black earth on either bank: the earth which was to give magic one of its most familiar names.

Almost every vegetable product grown in this area figures in magical rites carried out in the Middle East even today. Date palms, acacia trees, the sycamores, wheat, barley and millet: these are thought to be among the most powerful items in a magician's storehouse.

The Nile rises every year between the first and the sixteenth of July, bringing new life to the land dried up by many months of fierce heat. Its rising in flood by September is the signal for a festival in Cairo: the Feast of the Nile:

"Peasants," says Gaston Maspero,[44] "laden with provisions come from afar and eat together... the priests leave their temples, and carry the statue of the [Nile] god... along the banks of the Nile to the sound of chants and music."

The priesthood of Isis – foremost magicians of Egypt – were specially important at these events. Part of the "chant to the Nile" is given in a papyrus roll in the British Museum:

"Hail to you Nile... who rises to the Earth to give life to Egypt... men dance for joy when thou risest from the unknown... side by side one sees the men of the Thebaid and those of the North... when the horn signals that the Nile is risen, we sing to thee with the harp and beating hands."

Interpreted in magical terms, the rising of the river symbolised the marriage of Osiris with Isis: Osiris the Nile, Isis the Earth – the black earth of the area.

Modern Egyptologists claim that the ritual magic practices of Egypt must date back to pre-Dynastic or even prehistoric times.[45] Legend states that Shem, son of Noah, came to Egypt at the age of three hundred years, one hundred and ninety years after the Flood, and ruled the country for another hundred and sixty-one years. During this time, magic flourished there. Jewish tradition has it, of course, that Noah himself was a magician and that certain secret books were specially revealed to him.

Seal of Rameses II [See p. 49]

Innumerable stories are told in Egyptian and Greek writings about Egyptian processes for reviving the dead. While it is known that the Egyptians believed that the body would resurrect in another world, yet there are also clear indications that some of their rites were designed to revive the corpse. It is, of course, claimed that this was done not once, but many times. What makes this account interesting is the fact that one of the Pharaohs most famed for his magical learning actually caused the experiment to be undertaken in his presence.

He was Herutataf, son of Cheops (Khufu), and lived nearly four thousand years before Christ.[46]

Khufu, it seems, was one day discussing miracles with his son. Herutataf said that stories were all very well, but there were few people who had seen such things done. He then promised to show his father a man who could in fact perform the miracle of revivification of those who were not only dead, but had actually been beheaded.[47]

This magician was Teta, reputed to be a hundred and ten years old. He was versed in secrets from the famed sanctuary of Thoth. Even today it is not clear what they were. An expedition was accordingly prepared: the Pharaoh's son travelled down the Nile by barge, then on by litter, until the party arrived at the abode of Teta.

The account is filled with minute circumstantial detail, which seems to show that it probably took place, and that the legend is not merely one of imagination. We are told, for instance, that the sage was lying on a woven bed (probably similar to the *angaribs* which are still in use). Servants were rubbing his head and feet. Then follows an account of the meeting between the crown prince and the magician, in which the King's invitation was given, and Teta agreed to visit the capital. Leaning on the prince's arm, the sage accompanied the youth to where the boat was moored. Here he asked that his children and books be also brought, and this was done.

When they arrived at the Palace, the King ordered Teta to enter at once. As soon as he had been presented, Khufu asked why they had not met before. To this the sage replied that he came when called, and not before. "You have called, and so I have come."

Then Khufu addressed the magician again: "Is it true, according to what is reported, that thou knowest how to fasten on again to its body the head which has been cut off?" The ancient replied that he could do this thing.

The King asked that some condemned criminal be brought, but on the magician's intervention a goose was substituted.

He cut off the head of the bird, and laid it on one side of the colonnade, with the body on the other side. Teta stood up, and intoned some "words of power". The head and body then began to move towards each other, until they met, rejoined, and the head cackled.

Following this feat, Teta did the same with another bird, of a different species, and again, he severed the head of an ox, and caused it to be joined to the body.

This story, taken at its face value, might be thought to show that, powerful as he was, the Pharaoh Cheops had no magician in his retinue capable of duplicating this feat. History shows, however, that even while the Pyramids of Giza were being built, the magical and political power of Memphis – then the seat of government – was waning.[48] Ideas cultivated in Thebes, farther up the Nile, took their place, and the Theban deity Amen-ra (Jupiter) became one of Egypt's principal gods. The power of Thebes lasted in all for three thousand years.[49]

The effects of Egyptian magic on Greece were profound. For example, Papyrus No. 75, of Reuvens, is a long roll, having a demotic text of twenty-two columns, each with over thirty lines. On the reverse is a Greek translation. Among the drawings are a sceptred deity with an ass's head and one of Anubis, standing by a mummy stretched upon a bier.

Leemans gives a translation of the Greek text, which is crammed with magical lore, derived from Egyptian sources. Their headings may be briefly noted. Magical ceremonies of great thaumaturgic power, by means of love; the receipt for a remedy by one named Hermerius; a formula for happiness and future fortune; a method of producing a dream – then two more for the same purpose. Next comes a rite by which the operator can consult a divinity. Those who are given to bouts of unbridled temper may find their salvation in yet another process. They continue, almost interminably: from the making of a ring which will bring success to every enterprise, to the Sphere of Democritus. Then there is a method of causing strife between man and wife. Finally a means whereby a person is robbed of sleep until he dies is illustrated by a drawing of an Egyptian god.

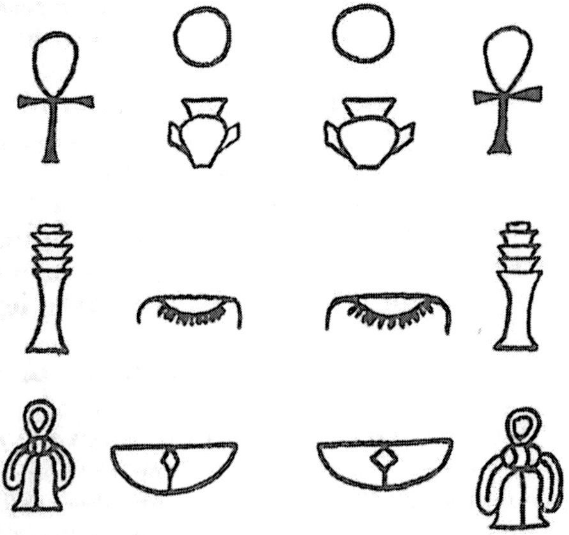

Magical design on the coffin of Priestess Ta-Ahuti (British Museum No. 24793)

It is thought that the author may have been one of the priesthood of Isis whom Porphyry criticises:

"How absurd a thing it is," he says, "that one subject to all the infirmities of humanity, should affect by threats to terrify not only demons or the spirits of the dead, but the Sun God himself, the Moon and other celestial beings. The magician lies in order to compel the heavenly bodies to tell the truth: for when he threatens to shake the heavens, or to reveal the mysteries of Isis, or the secret thing that lies hidden in Abydos, or to stop the sacred boat, or to scatter the limbs of Osiris to Typhon, what a height of madness does it not imply in the man who thus threatens what he neither understands nor is able to perform."[50]

And yet Chaeremon (first century AD), the sacerdotal scribe, mentions these things as having been high in the favour of the Egyptian priests, in their incantations.

We have it on good authority from Iamblichus that the Priests of Isis did in fact practise magic. He goes on to remark that the invocations of the priesthood to their gods did contain threats.

There is a strangely familiar ring about all this, to one who has studied the magical rituals of the West: especially those in the Jewish tradition. The following process, too, said to be ancient Egyptian in origin, will be familiar in tone to some readers:

"To be wrought by help of a boy, with a lamp, a bowl and a pit, I invoke thee, O Zeus! Helios, Mithra, Serapis, unconquerable, possessor of honey, father of honey.... Let the God whom I invoke come to me and let him not depart until I dismiss him...." Then the ritual proceeds "... fill a brazen cup with oil, and anoint your right eye with water taken from a boat that has been wrecked."

In spite of the many magical rituals recorded in such works as the *Book of the Dead* and other papyri, it seems probable that many which were used in ancient Egypt survive only as part of composite rites which have been handed down by Arab, Hebrew and other writers. One reason is that some of the miracles allegedly performed by Egyptian wizards are not catalogued among their own books of spells. It is likewise possible that many of the processes perished due to the Law of Transmission prohibiting their being confided to any but suitable adepts: and a limited number at that.

It was in the use of amulets that much of the religio-magical practice of the Egyptians excelled. Familiar to most people is the scarab: a model, often in clay or stone, of one of the types of beetle indigenous to Egypt. In addition to being a symbol of the Sun-god (hence of life), the scarab, when placed in a tomb, was believed to possess the power of bringing the dead to life again. All that was needed in addition to the scarab for recalling the life was a knowledge of the words of power, to say over the body.

This scarab-cult passed to Greece, whence we are given directions for charging the scarab with power before it is worn:

"Place the sculpted beetle, place it upon a paper table. Under the table there shall be a pure linen cloth. Under this place some olive wood, and set on the middle of the table a small censer wherein myrrh and kyphi shall be offered. And have at hand a small vessel of chrysolite into which ointment of lilies, or myrrh, or cinnamon, shall be put. And take the ring and place it in the ointment, having first made it clean and pure, and offer it up in the censer with kyphi and myrrh.

Anubis, God of the Dead

"Leave the ring for three days; then take it out, and put it in a safe place. At the celebration let there lie near at hand some pure loaves, and such fruits as are in season. Having made another sacrifice on vine sticks, during the sacrifice take the ring out of the ointment, and anoint thyself with the unction from it. Thou shalt anoint thyself early in the morning, and turning towards the east shall pronounce the words written below. The beetle shall be carved out of a precious emerald; bore it and pass a gold wire through it, and beneath the beetle carve the holy Isis, and having thus consecrated it, use it."

The spell in question was "I am Thoth, the inventor and founder of medicine and letters; come to me, thou that art under the earth, rise up to me, great spirit." It was further stated that only on certain days could the process take place: the 7th, 9th, 10th, 12th, 14th, 16th, 21st, 24th and 25th days, counting from the start of the month.

Two characteristics of ancient Egyptian magic which have descended to us in Western rituals sound the keynote of their spirit. Even in the days of Rameses II (over five thousand years ago) the belief in the mystic "Word of Power" was highly developed: just as magic itself was considered an art so ancient as to have no known source other than revelation by the gods. There is a strong possibility that some of these words – which were sometimes even then composed of unintelligible syllables – entered Egypt as a result of Mesopotamian conquests by various Pharaohs. Others, in all probability, were derived from Nubian magic, which still flourishes in Africa.

The second characteristic is associated with the above belief. In order to compel the spirits and gods to obey his will, whether for good or ill, the sorcerer had to be armed with Words of Power and a knowledge of the names of the gods. In this way he was able to take a dictatorial attitude towards deities, however powerful. There was no exception to the number and potency of the gods that could be "bound" or forced to act on the sorcerer's commands. In some cases, in fact, the magician actually identified himself so closely with the powers of the god invoked that he assumed his name, and issued commands on his behalf. Students of Medieval European magic will recognise this trait in some of the processes in the Western versions of the *Key of Solomon*, in which the operator communicates with the spirit not under his own name, but as Solomon himself.[51]

The "Words of Power", it may be assumed, are akin to the Semitic theory of the Most Great Name of God, which even initiates must not speak. It is thought that the Egyptians shared with other peoples the belief that a name – whether of a person or a god – was vitally connected with the powers, attributes and spiritual element of the named one. Is it entirely from modesty that women in many lands will not give their names to strangers? They are the "daughter of so-and-so", or "the wife of such-and-such a man". Anthropologists are familiar with tribal customs of wide currency, in which extraordinary precautions are taken to ensure that the real name of a person is not known outside his immediate family. In some cases, names are frequently changed. There is already a vast literature on this subject, and I cannot venture to add to it.

The magical word or name may not be understood by him who uses it, but it still possesses its original power. This belief may not have originated with the Egyptians: it certainly was current among them, as among later magicians in many lands.

In the Louvre there is a magical funerary papyrus dating as far back as Rameses II, in which barbarous words appear as names: "O Ualbpaga, O Kemmara! O Kamalo! O Aamagoaa! The Uana! The Remu!..."

Osiris *[See p. 53]*

Since similar words and phrases appear in most other ancient magical writings, it is probable that they meant no more to the priests than they do to us. Following up this line of research, and assuming that some Words of Power came from neighbouring lands, the Viscount de Rougé in the last century compiled a list of words – unfortunately unpublished – which seemed to show affinities with dialects spoken by the Nubians and others.

In the Harris magical papyrus there is a process by which the invocant, using certain names, actually takes on the shape of the god Amsu. There may be a clue here. It could be argued that the identification of the magician with a spirit or god in words and prayers might have been designed to cause him to become that god or spirit. At the least, he may have believed that he could "borrow" all the attributes and powers of the deity named, even for a short period. The ritual is designed to protect a man in a ship from any monster or hostile animal that might approach.

Taking a "hard egg" in one hand, the man says: "O Egg of the water which has been spread over the earth,[52] essence of the divine apes, the great one in the heavens above and in the earth beneath: who doth dwell in the nests which are in the waters, I have come forth from thee from the water, I have been with thee in thy nest, I am Amsu of Coptos, I am Amsu, Lord of Kebu."

Just as names contained magical powers in relation to the life on earth, so their potency was invoked in funeral ceremonies, and they were used in the imaginary encounters between the soul and the gods of the hereafter. No soul could hope to receive its just deserts and admission to the heavens until it had passed a very close examination, as is fully described in the *Book of the Dead*.

What of embalming, and the elaborately designed pyramids, both of which have been regarded as significant items in the magic of ancient Egypt? There is already a considerable literature in which such authorities as Flinders Petrie and Wallis Budge have fully described the embalming rites and their purpose. Briefly, the reason for preserving mortal remains is thought to be because contact, however incipient, remained to link the soul, ego (*ka*) and body after death. Lenormant states that there was an ultimate belief that the body would one day be resurrected in its former (though purified) form. It is, however, more widely held that the mummy was preserved as a hostel for the Ka. Again, the symbolic rites which were performed with the mummy – such as the "opening of the mouth" ceremony – seemed to be designed to reflect the events that were supposed to be happening to the soul in another world. It was, in fact, a sort of magical duplication of the soul's future life, on the familiar lines of sympathetic magic. There is a possibility, too, that a belief existed that certain organs in the body continued to function, in a different way from their normal role in life.

Books and pamphlets have been written in an attempt to prove that the pyramids represent symbolically both the *Book of the Dead* and the supposed Book of Thoth. There seems no doubt that the dimensions of some pyramids, and their internal arrangement and planning, are associated with mystical and magical concepts of dynastic religion. As to whether they are the key or not is a matter which is still open to discussion. Conventionally minded observers are, on the whole, inclined to regard the symbolism of the pyramids as natural projections from Egyptian belief and theology, rather than as signs placed there for any particular purpose other than to preserve the body from defilement. To take up any other attitude in the present state of knowledge of ancient Egyptian occult sciences would be tantamount to assuming that there was an intention by the Egyptian priest-magicians or their kings to transmit hidden knowledge to future generations. Since, however, there is no indication of a desire to make known their knowledge to others, let alone an inkling that the Pharaonic might would ever pass away, one might ask upon what premises such an assumption could be held.

In taking the stand outlined above, I exclude such supernatural "revelations" as were reported to me by one earnest occult student. He had had revealed to him in a dream – and partly through a spiritualist medium – that his "mission" was to go to Egypt, and camp in the shadow of the pyramids: when their occult power and intention would be made known to him. Being very wealthy at the time, and as keen as the next man for adventure, he did exactly as commanded. The only result was that the expenses involved were so great that he became impoverished. Equally unfortunately, no revelation resulted. When he returned to England, he found that his business had all but collapsed. It cannot, however, be denied that the experience had a very great effect upon him.

SINGING SANDS

In the El Meman chain, near the Red Sea, is the Jebel Narkous – Mountain of the Bell. Its rocks and pinnacles are so placed that when the wind blows from a certain direction, loud whispers are heard "proceeding from the rocks". This probably accounts for the ancient Egyptians being thought by less civilised Arabian tribes to have the power of raising the voices of oracles from the ground.

Many magicians claimed to be able to interpret the whispers: they were the voices of spirits, telling mankind what and what not to do. In any case, the effect on the visitor, even in this century, is eerie.

Similar tales are told of the Egyptian priests taking oracles from the Singing Sands. These sands still "sing", and probably there was at one time a regular system of interpreting the sounds. In this idea we may have a clue as to the source of some Dynastic Egyptian magical beliefs having come originally from across the Red Sea: just as we know that certain rites were derived from inner Africa. Desert people have many superstitions in connection with singing sands, which may be as old as the Egyptian ones. If, for instance, you hear them before the new moon, the signs are good for the tribe: if after, evil. Others are that such-and-such a journey is to be taken: and this being the case, further enquiries must be made of the sands as to the times and places to be visited.

I was told in Egypt just after the war, by a large variety of people, that a Libyan dervish had foretold war in 1937, and that he had warned the Senussi to prepare for the Western Desert campaigns. They would lead, he had said, to certain liberation from the Italian yoke. All this – and much else – he had heard from the Singing Sands.

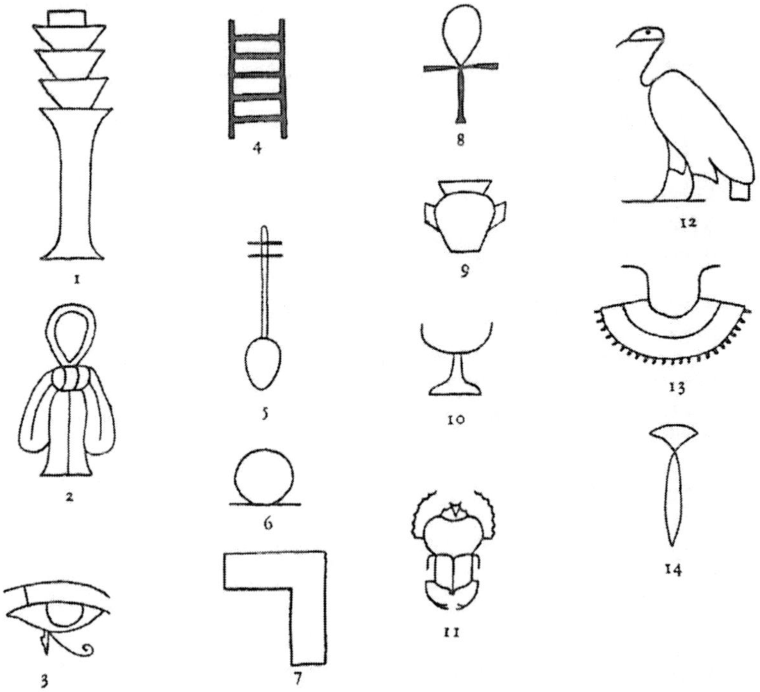

Egyptian amulets

(1) *The Tet*
(2) *The Buckle*
(3) *The Eye of Horus*
(4) *The Ladder*
(5) *Amulet of Nefer*
(6) *Amulet of the Shen*
(7) *Amulet of Safety*
(8) *Amulet of Life*
(9) *Amulet of the Heart*
(10) *Amulet of the Pillow*
(11) *Amulet of the Scarab*
(12) *Amulet of the Vulture*
(13) *The Collar of Gold*
(14) *The Papyrus Sceptre*

Near the *Kom el Hettam*, the mound of sandstone, which marks the site of the once-famous palaces and temples of Amunoph III, are two sitting Colossi. One is heard apparently to chant at sunrise. Others say that this is more like the sound of a breaking harp-string. Many explanations are, of course, given for this strange sound: that the Colossus was raised by Memnon, who had wonderful powers. He cured the sick miraculously, raised the dead, and daily at sunrise the winds made sure that certain words were repeated by his Colossus, giving the Salámát (greetings). I was even told that when Memnon and certain of his High Priests return to Egypt they will first come to converse with this Voice....

As opposed to this decorative and romantic story, the late Sir Gardiner Wilkinson explained that he had discovered a stone on the lap of the Colossus in question. Anxious to make some sort of test for himself, he ascended the figure and struck the stone with a small hammer. This sounded like brass being hit. Sir Gardiner therefore states that only the striking of the stone causes the statue to appear to speak.

Similar metallic noises may be obtained by striking parts of the high rocks at Tunbridge Wells, especially the Bell Rock. These phenomena, known in many lands, are most probably caused by purely natural factors, or else are contrivances arranged by former peoples as a supplement to magical rites. It is not usually thought likely that there is any direct extra-physical explanation.

At the same time their value as portents has often been shown. The story is told that where Napoleon cut the road between Savoy and France, about two miles from Les Sechelles, there is a gallery in a tunnel twenty-seven feet square and 975 feet in length. When the excavations for this were nearly complete and the tunnellers met in the middle, the intervening few inches were broken with a pickaxe. A sound like a great groan was heard. When this was reported to Napoleon his face went white: because he had been told by a magician that if such a sound were heard by or near him, the future would hold only defeat.

There is, of course, a scientific explanation for this happening. But the occultist would claim that the origin of a phenomenon need not be supernatural to make it valid as a sign. However, when a certain Mr Bakewell investigated the Napoleon Tunnel story he put the whole thing down to a difference in the temperature at either end of the tunnel.

Particular attention was paid by Egyptian magicians to the times and dates considered most suited to the carrying out of occult operations. This table gives the lucky and unlucky days, according to the ritual calendar of ancient Egypt. Days are marked in thirds; "L" means that the period indicated is fortunate, "U" stands for hours not under beneficent influences.

The Month of Thoth, starting on August 29th (1st Thoth is August 29th)

Day	*First third*	*Second third*	*Third third*	*Corresponding to:*	
1st	L	L	L	August	29
2nd	L	L	L	"	30
3rd	U	U	U	"	31
4th	U	U	U	September	1
5th	L	L	L	"	2
6th	U	U	L	"	3
7th	L	L	U	"	4
8th	L	L	U	"	5
9th	L	L	L	"	6
10th	L	L	L	"	7
11th	U	U	U	"	8
12th	U	U	U	"	9
13th	L	L	UU 53	"	10

Day	*First third*	*Second third*	*Third third*	*Corresponding to:*	
14th	L	U	U	September	11
15th	L	U	U	”	12
16th	U	U	U	”	13
17th	L	L	L	”	14
18th	L	L	L	”	15
19th	L	L	L	”	16
20th	U	U	U54	”	17
21st	L	L	U	”	18
22nd	U	U	U	”	19
23rd	U	U	U	”	20
24th	L	L	L	”	21
25th	L	L	L	”	22
26th	U	U	U	”	23
27th	L	L	L	”	24
28th	L	L	L	”	25
29th	L	L	L	”	26
30th	L	L	L	”	27

CHAPTER 6

Ju-Ju Land of the Twin Niles

"Mungo comes into him, and he is made..."

In the Sudan – that sprawling territory between Egypt and Ethiopia one-third the size of Europe – magic, black and white, still thrives.

It took me over a year to disentangle and assess the three main kinds of sorcery and witchcraft in this strange yet fascinating area. To the north, where the Haifa Cataract spills Nile water into Lower Egypt, temples and monuments tell a story of ancient Pharaonic ways still reflected in the habits of the local tribes. To the west, among the towering Nuba mountains, rainmaking and the black art, gum-picking and ju-ju go hand in hand.

To the far south, in the literally steaming Equatorial belt beyond the administrative centre of Juba, naked Nilotic people still adorn themselves with the sacred creeper, wreak revenge through magic, and have constant recourse to local oracles.

The main obstacle to piecing together confusing rituals was more than local reticence. This was not the first time a stranger had visited Nubia, seeking the lore of the magicians: nor would it be the last. In the more frequented places, therefore, there was a continual stream of warriors or their ladies, bringing reputed spells, or offering to conduct me to some sacred tree. Some of them claimed that the processes of liberating power hidden away in a miracle-working plant could be mine for a small present. For spears, money or razor blades a thousand spurious "spells" could be purchased daily from well-meaning, misguided or downright dishonest locals.

This was something to avoid. For, in Khartoum and Omdurman, twin capitals of the Nile's junction, travellers regularly bought "secrets" from the natives. A flourishing market in spells exists and thrives: so rampant, indeed, was this practice that I had to take an interpreter with me to some areas to explain my intention.

I told the Nuba chiefs that I was a different kind of traveller. My work, I said, was writing books, so that those who came after would read the history and customs of their people: and here – perhaps surprisingly – I found a ready audience. The reason was probably due less to my persuasive powers than to the fact that the elders of many Sudan tribes nowadays do feel the draw to the cities deeply affecting their young men. When they return, tribal youths only too often seem to have lost interest in local ways: to have grown apart from their own kin. Their new-found sophistication often makes them despise even those noble traits that Westerners themselves and others see in African society.

After I had mastered the technique of explaining these points I found Nubas and Shilluks, Nyam-Nyams and Hadendoas – whether from Arabised or Equatorial territory – generally anxious to explain their ways.

In the southern belt, there is no doubt that magic is something in the nature of an organised belief. Having their own temples, rites, secret societies, orders and degrees, the medicine-men seem to possess a spell for every occasion and for any human emotion.

Among the Nyam-Nyams – whose territory is cut by French and Belgian administered areas – some of the practitioners hold their rank hereditarily. Yet in many cases young candidates present themselves for admission into a magic circle: after which they are entitled to consider themselves as fully fledged sorcerers, and to practise on their own account.

Fine, upright, hardy men, the negroid inhabitants of the far south present something of an enigma, at least so far as their mental make-up is concerned. You will find them very adaptable to modern things: they drive motor-cars, learn English, adopt Christianity. Yet in the tribal areas even the most modernised native will show such a mixture of Western and African ways, that one sometimes cannot be sure of where his feelings lie.

One thing, however, was plain: most of the people still believe in their own form of Magic.

When the aspiring student presents himself to a witch-doctor for training, he is always questioned closely as to his motives. If the answers satisfy the master – or the magic council, as the case may be – he will be accepted upon payment of a regular fee. This payment is considered to be most important: not only because of the money involved, which is usually small (equal to a penny or so), but because of the first principle of *Nagua*, or wonder-working.

The reason given is that the "presiding genie" of Nagua – from whom all power is derived – demands a sacrifice of money, razor blades, or other small gift. This is oddly reminiscent of the more Western tradition of medieval magical ritual, in which regular sacrifices – or their equivalent – were made by the invocant. Similarly, when the witch-doctor (the *Irrah*) casts a spell for a client or exercises his powers in any way, he demands a coin: much in the same way as a gypsy asks for her palm to be crossed with silver before her power will work.

I found few witch-doctors reluctant to teach their lore to an outsider, once they were convinced that I myself did not intend to use magic in their land. Several stipulated that I should not practise the "art" within a hundred days' journey – to which I readily agreed. So seriously was the matter treated, even when I had been taught spells, that it seems difficult to believe that the practitioners themselves can disbelieve in magic.

The initiation starts with the master taking his pupil to a stream and making him bathe therein.[55] Together they enter a cave or retire under an overhanging bank, to assist the magic's spirit to enter their hearts. This points to some traditional association with a water-deity, now probably forgotten. When I asked the reason for it, they did not know, but all insisted that it was essential.

Next a flower resembling the common English primrose is picked and presented to the neophyte. After teaching him a number of simple spells, the tutor takes his student to a magicians' conference, there to watch the rituals of the art.

Typical of the spells is this one, for victory: "I am a Magician, all-powerful in spells. What I say comes true. I say, 'Give victory to so-and-so. He will have victory in all things.'" Then the magician goes on to detail the kind of success desired, with many an embellishment of the prowess soon to be infused into the lucky warrior or huntsman.

This was repeated seven times, the magician squatting on the bare earth. Before him stood the inevitable water-filled pot; in his hand the sacred whistle.

"When you say this," said the *Irrah* in explanation of the spell, "have a wooden whistle in your mouth: then blow it three times towards the points of the compass."

All spells are regarded as more potent when said over running water. The sound of my home-made shower-bath at once gave rise to the conviction that I was practising my "magic".

One of my informants, seized with the desire to make another man fear him, took me on a plant-collecting expedition. Four different kinds of leaf were found: to these he added a handful of ground nuts. This was boiled, with fat and two small barkless twigs, in a pot over a wood fire. As soon as the concoction boiled, he muttered constantly under his breath: "These are herbs, they have power: the nuts shall frighten my enemy. By the power of *Nagua*, the sticks are strong, they will beat the nuts; the water boils, boils like my rage. My rage upon the nuts, upon my enemy."

He informed me two days later that his enemy had come to apologise, and to ask for the spell to be removed. "And how did you remove it?" I asked. "By smearing the herbs, which I had buried, upon the footpath, of course," was the reply. "Otherwise he would have rapidly become worse than frightened, for my rage was great. Now he has even agreed to hunt for me, and to help me with the land."

Among this magic-ridden people, love charms are in great demand. One magician, offering to show me how to make one, asked whether they were in great demand in my country. The best I could reply was that they had been at one time. "If I went there, could I help the people with them?" came the query.

I shuddered at the thought of this practitioner – however charming on his home ground – with gazelle-horn cup, creeper skirt and string of bones in a Western metropolis.

He was making it in any case, and invited me to watch, with all the courtesy of one professional entertaining another. This was going to be an elaborate procedure: first the circle was drawn in a clearing, then the usual pot suspended from three sticks was boiled. Powdered peanuts, charcoal and sand were thrown in. Meanwhile the witch-doctor circumambulated the stew, carefully keeping within the protective circle, never taking his eyes off the mixture. After circling the pot about ten times, he threw twelve chicken feathers upon the bubbling surface, one at a time. About half a pint of oil completed the recipe. Taking up a small skin-covered drum, he beat it softly, alternately with the right and left hand. Then came the spell itself. "I am a magician, O pot, you contain the medicines of love, the spell of love, of passion. My heart throbs like the drum, my blood boils like the water." This he repeated thrice: then, gazing fixedly at the concoction, he intoned: "Bring my desire to me, my name is so-and-so, and my desire is one whom I love."

He assured me with the utmost solemnity that this spell, if repeated thrice on successive nights, would "bind" the beloved to him. And this was not all. "If the water is boiled until there is none left, and you carry two pinches of the residue wrapped in a leaf, it will attract the opposite sex every time you bring it out and lay it before you."

I asked him if this would not cause too widespread an effect. "No," he replied, "for they are not attracted until the spell is made complete by your looking at them, clenching both fists and putting them together, looking away and closing your eyes four times slowly. Each time you do it," he continued, "it becomes more effective."

But these spells are seldom practised by the laymen. For one thing, they are not told the full spell; secondly, a fairly long training is necessary before they will work. Aspirants to the respected rank of magician persevere in the observance of tabus and diet for at least forty to sixty days before casting a spell.

No magic-worker during the period of his study may look upon a member of the opposite sex for more than a few seconds – except after about seven in the evening. He eats certain things believed to bestow magical powers: especially green leaf vegetables, peanut paste and, sometimes, small birds. He wears a straw hat at night and sometimes two silver ornaments, such as pierced coins – Egyptian half-piastre pieces.

With these badges on the right side of the head or body, he enters a building or crosses paths with one long and one short step. During all this time, he devotes half an hour after sundown to softly beating a small drum. Just before sunset he spends at least five minutes gazing at the sky. In company he closes his eyes and bites his lower lip frequently. He is expected to talk little, except to those whom he sees acting in the same way.

Women do not practise magic as much as men. This, according to tribal belief, is not because they are any the less adept, but men are reluctant to teach them: there is a deeply ingrained fear of increasing power among women threatening to oust man from his paramount position.

The three cords – two red and one white – often worn by male witch-doctors cannot safely be worn by women, for fear of being detected as witches. Formerly, I was told, many women sported this insignia, which is believed to be a most powerful charm. The increase in power of their menfolk, and the measures taken by European governments against sorcery, have driven many of these customs out of currency.

Curiously enough, though reputed to possess by virtue of their secrets the ability to destroy life, the present activities of the Central African Ju-Ju men – so far as I could ascertain – seem mainly devoted to "White Magic". Most magicians hold that *all* death is due to magic being exercised against the deceased, from somewhere or other: yet few of them are ever notorious as death-dealers.

One of the greatest known methods of gaining magical power, say the southerners, is the "fish tabu". The intending magician asks for a fish to be placed before him by his wife, a relative or someone else in that order of preference. He then blinks his eyes three times slowly, "as though there is dust in them", frowns, and orders the fish to be taken away. Or he may merely touch it and leave the whole thing untasted. The reason given is that "the spirits preventing me from becoming a magician are attracted by fish, hide in it to get inside of me when I eat it – and are taken away when I refuse it".

The origins of these customs undoubtedly could be traced further back into history; though this would mean a great deal of research into tribal history and customs far beyond the scope of any one man, and through many territories of Central Africa.

Anyone can become a magician, they believe, but certain individuals are held to be better fitted for the task. The ideal sorcerer was described to me as of average height, fair rather than dark (possibly because some of their magic comes from the fairer-skinned Coptic Abyssinians), and between thirty and fifty or twenty-two to twenty-six years of age. People with red and full lips are also preferred.

I am convinced that there is often an element of auto-hypnosis in these magical arts. Sitting with his eyes unwinkingly fixed upon the surface of a pot of water, the operator's gaze nearly always seems to become vacant, as though in a trance. Then, while muttering spells repeatedly to the throb of the drum, and walking around and swinging his body from side to side, there is an atmosphere of vacancy and yet persistence very compatible with the hypnoidal state.

Much of Ethiopian occult lore has seeped through to the riverine southerners. One old man described to me the appearance and qualifications for a "born magician" which approximates closely with certain legends of that country.

The occultist, he said, may or may not know that he has the power. In either case he is to be sought and watched, for he is successful in life, and with very little effort can become a great magician. You will always meet him as a stranger, runs the legend; he is never a member of your own tribe, nor of your family – for in this case his magic would be of no use to you. He (or she) is of the opposite sex: tall, thin, young-seeming, the eyebrows being strongly marked, and "with a fixed gaze".

When one sees this man, he must be approached or spoken to on some pretext "and great advantage will come of it". There seems here to be some blending of that strange, legendary figure of the Middle East and Central Asia: Khidhr, Ilyas, or Enoch as he is sometimes called.

The typical magician seldom wears much more than a loincloth when carrying out his duties. Considered necessary, however, for daily use is a brimmed straw hat, with arrows drawn on the front.

He walks over a grave in order to gain magical power, carries pierced horns to make the magic circle, and perseveres in his dieting and concentration until – one day – "Mungo" comes into him, and he is made. This is the training and effort that it takes to make a good medicine-man in Africa.

Now *Mungo* is a sort of ectoplasm, believed to appear somewhere inside the witch, as soon as the magic has matured inside him. Its possession is known to nobody except himself.[56] It seems that this knowledge is thought to come intuitively – accompanied by a "feeling of no more fear, a lightness".

To sum up, one day after his diet and his drumming, his sky-gazing and blinking, having observed all the rites, the aspirant becomes aware that he is "ready for action". These basic ideas permeate Nilotic witchcraft among the Nyam-Nyams, Shilluks and others of Central Africa.

By contrast the magical operations of the Nubas of Kordofan – in the Sudan's far west – and the people whose homes border upon Egypt, adhere more closely to the ancient Egyptian forms in their occult arts.

In Kordofan, both men and girls perform ritual dances whose purpose may be described as magical. Like the Southerners, white powder or bone-ash is sometimes used to smear over the body.

In Taloda, shaven heads and horse-tail switches play an important part in ritual dancing, which is here performed communally by groups of tribesmen.

While hidden beliefs dating from dynastic times still lurk – particularly among the Copts – in modern Egypt itself, it is in the border areas of the Northern Sudan that the lingering superstitions and practices of four thousand years ago may be found.

No man or woman can be seen without the traditional charm – a *Hijab* – for strength, or against the Evil Eye.

Mummy dust is greatly prized: the crumbling temples, such as that of Semna near the rushing Nile, are supposed to have been the seat of miraculous cures. Spells used by the nomad tribes seem to be phrased in a tongue which may be that of the Pharaohs. There is no doubt that they themselves attribute the reputed efficacy of their magic to Pharaonic origins.

In the area of the former goldmines once worked by ancient Egyptians, Romans, Greeks and Arabs, many a tale is told of those among the Hadendoa – Fuzzy-Wuzzies – who are reputed to have learned the dark arts through a prolonged sojourn among myriads of bats nesting in abandoned mine-workings.[57]

Much remains to be studied before an effective assessment of African magic can be made: until then, notes such as these are all that can be offered. Does Central African magic work any wonders? Or does it perform any useful social function? I can give no better reply than that of a French officer of thirty years' Equatorial experience: "What can I say, monsieur? When one has lived with a thing, seen it every day for a lifetime, its demands provoke acceptance of much we cannot bring ourselves to believe in the West."

Vast controversies have raged over the supposed possession of special and psychic powers by the Africans. To study them in more detail would involve collecting and sifting large quantities of material which are not strictly relevant to the main purpose of this book. In the chapter on ancient Egyptian magic, we have noted that there are indications that the southern countries of the Nile have played a part in the transmission of magical arts westwards. From this point it is but a step to link up with hundreds of occult rites which are in use or were formerly practised by other native African peoples.[58] The most that we can do, however, in the present book is to note outstanding characteristics among the magic of African populations even farther southward than the Sudanese.

The peoples loosely known as Kafirs (from the Arabic *Káfir*, "infidel") possess a rich store of knowledge and belief in things occult. Like other magical systems, they possess rites for divination, diagnosis and cure of disease, and communication with spirits. Add to this their belief in amulets and talismans, plus the practice of thaumaturgy, and you have a picture of the supposed powers of shamans, medicine-men, witch-doctors – call them what you will – everywhere.

A man's picture, effigy or even shadow can be "worked upon" by magic, say the Kafirs, in common with the Japanese, British witches, Chaldeans or Egyptians. Illness, as in the case of primitive (and even later) Semitic ideas, can be transferred to animals: scapegoats, too, are offered as sacrifices. Wizards, like Teta and others, can revive the dead, even from their graves. Wealth can come to a man through magic – but the snag here is that a man suspected of getting rich quick through supernatural means may find himself on trial, like the witches of Spain or England in former times. His trial, like theirs, will involve ordeal by fire or water: even, as with the ancient Greeks, by poison. As the medieval witches were supposed to covet human babies for their dark art, so do Kafir sorcerers the same. All these resemblances, and many more, are there for the culling.

While it would be difficult to establish whether these and other practices originated in Africa, or spread there from other continents, nevertheless I think that the interesting facts are these: (i) that here we may have rites which still linger, though they have died out elsewhere; (ii) they seem too widespread and similar to other countries' magic to have been developed independently, and to have grown up in a manner parallel to their appearance in other lands. Witch-doctors wear special regalia. They make brews closely resembling those of Oriental and Western magic. They divine by bones, the Amazulu crystal-gaze, exorcism and other demon-expelling processes are common. Is it likely that all these facts are mere coincidence? If they are, it is remarkable enough. If they are not, they are more than deserving of closer attention. And this attention would be rewarding, no matter whether you approach the subject from the viewpoint of occultist, sceptic, scientist or mystic. But that would have to be the subject of a further book.

CHAPTER 7

The Fakirs and their Doctrines

"The Perfect Man gains his power through developing the mystic force inherent in the body. This is centred in the Five Secret Organs: the Lataif. These are: the Heart Centre, the Spirit Centre, the Secret Centre, the Hidden Centre, the Most Mysterious Centre..."

—*Sheikh Ahmed El-Abbassi:* Secrets of Sufi Power, *a development of Shah Muhammad Gwath's* Secrets of the Mystic Way *(Asrar-ut-Tariqat, of the Naqshbandiyya Order)*

THE WEST, WHICH prides itself with some justification upon having rescued from oblivion many aspects of oriental culture and learning, has been profoundly influenced by *Tasawwuf*: the doctrine of the Fakirs.[59] Yet how many people, apart from a handful of orientalists, can say what this is?

Yoga, Shinto, Buddhism, Taoism and Confucianism, all have their devotees in Europe and America. Yet Sufism – the ultimate mystical sanction of the Arabs, Persians, Turks and the rest of the Muslim World – remains the last closed book of the mysterious East.

Is Sufism a religion? An occult cult? A way of life? It is, in part, all of these things – and none of them. Among the four hundred million followers of Islam, Tasawwuf commands a power such as no political, social or economic creed does here or elsewhere.

Organised in a semi-monastic, semi-military fashion, this amazing philosophy was shared by elements as diverse as the ancient Arab alchemists – the Brethren of Purity – the Mahdist warriors of the Sudan and the greatest classical poets of Persia. Under the banner of the Fakirs (literally "the humble ones"), the Turkish Empire's dervishes stormed Vienna. Urged on by Sufi mystical poetry (and, it is claimed, supernatural power) the Afghans conquered India.

Then, on the other side of the coin, Sufi literature and culture were responsible for some of the outstanding architecture and art of Asia.

What are the origins of this strange cult, which even modern researchers acknowledge to be still the strongest single force in the Middle East today? In spite of the fact that a considerable literature on the subject exists in oriental languages, nothing is known with complete certainty as to the very beginnings of the cult.

Sufi historians trace their foundation to Muhammad himself, but it has been stated that this esoteric cult stems from man's earliest strivings to liberate his ego from material things.[60] This, in fact, is the main aim of the movement. Sufism is a distinct and very complete way of life, setting as its goal the realisation of man's (and woman's) believed role in life.

Man, argue the Sufi saints, is part of the Eternal Whole, from which everything is derived, and to which all must return. His mission is in preparing himself for that return. This can only be achieved through purification. When the human soul is correctly harnessed to the body, and has obtained complete control over it, then man appears in his perfect form: the Perfect Man, in fact, emerges as closely resembling the superman, possessed of amazing powers, who figures in the aspirations of Eastern and Western occultism alike.

There are distinct steps by which a "seeker" progresses towards this end. Organised in Orders resembling the monastic orders of the Middle Ages (alleged by some to have been modelled on Sufism), the first condition of enrolment is that the recruit must be "in the world but not of it". This is the first important respect in which the cult differs from almost every other mystical philosophy. For it is fundamental that every Sufi must devote his life to some useful occupation. His aim being to become an ideal member of society, it naturally follows that he cannot cut himself off from the world. In the words of one authority:[61]

> Man is destined to live a social life. His part is to be with other men. In serving Sufism he is serving the Infinite, serving himself, and serving society. He cannot cut himself off from any one of these obligations and become or remain a Sufi. The only discipline worth while is that which is achieved in the midst of temptation. A man who, like the anchorite, abandons the world and cuts himself off from temptations and distractions cannot achieve power. For power is that which is won through being wrested from the midst of weakness and uncertainty. The ascetic living a wholly monastic life is deluding himself!

Though the word "Fakir" has come to be used in the West as denoting a kind of itinerant juggler or wonder-worker, its real meaning is merely "a humble man". Humility of the Seeker is the first requirement. He must renounce his struggle for mere worldly aims until he gets the reason for life into the correct perspective. This is not, in fact, contradictory. For a man may legitimately enjoy the things of the world, provided that he has learnt humility in their application.

What has given Sufis – in their role of fakirs or dervishes – that halo of invulnerability, infallibility and superiority is the application of this doctrine. There is no doubt at all that the concentration of mind achieved by Sufis is responsible for what could be classed as truly supernatural manifestations. There are instances, recorded with as much historical accuracy as one may expect anywhere, of the strange power of some of these men. Approaching the question in as scientific a manner as possible, many are the instances of bogus Sufis merely playing upon the gullibility of the masses. On the other hand, tens of thousands of unbiased people are convinced of the fact that Tasawwuf can bring power of an unheard-of degree to some of its practitioners.

It is necessary to point out here, as in other parts of this book, that such manifestations may, if true, merely be the application of secrets of nature which are as yet imperfectly understood by orthodox science.

What are the miracles and powers attributed to the Sufi saints? While there is almost no thaumaturgic phenomenon which has not been claimed by some authority as performed by dervishes, some[62] miracles are more characteristic of the cult than others. The first one (in conformity with the belief that time is non-existent) is the annihilation of conventional time. Stories – some of them on the authority of meticulously accurate historians – covering this phenomenon are many and varied.

Perhaps the most famous is the case of the Sheikh Shahab-el-Din. He was able to induce, it is said, the appearance of fruits, people and objects absolutely at will. It is related of him that he once asked the Sultan of Egypt to place his head in a vessel of water. Instantly the Sultan found himself transformed into a shipwrecked mariner, cast ashore in some totally unknown land.

He was rescued by woodmen, entered the nearest town (vowing vengeance against the Sheikh whose magic had placed him in this plight) and started work there as a slave. After a number of years he gained his freedom, started a business, married and settled down. Eventually, becoming impoverished again, he became a freelance porter, in an attempt to support his wife and seven children.

One day, chancing to be by the seashore again, he dived into the water for a bathe.

Immediately he found himself back in the palace at Cairo, again the King, surrounded by courtiers, with the grave-faced Sheikh before him. The whole experience, though it had seemed like years, had taken only a few seconds.

This application of the doctrine that "time has no meaning to the Sufi" is reflected in a famous instance of the life of Muhammad. It is related that the Prophet, when setting out on his miraculous "Night Journey", was taken by the angel Gabriel to Heaven, to Hell and to Jerusalem. After four score and ten conferences with God, he returned to earth: just in time to catch a pot of water that had been overturned when the angel took him away.

In addition to the non-existence of time, space plays little part in preventing the Sufi adept from travelling where he will. Transportation of many of the most famous Sufi teachers is said to have been a common event. Sufis have been seen at the same time in places many thousands of miles apart. Sheikh Abdul-Qadir Gelani – one of the most celebrated saints of Sufism – was believed to have travelled thousands of miles "in a flash", in order to be present at the funeral of some fellow adept.

Walking upon the surface of water, and flying enormous distances in the full view of people on the ground, are other wonders said to be regularly performed by the initiates.

Miracles, as such, are thought to be possible only to prophets. But wonders (*karámát*) are held to be possible to a great number of Sufis. The activities of magicians – which are generally a form of deception worked upon gullible people – are classed as *Istidraaj*, signifying mere conjuring tricks and works of stealth. Magic proper, by which is meant thaumaturgy through the aid of spirits, is an entirely different branch of occult science.[63]

ORGANISATION OF THE ORDERS

Mystical Orders of this type lay down rigid rules in a set pattern for aspirants to Sufi power. Apart from those who pursue the cult alone, all new recruits must be accepted according to a formula by a *Pir*, or teacher. Sons follow in their fathers' footsteps in entering the Order to which their parent belonged; and only those who have been recommended by certain sponsors may be accepted as disciples into the first degree of "Salik": Seeker.

Orders, which are named after their founder (Naqshbandíyya, Chishtíyya, Qádriyya, etc.) are organised in groups studying under acknowledged masters. Promotion from one degree to the next is through a patent or declaration by the master of the group to which the acolyte belongs. In order to study a particular branch of the art, students may travel from Morocco to Java, or from as far afield as China to Libya, to join the *Halka* (circle) of a celebrated teacher. Then, if the latter agrees, the candidate will be placed on probation for some months. Living a life of poverty, dressed perhaps in saffron robes and performing menial tasks, the seeker during the period of his studies must remain attached to his master with a devotion which far exceeds even the most rigorous discipline of any military force.

He must take part in the ritual recitations of certain holy and secret scripts, must observe the Five Ritual Prayers and ablutions, the annual month of fasting from dawn to sunset, and read the works of the masters.

THE ORDERS

Several distinct Orders or *Tariqas* ("Pathways") of Sufism are known. All trace their origins to Muhammad himself, and also to his companions. It has been asserted that they originated in a mystical fraternity among the Prophet's immediate followers – the *Ashǻb-Us-Safá*, or Companions of the Bench. These men, about whom very little is definitely known, immersed themselves in good works, contemplation, fasting and prayer. Even the derivation of their name is shrouded in mystery.[64] The widest held theories, however, state that they are either named after their woollen robes (*Souf*, wool, in Arabic), or from "*Safá*", purity.

The main orders today are the Naqshbandíyya, Chishtíyya, Qádriyya and Suharwardíyya. Each is self-contained in itself; none is inimical to the others: saints and practices are sometimes held in common; the objectives of mankind, and particularly of the Sufis, are almost identical in each.

There are a number of other Orders, scattered from Morocco to Java, through India, Afghanistan – anywhere, in fact, that Islam has spread. In all cases, rites and writings are highly symbolistic.

In every case admission to an Order depends upon sponsorship and initiation.

Sufis traditionally hold an important, if undefined, place in both society and history. The Dervishes of the Sudan were – and still are – a Sufi Order, organised as a militant and nowadays philanthropic entity. In the days of the Ottoman Empire, the greatly feared Jannissary[‡] shock-troops were a military Sufi fraternity, connected with what are today known as the Naqshbandíyya. The present King of Libya, Sayed Idris, is the Chief of a Sufi order, and most, if not all, of his subjects consider themselves Sufis. The Fakir of Ipi – that "Firebrand of the North-West Frontier of India" – is a Sufi leader. These brief facts may tend to give the impression that there is much militarism in the different Orders: perhaps the explanation may be that other aspects of the cult are less well known in the West; reference to them out of context would serve only to confuse the reader.

OBJECTS OF SUFISM

The theory of Sufism is that man, in his ordinary state as part-animal, part-spirit, is incomplete. All Sufi doctrine and ritual is dedicated towards making the Seeker (*Sálik*) pure, and therefore *Insán-i-Kámil* – a Perfect Man, or Complete Man. It is envisaged that a person may be able to achieve this state of Completeness by himself, or even through means other than Sufism. Yet it is contended that Sufism is the established way, with its prescribed method and the guidance of the Masters who have already trod the Path.

‡ From Persian *Ján-nisar*, "Life-scatterer".

When the aspirant has attained the state of completeness which is the goal of the cult, he is then in tune with the Infinite; and those strivings and uncertainties to which he, as a mere imperfect mortal, has been subjected, are no more. This ultimate stage of achievement is known as *Wasl*, "Union".

The monastic life, however, is strongly eschewed by all Sufi thinkers. They reason that if a man deprives society of his service and activity, he is being anti-social. Being anti-social is against the Divine Plan. Hence he must, in the words of the First Principle of Sufism, "Be *in* the world but not *of* the world!"[§]

The hierarchy of Muslim Sufi saints, therefore, are known by their occupations as well as by their titles. Hence, one (Attar) was a chemist; another (Hadrat Baháuddin Naqshband) was a painter, and so on. Certain kings of India and Persia, upon becoming Sufis, took up some extra occupation to pay for their own upkeep, while still remaining rulers and taking nothing from the treasury on their own account.

THE INVISIBLE RULERSHIP OF SUFISM

Chief of the entire Sufi system is the *Qutub*: he is the most enlightened of all Sufis, has attained the degree of *Wasl* (Union with the Infinite) and holds power over, according to some, the entire Sufi organism. Others say that the Qutub has considerable political or temporal power as well. In any case, his identity is known to very few. He maintains communication only with the Leaders of the Orders.

Conferences are held telepathically, or else by means of "time and space annihilation". The latter phenomenon is said

§ "*Dar Dunya Básh: Az Dunya Mabásh!*"

to mean that Sufis of the degree of Wasl are able to transport themselves anywhere instantaneously, in physical form, by a process of decorporealisation.

The Qutub is attended by four deputies – the *Awtád*, or Pillars, whose function is to maintain knowledge of, and power over, the four corners of the earth, and to report to him constantly the state of affairs in every country. Subservient to the Awtád are the forty *Abdal* ("those who have become spiritually changed"), and under them, in turn, seventy Nobles, who in their turn command three hundred Lords. Sufi saints who do not hold an actual office in this hierarchy are termed Saint: *Wali*.

ENTRY AND INITIATION

Entry into an Order is made through one of the many hundreds of branches (*Halka*) – also known as Circles – which flourish throughout the East. Although explanations of the more esoteric aspects of the cult are not forthcoming to any but initiates, it is important to note that his membership of an Order is usually not kept a secret by an initiate.

In some places men take their young sons to be present at the rites of the Order; hence many grow up with a curiosity about Sufism; and it may be said to be unusual for the son of a Sufi not to join the Order himself.

When a candidate for the lowest degree (that of *Salik* – seeker) is presented, he may be allowed to attend meetings for some time before being presented formally by his sponsors for enrolment. Acceptance by a Chief, or *Pir*, does not necessarily mean that promotion is likely to follow. This is one of the truly extraordinary facets of Sufism, as opposed to other mystical or secret fraternities. Promotion or elevation in the

Order, or even the passing of secret knowledge, come to a person automatically as soon as he is ready for it.

Unless the aspirant is "Mature" (*Pukhta*) for enlightenment, he will never progress. Once he has been initiated, however, he will most probably be on the Road to Success, and if he adheres rigidly to the rites and practices of the Order, he will be able to benefit from them. In other words, if – as sometimes happens – a person other than an initiated Sufi attends a Sufi *Halka*, he may hear all that is being said, he may take part in all the repetitions of sacred formulae, he may even join in the ritual circumambulations: but he will derive no enlightenment, no benefit, no understanding therefrom.

A striking example of this is the Monastery of the Maulavi Order in Cyprus, where anyone at all may attend the strange ceremonies of the "Dancing Dervishes" – and the latter are in no way put out by the presence of infidels, uninitiates or even detractors. It is their unshakeable belief that their ceremonies and repetitions of formulae (*Dhikr*) are efficacious only for those who are initiated.

Newcomers, having been introduced into the circle of Sufis, generally attend for several sessions of recitation, repetition of holy phrases, singing or dancing, depending upon the Order in question. In relation to music, some Orders employ music, others do not even permit recitations, except *sotto voce*.

At a convenient moment in the proceedings, the candidate is presented to the Chief of the Circle. He may then be asked certain questions to determine his suitability. If he is accepted, the Chief takes him by the hands and whispers to this effect in his ears. The recruit is then known as a Seeker, and the only remaining rite to be performed to complete his enrolment in the Order is the Great Oath. In this the Salik undertakes to obey his Pir, absolutely and without reservation.

While nearly every Sufi following the Path is a properly coached and entered Member of his Order, one other form of Sufism is known. This, called *Uwaysi*, is practised by those who, while following established Sufi patterns of discipline and thought, are yet affiliated to no Order. The name is derived from one Uways ul Qarani, of Yaman, a contemporary of Muhammad, who is said to have been in spiritual contact with the Prophet in spite of never having met him.

Two important facts about Sufism are exemplified in this Uwaysi doctrine. First, it shows the spiritual or telepathic link which forms a significant part of the cult. Just as time has no established meaning to the Sufi, so it is possible for one of their number to be in communication with another who may be far away – or may even be dead. Hence we find important Sufi saints claiming inspiration and co-operation with others whom they may never have met; or else from the spirit of one long dead. Secondly, it is acknowledged by Sufism that progress may be made in the Path by one who is not under direct or constant instruction from his Pir or master. At the same time it is emphasised that such cases are rare.

THE SUFI PATH

Following his acceptance by the Chief of the Halka, the Seeker gains the title of *Murid*: disciple, and must then embark upon the rigorous preparation which will lead him to Stage Two: that of *Tariqat*, or potentiality. This latter forms the first real degree of Sufism, and denotes spiritual progress.

Between the First and Second Degrees, in addition to obeying every instruction of the Master, the disciple must not omit any point of the ritual observance of formal Islam. In addition to reading certain prescribed books, he spends as much time as he can on the recitation of dhikrs.[65] These formulae are designed to remedy any defect in belief or ability that may have been discerned by the Pir. This is considered to be the period of rededication to the theme of "Be *in* the world, yet not *of* the world". The intention and aim of every Seeker at this stage is to concentrate upon the thoughts and personality of the Pir. In his turn, the Pir turns his thoughts regularly towards those of the disciple, sending him vital spiritual energy, to fortify him in the battle against the "Self". By the Self is meant the things of the flesh which detract from true spiritual progress.

In the stage of *Muridi*, too, the Seeker may take part in the nightly meetings of the Dervishes (Sufis), in their halka, or monastery. Present at such meetings, and repeating the same dhikrs, may be Sufis in several different stages of advancement. But this will not affect the potency of the dhikrs or the progress of individuals, because it is held that the same dhikr may be of great value in any one of the stages. This is, of course, determined by the Pir.

When the disciple merits the title of Tariqat – either because his Pir decides so or because he himself has reached the stage of knowing that he has progressed – he transfers his attention from the thoughts of his Leader to those of the actual Founder of the particular Order. At this time, however, the Leader keeps his own thoughts focussed upon the disciple, to reinforce his spiritual powers.

It is at this stage that the disciple may be allowed to pursue certain thaumaturgic practices, if his Pir decides that it be permissible. His abilities in occult knowledge and actual magical phenomena are great: but he may employ them only with consent.

These Sufis are now in the Stage of *Safar-ullah*: the Journey to Knowledge. They must concentrate upon the achievement of one-ness with the spirit of the Founder of the Order, whom they now call Pir, in place of the Leader whose disciple they are. The Leader himself is now known as Sheikh, or Murshid.

They travel, often to far countries, at the behest of the Murshid. Preaching the cult is not allowed, unless they are asked about it, and unless they feel that their questioners may be able to profit by such knowledge. Pilgrimages to Mecca, Medina, Jerusalem and to other shrines are undertaken. This stage generally takes far longer of attainment than the previous one.

It is known and recorded, however, that promotions from a low stage to one of the highest may take place without the intervention of the Murshid.

After Tariqat comes Stage Three: *Arif*, the Knower. At this point the Seeker dedicates himself to the attainment of unity with the thoughts of Muhammad, and has graduated beyond the mind of the founder of the Order. This part of the road is known as *Safar li-Allah*: the Journey Away from Neglectfulness.

Occult and all supernatural powers are very marked in the Stage of Arif. The spirit has been all but purged of the detrimental physical aspects and lusts. The "Self" is well under control. All that remains is the Summit – the Degree of *Fana*, or Annihilation. This means the total destruction of all thoughts which separate the Seeker from the full knowledge of all things. Farther than this he cannot go – except to Stage Five; which involves a return to the baser life, in order to purify others.

MIRACLES OF THE SUFIS

Kamáluddin, one of the most important of the Sufi historians, gives a typical example of raising of the dead, as familiar to students of the Naqshbandi Order.

Qaiyúm, a Naqshbandi leader, is stated to have revived his granddaughter, even though her death had been certified three days before. The saint maintained that she was still alive. It was only when the body was actually showing signs of decomposition (of rapid onset in the Indian climate) that he simply called to her... and she is claimed to have sat up immediately.

A large number of miracles are reported of the best known woman Sufi, Rabii'a al-Adawiya, in the eighth century.

Her main teaching, as expounded to the few who know her well, was that prayer and the recitation of formulae were the Gateway to Knowledge and hence to power. She was disinclined to concentrate upon the generally accepted use of prayer as a means towards forgiveness and salvation.

Using the formula *Lá-illáhá-illa-alláh* ("There is no God save Allah, the One"), she is reputed to have made fires without wood, obtained food without leaving her house, and been supernaturally supplied with sufficient gold for her needs.

She was sold as a slave early in her life. One day her master said that he once noticed that a lamp seemed suspended above her, yet without support of any kind. This experience so troubled him that he immediately set her free, without saying anything to anyone.

Sufi miracle-workers, in addition to the observance of the ritual prayers and ablutions, employ several principal dhikrs which induce the concentration of mind that enables occult phenomena of almost every type to be produced. Among these achievements are the ability to relieve pain and destroy disease, transportation anywhere in the twinkling of an eye, knowledge of future events and also of what anyone is thinking, even though that person may not be present.

DHIKRS OF THE SUFIS

All recitations are performed in a state of ritual purity. The face, arms, feet and mouth are washed. If the Seeker has slept since his last dhikr, he must have a bath. Any other pollution must also be removed by complete immersion.

Dhikrs are generally said during the hours of darkness. When a supernatural result is desired, the dhikr must dwell upon some facet of the Divine power allied to the effect to be accomplished. Thus, when a Sufi wishes to cure illness, he prepares himself by repeating a dhikr consisting of the Name of God which denotes healing. By this means the Sufi intends to collect in his mind a tremendous potential of mental force associated with healing. This he projects towards the object of his attentions, at the same time concentrating upon the desired result.

When a Sufi's aid is invoked to ensure, for example, success in any venture, he will purify himself and spend three nights, culminating on a Thursday, reciting the simple formula *Ya Fátih* ("O Victor") – one of the Attributes of the All-Powerful. On Thursday (the "powerful" night of the week) the full quota of power will have been built up in his mind: this, at any event, is the theory. He may also give the person a talisman or amulet with the dhikr written on it, to wear on his arm. Even today, these dhikr amulets are widely worn among all classes in the Muslim East. It is not uncommon for Sufis to receive a visitation from some important member of the Order – perhaps long dead – advising them as to the best course to take in any matter upon which they are uncertain.

At the outset of his training the more esoteric aspects of Sufism are of less concern to the Seeker than the attainment of progress through implicit obedience to the formulae of the cult. The root of all such progress is Dhikr. Having either been given a set dhikr to repeat (if he is under the direct guidance of a Sheikh), or having selected one himself (if he is an *Uwaysi* working towards the goal alone), his task is to repeat it with meticulous regard for the times and frequency of its saying.

If the formula is said under the breath ("Dhikr khafi"), a rosary with ninety-nine beads is used, one bead being told after each repetition. In the case of the "Dhikr Jali" (loud repetition) the rosary is often not used. When not attending an actual halka ("circle") meeting, the Seeker generally goes to some quiet place, or spends his contemplation-time in a room set aside for the purpose.

There is, too, the exercise known as *Fikr*, which consists of meditation: concentration upon some power that is desired, or upon the immensity of the Universe. When Dhikr and Fikr have been indulged in to such an extent that they become second nature, the Superior Form of Dhikr becomes necessary. This is the control and concentration of breath: the mind is concentrated upon a single idea, and the original Dhikr formula or another one is recited, this time in set rhythm corresponding to the breathing.

When the Dhikr has so sunk into the mind that it is being automatically repeated without conscious effort – then the "Superior Form" is used. According to Sufi doctrine, mastery of the thought processes and their linking with the body have been achieved.

The purpose of this Superior Form is the production of the next – and highly important – phenomenon: ecstasy. While it is conceded that ecstasy can come without the Dhikrs, yet it is claimed that it cannot be induced so readily by other means. In the state of ecstasy, which may be followed by unconsciousness, the mind undergoes a transformation whose nature is not described. True ecstasy is known by the technical term *wajd*, and paves the way to *Khatrat* – illumination. Here the mind and soul are liberated from the body, and knowledge and power take the place of the base thoughts of which the mind has been purified. In the Chishti Order, music is used to induce the ecstatic state; some orders claim that their members fall into a trance after looking into the eyes of their Sheikh. The so-called Dancing Dervishes accomplish trance and ecstatic phenomena through monotonous circumambulations; and this is most marked in the Maulavi Order, most popular in Turkey. In the ecstatic state Sufis are believed to be able to overcome all barriers of time, space and thought. They are able to cause apparently impossible things to happen merely because they no are longer confined by the barriers which exist for more ordinary people. Certain it is that some of their supernatural activities are difficult, at the present stage of knowledge, to account for. It will be observed that the general principles to be found in very many systems of religious and occult practice are strangely similar. The principles of leadership, discipleship and discipline, contemplation and monoideism can be found in the secret and not so secret rites of nearly every people.

If the wonder-workings of the Sufis and Hindu *gurus*, the African witch-doctors and the Amazonian medicine-men are to be investigated in a spirit of true science, there can be no question of belief or disbelief. We must admit that we have not conclusively shown that secret esoteric lore does not exist. Neither can we explain the similarities on a basis of psychology: that these rites are only symbolic of man's limited and natural strivings for superiority alone. The scope for investigation is extraordinarily wide.

I AM:
(Sufi poem of Mirzá Khán, Ansári)

How shall I define what thing I am?
Wholly existent, and yet non-existent, through Him, I am.
Whatever becometh naught out of entity,
The signification of that nothingness am I.
Sometimes a mote on the disc of the sun;
At others, a ripple on the water's surface.
Now I fly about in the wind of association:
Now I am a bird of the incorporeal world.
By the name of ice I also style myself:
Congealed in the winter season am I.
I have enveloped myself in the four elements;
I am the cloud on the face of the sky.
From unity I have come into infinity:
Indeed, nothing existeth, that I am not.
My vitality is from life's source itself;
And I am the speech, every mouth within.
I am the hearing-sense with every ear;
And also the sight of every eye am I.
I am the potentiality of every thing:
I am the perception every one within.
My will and inclination are with all;
With mine own acts, also, satisfied am I.
Unto the sinful and vicious, I am evil;
But unto the good beneficent am I.

Occult phenomena associated with degrees of the Sufi Path:

1. *Mujiza* (Miracles). Performed only by prophets.

STAGE 5 —*Baqa* Degree of Wali (Saintship). State of *Masaviut-Tarafain,* or 'Equiposed between the Two Forces'.

Known as the Safar - Billah: Sufi returns to the ways of man to guide men.

2. *Karamat* (Wonders). E.g.: walking on water, prediction of the future.

STAGE 4 —*Fana.* Annihilation. The Summit. Truth is reached and Fana achieved in strict solitude and concentrated meditation. Seeker achieving spiritual oneness with the Spirit of the Prophet.

Known as the Safarli-Allah: the travel away from neglectfulness.

3. *Mu'awanat* (Supernatural Thaumaturgy). E.g.: flying, annihilation of space.

STAGE 3 —*Arif* (Knowledge). Attainment of spiritual and occult powers.

Seeker achieving unity with the spirit of the *Pir* (founder of the Order).

Spiritual power projected into Seeker's mind by his Sheikh (leader).

Stage of Safarullah: the Journey to knowledge.

4. *Sihr* (Lawful or 'white' magic; performed by permission of the Sheikh).

STAGE 2 —*Tariqat* (Potentiality). The first real stage of Sufism. Dedicated to one-ness with the spirit of the Sheikh or Murshid (spiritual leader).

During this period the Seeker follows his Sheikh in all things, blindly adopting certain recitations and spiritual exercises.

Period of rededication to the theme of 'Be *in* the world, but not *of* the world'.

STAGE 1 —*Muridi* (Discipleship). Accepted by master as suitable candidate for the Sufi Path.

Salik: Lit. 'Seeker'—generic term for Sufi in the Sufi Path.

Diagrammatic Representation of The Sufi Path (Tariqa-sufiyya)

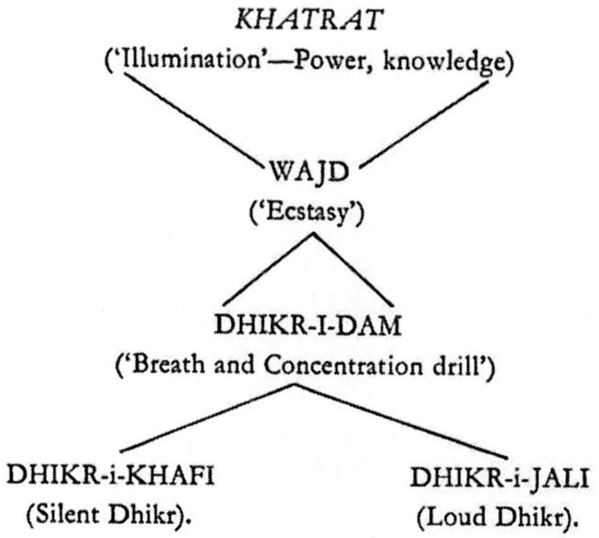

(Representation of the steps to Illumination through Dhikr (Repetition) of the three types, according to the secret lore of Sufism.)

ORGANISATION OF THE CHISHTI ORDER

<table>
<tr><td colspan="2">GRAND MASTER</td></tr>
<tr><td colspan="2">PIR (Chief of the Monastery)</td></tr>
<tr><td>Pilgrim Sufis
(organisers of the local Halqas – circles – and administrators)</td><td>Dweller Sufis: (i) Workers
(ii) Associates
(iii) Recluses</td></tr>
</table>

Five Halqas, under the Pilgrim Sufis, organised into guilds and centres for the further dissemination of the lore through lay associates in each town and village within the Monastery's jurisdiction.

Esoteric Saintship.

QUTUB—The Axis. Head of all Sufis.

First Imam ('leader') | Second Imam (assistants to Qutub)

O O O O

The Four Awtad ('Pillars') corresponding to the four points of the compass.

O O O O O O O

The Seven Abdal—deputies of the Awtad, and responsible for the affairs of the Seven Continents.

O O O O O

Five Amd (Supporters), assisting Abdal.

Seventy Nobles, represent territories.

Three Hundred Chiefs of lands smaller than nations.

Saints, without territorial jurisdiction.

Seekers, working under saints.

Laity and affiliates.

Theoretical Diagram of the World Sufi Hierarchy

THE ELEVEN SECRET RULES OF THE INITIATE IN SUFISM

Characteristic of all Sufi Orders are the Rules laid down by the founder – and sometimes added to by his successors – for the conduct and concentration of Seekers. These are the indispensable Rules of the Naqshbandi Order:

1. *Awareness of Breathing*. The mind must be attuned to be secretly aware of everything, even breath. At the same time, the mind must pulsate with thoughts of the Infinite (divine essence and omnipotence).
2. *Travel in One's Own Land*. It must be remembered frequently that the Sufi is a "traveller" – along the Sufi Path.
3. *Watching the Feet*. When walking, the Seeker must glue his gaze upon his steps. The secret meaning of this is that he must be aware of where he is going, in a metaphorical sense.
4. *Solitude in Company*. The mind is to be repeatedly concentrated so that, even in company with others, in the midst of distractions, the Sufi may keep his thoughts relevant to his task.
5. *Remembering*. The Sufi must never forget that he is a dedicated person.
6. *Restraint*. This refers to short prayers which are used to punctuate the repetitions of the Dhikr.
7. *Awareness*. The mind must become aware that there are many distractions. These are to be combated.
8. *Recollection*. Concentration must be possible through thinking this word, and without words.
9. *Pause of Time*. During pauses in thinking, the Sufi must recapitulate his actions, and examine them.

10. *Pause of Numbers.* Awareness that the required number of repetitions of the Dhikr phrase have been completed.
11. *Pause of the Heart.* During this pause the mind is trained to visualise the Seeker's heart bearing the Name of Allah.

CHAPTER 8

The Arabian Contribution

"In the name of Sulaiman, son of David (upon whom be peace) who made all the Jinn subject to him: I do hereby, and in the name of King Sulaiman, and by his seal as my oath, bind myself to use the power that thou shalt give me in the way I think to be for the best, and to keep my power secret from all."

—*Magician's oath:* Book of the Sevenfold Secret, *First Gate*

LITTLE IS KNOWN of Arab magical practices before the rise of Islam in the seventh century of this era. According to Arab tradition, Solomon left a vast heritage of his spells and powers to a number of initiates, who guarded the secrets in out-of-the-way oases. Other magicians, armed with magic words, talismans and spells, filled vast caverns full of treasures and exercised their power as a sort of occult elite, over the entire world.

Before the advent of Islam, the Semitic traditions shared by Arabs, Jews, Assyrians and others were embodied in the rituals and symbolism of the idolatry of the Temple at Mecca: the mystic Kaaba, which Muhammad purified and rededicated to monotheism after the success of his mission.

Among the three hundred and sixty spirit-gods set up there were Al-Lát, Manát, 'Uzza and Hobal: demons and gods who "gave oracles and decided the ways of man". Their priests were drawn exclusively from the tribe of Quraish, the royal clan. We have sufficient knowledge of the pre-Islamic Arab sorcerers to know that their methods closely resembled those of the other Semitic nations. Where the Arab contribution becomes interesting is during the period after the all-conquering clans swept out of the desert, and the epoch of assimilation with other systems came to the fore.

The story of Arab-Islamic magic follows the pattern of Arab civilisation. Under the early caliphs of Syria, Spain and Egypt, the staggering mass of written material captured from the heritage of Rome, Greece, and all the other conquered nations was translated into Arabic. Scholars – frequently at State expense – systematised the teachings of Aristotle and the other Greek writers, summarised ancient histories, organised the codes of law, religion and ethic. At the flourishing universities of Kairouan, Azhar, Cordoba, Baghdad, doctors worked on medicine, magic and alchemy. Jewish and Chaldean magical beliefs were "boiled down" and studied.

What was the Arab-Muslim attitude towards magic? Taking, as always, their lead from the Qur'an, the sages accepted the theory that magic, in one form or another, was a definite force. Some of the world's most interesting magical treatises come from the pens of Arab-Muslim writers between the twelfth and sixteenth centuries: and it was partly through their work with learned Jews in the Arab-Spanish universities that much of oriental lore entered Europe.

Fakhr-ed-Din El-Rázi (Rhazes) outlined one of the first Arab systems of magic. According to him *Sihr* (magic) is to be divided into three *Naw'* or categories:

First comes Chaldean magic, which meant to him largely a star-cult, and included astrology and spirits attributed to forces of the stars.

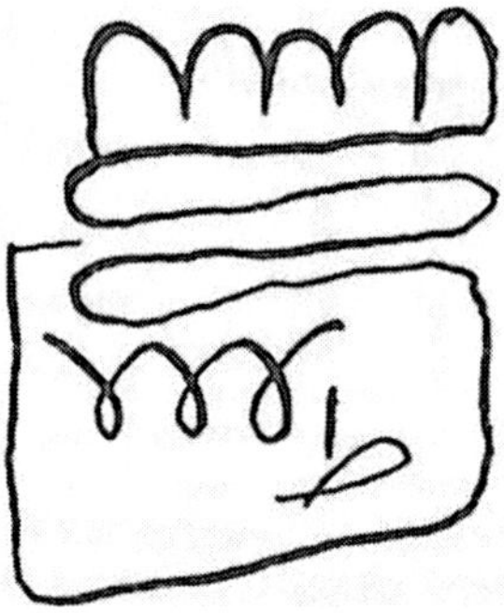

Arabian spell to dry up rival's well or cistern – after Ibn Khaldún [See p. 110]

Secondly, he says, there is true spirit-magic, which may be a form of spiritualism, together with hypnosis. It also dealt with the interaction of the human soul upon its host the body, and upon the bodies of others. Contact with other human spirits and their employment forms a part of this section. Finally, there are miracles, which are vouchsafed only to prophets, according to the Muslim belief.

Legend has it that there were two angels, Hárut and Márut, who learned magic, and transmitted its knowledge to mankind, and this thesis is basic to all Arab magic. There are also such things as Jinn (genii), which may be part spirit and part something else. Both the angels and genies are mentioned more than once in the Qur'an. Another form of magic treated by Arabs is *Maskh*, the art of transforming men into animals which is known in the West as lycanthropy.

The classical books of Arab researchers in many other fields than the occult record magical beliefs and processes. Such authorities as Tabari, the historian, speak of magic, while the *Social Philosophy* of Ibn Khaldún mentions certain rites seen and recorded by him. Even the philosophical writings of Al-Ghazzali, father of modern logic, make it clear that the Arab masters had given the subject serious thought.

Ibn Khaldún, the social philosopher, gives one of the most refreshingly unbiased accounts of a thinker faced with magical beliefs. Writing in the fourteenth century, he says that there were two types of magic: (i) Pure Magic; (ii) Talismans.[66]

Pure magic he defines as some force which comes straight from within the magician, without the intermediary of any "helper" (*mua'win*). In this form there is no question of spirits being used or conjured.

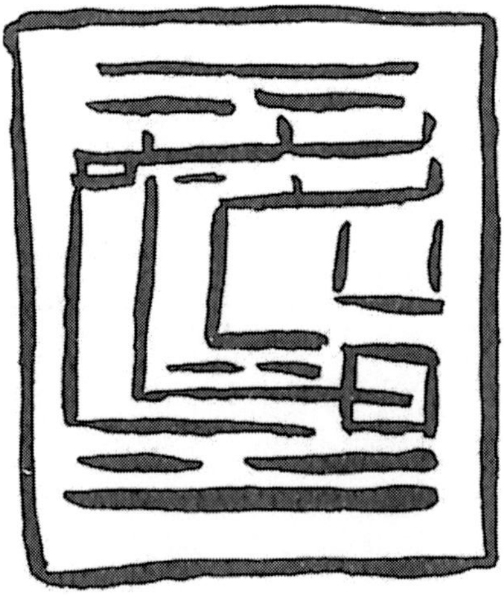

Stylised "power spell" in Chinese brushwork, inscribed on paper with peachwood stylus. The wording is Arabic: "O Tribe of Hashim!"
—Author's collection

This is perhaps an echo of the *mana-akasa* belief in a widespread almost untapped occult force, which is there to

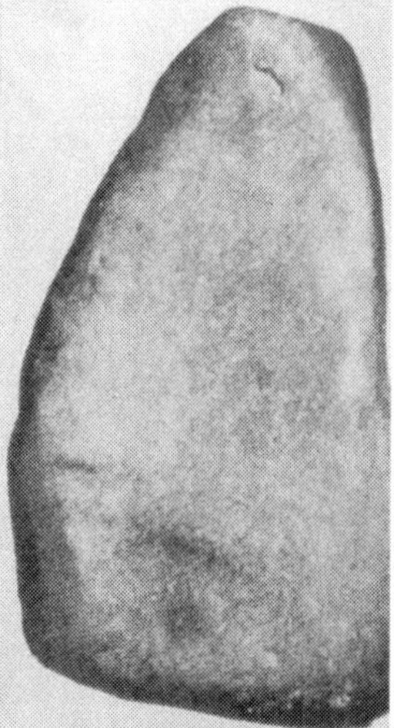

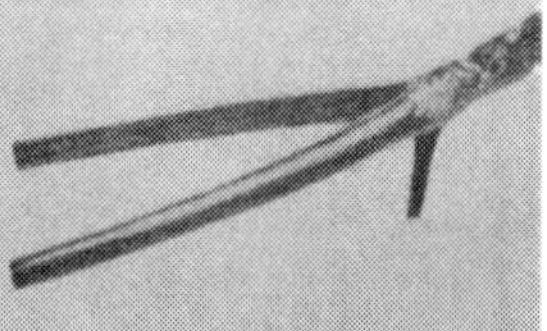

Top, left: The inexplicable foam below Paphos cliffs (Cyprus) "from which Venus rose" (Ch. 4)

Centre, left: Grave-shrine of Baba Wali Saheb in Kandahar. Said to have the power of rendering weapons invincible (Ch. 7)

Bottom, left: Kurdish ritual sword-dance, terminating in "ecstasy and revelations". A remnant of the pre-Islamic Peacock cult (Ch. 11)

Top, right: The earliest form of Venus, (Aphrodite). Around this grey monolith, brought as their goddess by the Phoenicians from South Arabia, was built the Sanctuary of Paphos: greatest pilgrimage centre of the ancient Mediterranean (Ch. 4)

Centre, right: View of the mystical Shrine of Venus-Astarte (Aphrodite) at Paphos, on a coin of Bylbus (Ch. 4)

Bottom, right: Red-lacquered Chinese spirit-writing instrument, resembling a divining-rod. The head represents a dragon (Ch. 17)

Top, left: Aqil Khan, the alchemist who instructed the author (Ch. 14)

Centre: Indian Sadhu, demonstrating the use of an "invocatory shell" (Ch. 13)

Bottom, left: Himalayan magician, with magical staff. His clothes are purposely tattered, to indicate humility (Ch. 9)

Top, right: Afghan Fakir, credited with immense psychic powers, and specializing in the hypnosis of animals (Ch. 7)

Bottom, right: Persian wizard, in the patched robe of a Sufi Order. The wand, dagger and sling are part of his magical accessories (Ch. 11) be used, and neither good nor evil: almost a psycho-physical force. The second form, which is summarised in the term Talismanic, implies the necessity of making contact with and use of some other force.

Ibn Khaldún was the first to notice that there is some link between the hypnoidal state and the ability to make use of some sort of power. He says that the pentacle-drawing and other rituals must work up the magician's emotions to a high pitch. If this is not achieved, there will be no result. This is the first scientific comment to be recorded in the study of magic.

This background of intense intellectual activity, covering a study of various systems, produced a wide variety of talismans[67] and other wonder-working items.

Talismans must be made at certain times. They are to contain either or both of the magical metals iron and copper. Their symbolism is a powerful agent for compelling the subservience of spirits. Those who desire to cause discord, for example, must make their talisman square when the moon is in Aries. But one made in Aries, and of circular shape, will compel a spirit who has knowledge of hidden treasures to appear and divulge his secrets. The word ATHORAY, which is under the aegis of the Pleiades, when inscribed on a copper tablet, gives powers far beyond the ordinary to sailors, soldiers and alchemists. Buildings, wells and mines may be wrecked by a magical talisman made of the same material, with the word ADELAMEN and the sign for Taurus written thereon. This is also thought to be powerful for any form of evil magic. ALCHATAY, made under Taurus, with its sign and this name upon it in black on a triangular piece of iron, is carried by travellers, and is said to cure many illnesses. ATHANNA, written with the sign of Gemini on a crescent-shaped tablet of iron and copper, helps besiegers. Used in evil magic, it can destroy harvests, and is effective for revenge.

ALDIMIACH, also under Gemini, and composed in the same way as the former talisman, is used for love and friendship.

It was recommended that a complete set of these signs should be written on white paper with jet-black ink, and carried on the person. Then, when the moon or sun was passing through the appropriate signs of the Zodiac, the latent virtues of the talismans would start to operate, and the requisite benefits would be felt and seen.

There are still other variations on this astrological lore: Almazan, under Leo, causes men to quarrel, and women! It is a bad sign for travellers, and a general promoter of discord as a talisman. Algelioche, also under Leo, being at a fixed position, promotes love and benevolence. Azobra, from the mane of Leo, is good for voyages and to regain lost affections. Alzarfa, from Virgo, is fortunate for gain; Achureth, from Virgo, keeps love and cures the sick, though it does not help land travel. Those who want to find a treasure made their talisman with the name of Agrafa, under Libra; and Azubene, with affinity to Scorpio, was unfortunate for sea travel.

Talismans in copper and lead made under the power of the Crown of Scorpio and engraved with the name Alchil were supposed to favour fortune in general, and travel.

The following Arabian talismans complete the list given in several magical books: they were widely current at one time in Europe.

Allatha, the tail of Scorpio, is unlucky for travel or new friendships, and so is used in hate magic. Abrahaya destroys ill-gained wealth and incites people to gamble. Abeida helps harvests and travellers, but causes divorce and discontent if used with vicious intent. Sadahecha, which comes under Capricorn, ensures good health, while Zabodola cures certain diseases. Sadabeth is the Star of Fortune, and its talisman should be worn by all who seek conjugal loyalty. Sadalabra, in conjunction with other hate-talismans, is useful for revenge, destroys enemies and also causes divorce. Alfarz, on the other hand, helps one to meet one's life partner, and brings good fortune in general. Albothan, which is governed by the force of Pisces, brings safety in strange places: it is one of the protective charms worn by magicians while at their work. It promotes harmony, and makes married people happy.

Arabic magic is highly symbolised. Many of the traditional signs of the wizards – the pentagram, Seal of Solomon and Shield of David, the Eye of Horus and the Hand of the Moon god – are in constant use among Arab-Islamic sorcerers.

One curious belief deserves mention here. In the case of the swastika – that symbol of the sun and of life among peoples from time immemorial – the Arabs have decided that a special virtue resides in its form alone. If that form is allied to a meaning assigned to it by thought-force, then the force becomes doubled. Should the meaning be trebled, so is the force which is at the command of the magician through the very symbolism of the swastika or other magical device. In the seventeenth-century Arabic work *Tilism wa'l Quwwa* (Power and Talismans)[68] we find an expansion of this theory. The Christians, says the anonymous author, took the sign of the Cross as their emblem. Now we know that from time immemorial the Cross has been used in magic to portray the Sun and also that it "contains within it virtues of a kind of which we are uncertain". It was potent before Jesus. After the Crucifixion, it was adopted, and thus has a double function and potency. "The same is true of the Swastika".[69]

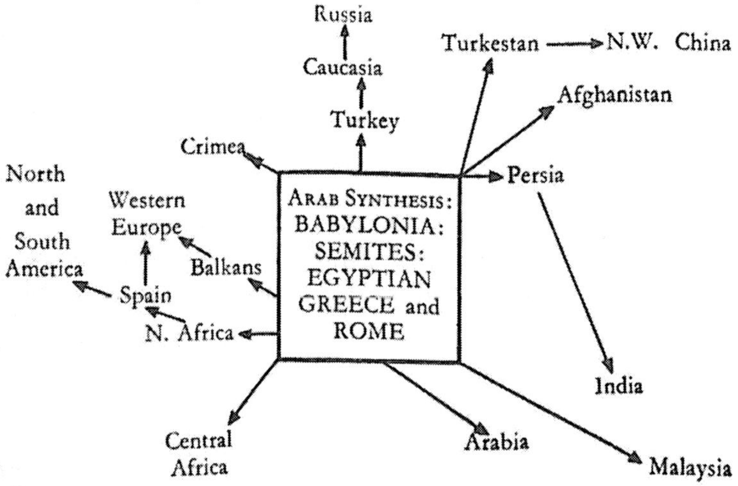

Chart illustrating Arabian rediffusion of the magical arts inherited from Near-Eastern civilisations: eighth to fifteenth centuries, AD.

Where the Swastika originated is not known. In China, it is still extremely common (under the name of *wan*) and is thought to have been adopted under Buddhism, which possibly points to an Indian source: "the accumulation of lucky signs possessing ten thousand virtues, being one of the sixty-five mystic figures which are believed to be traceable to every one of the famous footprints of Buddha". It is also current in other lands which have Buddhist traditions.

"It has been identified with the Hammer of Thor" – whence, possibly, the German Nazis adopted it, as an "Aryan" symbol – "the Zeus or Thunderer of the Scandinavians".

The name which we use for it is derived from two Sanskrit words *su* ("well") and *asti* ("it is"), meaning, it is well.

There are many varieties of the cross-swastika: among them the fylfot which is the emblem of the Isle of Man.

There have been several Arabian adaptations of the swastika-symbol to powers, invocations and names. In one, the phrase *Ya Ali* ("O, Ali!"), an invocation to the Fourth Caliph and Companion of Muhammad, is seen. This is current among followers of the Shiah rite, who revere this personage very highly. Again, in Persia, the symbol was used to enclose the Persian invocation to the Four Caliphs: *Yá Chahár Yár* ("O, Four Friends"). In this case the arms (or legs) of the figure, as with the former one, give the impression of clockwise rotation. One calligrapher, knowing of the meaning of the *Chahár Yár* phrase, prepared a version of my name for a seal, in which were two swastikas rotating in different directions. The last one contained my title: *Sayed Shah*.

So much for the talismanic aspect of the Arabian contribution. Characteristic of the employment of demons and spirits – as opposed to the talisman theory or "second force" of Ibn Khaldún – is the intricate question of the knot spell.

An important reference to the making and use of knots as a vehicle for curses is found in the Qur'an:[70]

> *The Daybreak:*
> Say thou: "I take refuge with the Lord of Daybreak
> From the evil of all He hath made,
> And from the evil of the dark one when it spreads
> And from the evil of those who blow upon knots
> And the evil of the envious when he envies."

This clearly refers to the ancient Semitic knot-lore which is quoted in the *Maqlu* (Burning) Tablets:

> "Her knot is loosed, her sorcery is brought to naught, and all her charms fill the desert."

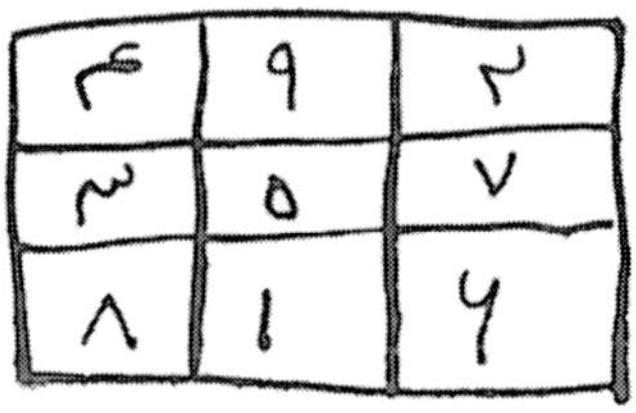

Magic square for easing childbirth. From Al-Ghazzali's Deliverance from Error. The numbers are:

4 9 2
3 5 7
8 1 6

[See p. 110]

Muslim tradition tells a curious tale of the Prophet Muhammad being bewitched by a Jewish sorcerer using this method. Nine knots were tied in a string, each knot "binding" a curse, and the thread was then hidden in a well. Only the archangel Gabriel's timely warning, we are informed, disclosed the hiding-place of the death spell. Such spells are countered by untying the knots, one by one: but in this case the chroniclers affirm that they unravelled themselves at the Prophet's command.

Just as evil can be "bound" into knotted thread, so can good be done by the same means. Among the Central Asian tribes, illness is cured by "blowing upon knots"; and there is a regular ritual attached to the whole thing. A three-coloured cord is spun, in green, blue and red; one knot is tied every day. After seven days the spell is buried in an inaccessible spot, and the disease will then disappear.

Many of the stories in the *Arabian Nights* have as their basis the magical beliefs of the Arabs and Chaldeans in the jinn and their powers. Just as the Western witches supposed that they could, by performing certain rites, gain the services of a powerful demon, so do traditional Arabian and Islamic writings tell of the wonders of Jinn-land and the country of the fairies (Peristán). The method of conjuring jinni by talismans is widespread. Briefly, though there are variations, this consists in making a talisman and perfuming it with the requisite incense, as the first step. After this has been done, the jinn is conjured in the name of Solomon, and threatened with Solomon's wrath (i.e., being sealed in a metal bottle) if he does not appear. If the correct number of repetitions have been made, and certain other requirements complied with, the jinn will come and serve the invocant.[71]

Muslim theologians are somewhat at variance about the question of the Word of Power and its uses. Some contend that such a word, though it exists, is known to nobody on earth: hence its use is a question which does not arise. Those who follow Ibn Khaldún and Geber (the latter is said to have written five hundred books on magic) maintain that the Word has been revealed and that this name (*Ism-el-Ázam*) is the one which alone compels the obedience of the genies. Students of the occult like Geber (Ja'afir Abu-Musa), however, make a point of distinguishing between magic and sorcery. The latter (*kahána*) uses talismans alone, without the Name of God, which cannot, they affirm, be used for evil ends.

There are other traces of Egyptian and Babylonian magic in Arabian occultism as passed to Europe in the Dark Ages. Either from here or through the Indian connection (possibly both) the Arabs felt that the magical circle *al-Mandal* was necessary in all conjurations, to protect the operator from the wrath of Satan – Satan, of course, being the originator of black, as Solomon was of white, magic.

Among the best-known writers, either on current magical practice or its theory, were At-Tabari (*Tafsir*), Er-Rázi (*Mafatih*), and Al-Zamakhshari (*Kashshaf*). Their works are generally neglected by Western students of the occult. In fact, their material is not available for study in Western tongues in accurate translation.

CHAPTER 9

Legends of the Sorcerers

"We saw with our own eyes one of these people making the image of a person to bewitch... a demon comes out of his mouth... many evil spirits come down, and the victim is attacked by the specified evil."

—*Ibn Khaldún:* Muqaddama
(fourteenth century)

THE MYSTERY OF EL-ARAB

The nomadic Arabs of the Hejaz today are anything but a superstitious people. The rigid and unimaginative impact of puritanical Wahabism, as preached under the present regime, leaves little room for anything other than a strictly literal interpretation of life. The one exception that I found there – during over a year of recent wanderings – was the story of El-Arab.

El-Arab was, it seems, either a great fraud, a great magician – or the first man to make use of electricity. Three or four hundred years ago he appeared, in the form of a wandering anchorite, and sought refuge in a small village. Following a dispute during which his interpretations of theology seemed too liberal to the local residents, he was driven forth into the wilderness. It seemed, however, that El-Arab had taken a liking to the spot. From the sand-dunes about a mile away he is said to have directed long lightning-flashes at the unhappy inhabitants – until they rather unwillingly invited him to take up his residence among them.

There were no more religious discourses. Instead, El-Arab ("The Arab" – that was the only name he would give) spent his time demonstrating his lightning, and enlarging upon his theories. According to his teaching, lightning, like everything else, had its real uses. Things which were not put to a use were simply being wasted. He, El-Arab, had learned how to master it, and to bend it to his will. When he was charged with sorcery he merely laughed. He used to demonstrate to travellers the lightning: imprisoned, as he said, in clay jars. Very little more is known of his activities, except this: when anyone was anxious of news from some far place, El-Arab would slightly open one jar, and call upon the lightning to bring back tidings, aiming it in the general direction of the desired news. There would be a puff of smoke, a sharp crack, and lightning would fork forth from the vessel. Then he would open another jar ("into which the lightning, swifter than light, had returned"), and behold, within would be seen a green glow. This El-Arab would interpret, and give the desired information: "which always turned out to be true".

In his normal life there seemed nothing at all odd. And the strangest thing was that travellers used to follow the light when lost in the desert – and reach the village in safety.

When he died, El-Arab was said to have lived in the settlement for nearly two hundred and fifty years. Small wonder that generations had grown up regarding him as nothing extraordinary, lightning and all. But there was a rude shock when he died. As is customary when a revered man dies, his body was buried on the spot: under the desert sands in a dune near the village well. When the mourners returned to their village it was seen that El-Arab's house had disappeared! This phenomenon had not only never been seen by the local people – but they had never even heard of such a thing. And so it is still talked about. As one man said to me: "It may seem strange – but again, there has only been one El-Arab. Had there been two, it is likely that the second would have departed in the same way."

From a scientific point of view, several things strike the student of oriental tales about magicians. It comes, first of all, as something of a shock to note that so very little has been done in sifting the magical lore of the East to ascertain, where possible, fact from fancy. In many cases there seems to be an underlying stratum of truth in these stories – particularly those concerning individual magicians. This does not necessarily mean that they are entirely true: it does mean that there is still much to be learned from oriental magic. Reading accounts of reputed sorcerers and talking to the people among whom they have lived, one is driven to the conclusion that, in general, the people of the East are not more easily deceived than those of other lands. In the tale just quoted, for example, the Arabs who retail it are not content with marvelling at the seeming miracles of El-Arab. History has shown them to be an essentially practical race: hence, as would be expected, they are more interested in *how* he gained his power – and whether it can be duplicated. This, it will be observed, is the essence of the scientific, rather than the philosophical, attitude. Naturally, the Arabs of that area lack even the basic scientific knowledge to carry speculation beyond semi-medieval scope. It is their attitude, however, which counts.

For the purposes of study, therefore, it is interesting to collect these same tales of sorcery.

SADOMA OF BAGHDAD

A magician greatly in demand in the days of the early Caliphs of Baghdad was known as Sadoma. It was his wont to travel miles out into the trackless desert "there to commune with spirits". Many times he came across travellers, seeking water and almost at their last gasp. It is reported that, although he carried no food with him, he was always able by supernatural means to produce water and choice fruits to revive the starvelings. There are several records of this type of wizardry. One such magician (whose food was carried into the desert for him by the magical *Roc* bird, familiar to readers of the *Arabian Nights*) was able to make stranded travellers eat, even though they were unconscious when found.

Other travellers – even today – relate that, having sunk into a stupor through lack of food, they slept. When they awoke, these people claim, it was as though they had seen in a dream the right road home, printed across the desert sands. And their strength had returned. Apart from the legend of Sadoma, it is possible that the subconscious mind was in some way stimulated during the sleep, and that that strange sixth sense which desert people acquire came to their rescue.

Emotion, of any kind, seems often to raise mental powers to a higher pitch. This, at any rate, could be an explanation for many of the phenomena of magic. It is usual to state that the emotion (cupidity and power-lust) is what drives man to theurgic acts. Psychologists – and historians – claim that a slight unbalance of the brain is enough to make a man believe that he can control nature: because he wants to do so more than anything else. This theory is as good as any. It is interesting, nevertheless, to note the *magical* attitude towards the situation. It is only when emotion is roused to a greater than natural pitch, say the magicians, that man is capable of rising above the natural order of things, and wreaking his designs upon nature and other men alike. Again we come here close to semi-religious and frenzy states.

This pattern is followed in the local tale of the Altankol – the Golden River – in Tibet. Running into Lake Sing-su-lay, the stream carries with it particles of alluvial gold, which are trapped in goatskins staked in the waters. But legend has it that a certain Tibetan magician swore that he would gain control of the gold, so that it should be available only to those who were worthy of it.

As a result, we are told, a pact was made between the magician and the River God. Now, whenever danger threatens the country, the gold stops coming. It is claimed that during several campaigns with China this discrepancy in gold was noted both before and after the event.

SILTIM THE WIZARD

Siltim, an Arab sorcerer, had cultivated the art of taking any form he chose. Falling in love with a beautiful girl who disliked him, his love reached such heights that he retired to a desolate riverine spot to nurse his feelings.

After a period of two years, in which he was said to have learned the language of fishes and been able to project his powers far away at will, he discovered how to summon the girl to him, in the dead of night. She was aware of visiting him. Her stories of her dreams might have been believed, but she held that the magician lived in a wondrous palace, whereas it was known that he had nothing more than a hut on the riverside. Relatives became anxious in due time, and one of them travelled to the hermit's hut to charge him with sorcery. This he freely admitted, and stated that he had the power to convert his home into a marble palace. As soon as the visitor returned to report, the girl actually vanished. And so did Siltim. This tale is typical of the "emotion-concentration" element common to very many branches of magic.

Many stories have been handed down in the East relating to the search for the Elixir of Life, by which immortality could be secured. Many of them centre around the heart or the liver, and some are clearly symbolical. The following very popular tale seems to combine philosophical and occult elements, and may be in some way based upon some real occurrence.

A wealthy landowner married the daughter of a Persian prince. Soon after the wedding the husband spent much time away from home, engaged upon pilgrimages. One room in the house remained locked.

Although warned never to pry into the secret, the young wife found that her curiosity could not be contained. One day a travelling locksmith called, while the husband was away in Syria. He was commissioned to open the door. Excitedly, the lady accompanied him. To her horror, as he tried the first key the man collapsed at her feet, uttering terrible shrieks. When the servants ran to their mistress's assistance, the locksmith was found to be dead.

On the husband's return, of course, the princess had to admit her guilt. She was then told that he had been engaged upon experiments whereby the panacea of perpetual life might be produced. He had almost succeeded, according to the tests set forth in an ancient manuscript. Only one small part of the experiment remained to be done: yet this unfortunate interruption (as is the case with most magical rites) had rendered all the work null and void. The part of the process which was incomplete was the adding of the heart of a locksmith.

But this was not all. A large gash was seen on the left side of the dead man's breast. Inside the locked room, all had been turned to ashes. While the couple stood looking at the devastation, a mocking laugh floated down from the ceiling.

The story ends on the melancholy note that the husband went mad, and then the wife. And as each died, within a few months of each other, it was found that their hearts had been removed. That is why a house in Old Teheran is still called the Mansion of the Three Stolen Hearts.

Magicians – especially when they are itinerant cheats – often have an eye to topical matters, as well as playing their part in aiding those suffering from traditional diseases and ambitions. During the last famine in India, a little-known Bombay wizard – whose main theory was that nakedness was akin to godliness – became rich overnight.

Charms made by him with "Himalayan leopard powder" – or so he stated – ensured that their possessor could not be harmed by hunger or disease. Thousands of people did, in fact, die: but not the magician. He could afford to buy black-market rice. Neither did one woman who reported his wonders to a certain Maharaja. Nothing was to be done in his State, declared that Prince, until the magician had been brought before him.

After a considerable amount of persuasion, the sorcerer was placed next to his Highness in his court assembly. Every word that he said was taken as gospel. Loaded with honours and possessions, he stuck out until the last against the wearing of clothes. When he was last heard of, his self-esteem had so grown that he would speak only twice a day. Every word was recorded with a pen of gold. California is not the only place where strange cults can spring up. If the reader thinks that Britain, too, is immune, let him read the boasts of those who claim to teach esoteric "Eastern" lore and may or may not know anything about it.

This story is first-class material for future myths and legends. Unless the magician is discredited, it is likely that his exploits will become famous.

I have been able to collect interesting material of a vampire-legend in the making which seems unusually interesting.

There are many tales circulating in India about a certain "English Vampiress", who is said to have eaten raw flesh, and to have drunk the blood of humans whenever possible. Is this story true? Is it just another of those blood-curdling tales spread by anti-British agitators (like the "Belgian babies" horror of the First World War)? The truth is somewhere in between. It forms one of the most classical examples of legend-development that I have ever encountered.

An English widow – her husband had been killed in 1916 – lived in Bombay, and spent the hot season in the hills. She is said to have been, outwardly, quite average in appearance. The only thing about her attitude to life that seemed marked was her belief that she was irresistible to the opposite sex. Even that is not unknown.

A Maharaja who was staying one year at the same hill station was in the habit of giving magnificent parties. One night, after one such entertainment, this woman ("Mrs W") and a friend ("Mrs S") were travelling home in a ricksha. The ricksha in front of them was upset against some rocks, having taken a corner too fast. Several people were injured. The two women stopped their ricksha, and went to see if they could be of any help. Neither of them, be it noted, was involved in the accident, or hurt in any way.

When they got back to their hotel, Mrs S. noticed that her companion's mouth was covered in blood. Later the story circulated that Mrs W. had been seen sucking the blood of one of the victims of the accident: she was a vampire. She died some months later, and hence the legend has grown and will probably continue to grow.

By chance, however, I was able to meet Mrs S. and ask her what she knew about the whole thing. Here is her story:

"I asked Mrs W. that very night why there was blood on her face. At first she said that it came from one of the victims, and that it had got on her face by accident.

"Three days later, however, when the rumour was going round that she was a vampire – repeated by some of the survivors of the crash, and not by me – she came to me to make a 'confession', and said that she was going to return to England for treatment.

"I asked her if she was a vampire, and she said that she was not. The truth was that, when a child, she had suffered from some illness which made it necessary for her to eat raw meat sandwiches. She became so used to them that she could never eat cooked meat. Her doctor regarded this as more or less harmless, and a psychological state. So the diet was continued. When she went to India, she found that it was difficult to get raw meat, though she had a great longing for it, and in the end managed to arrange a supply. But she used to 'ration' herself, as much as possible. On the night of the crash, she said she had not had any for weeks, and the sight of the thing as she bent over the injured man was too much for her, so she touched her face to his, as if to kiss him. An Indian present, who may have known about her liking for red meat, started the rumour."

Human vampirism, therefore – if it has ever existed – might be ascribed to a psychosis, or an appetite engendered by conditioning to raw meat. That raw meat has been eaten by man is well known. A relatively recent survival of this practice is contained in the accounts of the famous Scottish man-eater Sawney Beane and his family.

There may be certain main principles involved in magic: there certainly is no clear unanimity among magicians as to the reason for the use of symbolic words, devices and writings.

Probably still alive and doing a remunerative business is a certain Tibetan holy man – he repudiated the title of "lama" with some contempt – who sold, for the equivalent of five shillings, a "Scroll for the Purification of the Soul". This, he said, is essential before anyone can become fully human, let alone be able to study or appreciate the wonders of magic. Celebrated as a sorcerer, he would not talk of his spells, and denied that he was three hundred and five years old. "Listen not to what people say about me," he said, "for I am not only not over a hundred years of age: I am not yet born!"

The scroll – of which I have one – consisted of bleached leaves, which had to be worn for several days before being written on by the wizard. This ensured the penetration of the scroll by the aura, and guided his hand. I had to stand behind him for about fifteen minutes to have my scroll completed. During this time he kept up a constant flow of conversation with someone who was "a city dweller four days' march from here, and somewhat indistinct owing no doubt to high winds". The finished work was wrapped in a piece of dried skin and tied with gut. When I brought it back to England it was useful as a barometer because the gut invariably became damp four hours or so before rain.

The holy man told the writer that the paraphernalia of magicians – especially those who foretold the future – were all so much window-dressing "only to impress those who demand such things, and I have heard that this is also so in the West". He stated that the only genuine costume for a magician was such as he himself wore, and he begged me to take to it without delay, so that I would feel the beneficial influence which would thenceforward guide my life.

On his head was a pancake-type hat of snow leopard fur – no longer snowy – and in his ears great unpolished lumps of amber. A long, heavy string of similar lumps interspersed with pieces of rough jade hung round his neck, over a dirty, yellow fur-lined coat, which reached to the ankles. From his waist hung a large green skin bag, embroidered in the same colour, and dotted with red glass beads. A deep leather fringe completed this. On his feet were a pair of embroidered turned-up-toe slippers, tied securely with gut. His winter boots were suspended around his neck.

He refused to part with the jade and amber rings on his fingers. These, he said, were his "luck", and destroyed such things as mountain demons, various kinds of enemies, and the werewolves who attacked travellers.

His last words to me were a warning against washing the body. "The hands may be washed, but the body – never." In this, at least, he seemed to be a devoted follower of his belief.

There are many stories current in Egypt about magicians of the Middle Ages, and their attempts to find the Elixir of Life, or the Philosopher's Stone. One of the most interesting of these was told me in Cairo, and I noted it not for its plot so much as for certain elements therein.

Scattered among Arabic and Persian alchemical and magical writings there are references to "the golden head" and yet never an indication as to what this was. Here I found a definite reference to it at last.

A famous Cairene sorcerer – El Ghirby – concentrated his activities upon the finding of hidden treasure. To this end he learned, by means of an old man's advice, how to transmute clay to gold. This, however, could be done only once. When transmuted the head became an oracle, or possessed by a spirit. One of its powers was to declare where hidden treasures could be found.

It seems that El Ghirby had already used the head for ordinary divination, and that it had given oracles as to many and strange things. Sure enough, once transmuted, the head began to speak, "though its eyes and lips moved not at all", and gave him minute directions as to where the first treasure was to be sought. When he had brought this back to his house, El Ghirby again consulted his oracle. According to the testament which it is claimed he left behind, the Head refused to tell him of more than one treasure a month. He composed himself to wait. But again the Head cheated. It told him about a treasure, vaster than man could even imagine: but it was sunk eight hundred feet below the bottom of the sea! In the ensuing altercation the Head threw a jar at El Ghirby's head, which smashed itself in the street, and attracted neighbouring attention.

This passed off quietly enough: but the quarrels between the spirit of the Head and the magician became more and more frequent. It was generally assumed in the locality that the man was mad. One day when a certain inoffensive jeweller was passing, a particularly large jar flew through the window of the Ghirby mansion, striking the jeweller on his neck. The matter came to court.

In his defence the magician denied the charge of assault, and explained about the head. He was sentenced to six months' jail. When he returned home, the Head seemed better behaved. It advised him to make the Elixir of Life, and even supplied full details of the ingredients and method. Before long word came to the magistrate who had sentenced the sage. As a man in his seventies, this was a discovery that he could not afford to ignore. In return for a free pardon and a document explaining that El Ghirby was sane and blameless, a phial of the precious medicine changed hands. That same night, the Head addressed the sorcerer:

"I have just heard that the magistrate has taken the potion. This means that he will have at least sixty more years of life. But I forgot to tell you that they are *your* years! You will die in the morning, as soon as the magistrate's Elixir begins to act!" It is said that El Ghirby had hardly time to write out a confession of the whole affair, and throw the Head into the Nile, before death overcame him.

CHAPTER 10

Calling the Spirits

"Abjad, Hawwaz, Hutti, Come Thou, Spirit: for I am Solomon, son of David, Commander of the Jinn and Men! Come, or I will imprison thee in a metal flask!"

—*Abu-Hijab's* Calendar of Genies

The belief in the existence of spirits and other formidable forces is only one step from the desire to call them, bind them, and make them do the sorcerer's bidding.

It is customary – at least among older writers – to divide this spiritism into groups, or subjects, for the purposes of study. One might say that spirits can be distinguished as good and evil, as human souls and those who have never had a corporeal form. Again, some spirits are made to appear in human, some in animal, others in more alarming, shapes. But this method of examining spirits, if you consider it well, does little to contribute towards actual knowledge of the art.

What is interesting is that evocation itself – whether Christian, Buddhist, Arab, Egyptian or Chaldean – comes within an accepted framework of method and ideas. There is the consecration of the operator, his implements (if any) and, generally, the magical circle. There is the actual invocation and the evocation. When the spirit has appeared, there follows the phase of command or enquiry. Finally comes the inevitable Licence to Depart, without which the operator may be harmed by the apparition. Two things are often considered indispensable: some connection with death or the dead, and the possession of Words of Power.

A great part of the importance and interest of spirit-calling from our point of view is because a very large part of almost all magic is dependent upon spirit aid: whether it be curse, blessing or merely magical power over and beyond that held by others. One might even define magic as the alleged art of gaining power through supernatural (spirit) powers. Hence spirits – or some hitherto unidentified force conveniently so termed – form the very heart of magic, whether ceremonial, popular or superstitious.

It is generally overlooked that "spiritualism" – the evocation of the spirits of the dead – as known in Europe and modern America, is only one branch of magic: a branch which is traditionally exercised by witch-doctors in Africa, tribal Amerindians, and Shamanic operators in China and Japan,[¶] not to mention a score of other communities.

The raising of spirits, especially those of dead relatives, is supposed to need much dedication and preparation. While it has always been conceded that there are some (like modern mediums) to whom such powers come more easily, yet it is sometimes forgotten that the books of the magicians give detailed accounts of the procedure, which can be followed even by ordinary people.

It was considered necessary sometimes, in processes attributed to the Chaldeans, to know the birth date of the person to be evoked. If a horoscope were available, so much

¶ Compare the account of spiritism and "automatic writing", s.v. *China: Spiritism*, chap. 17, *infra*.

the better. This meant that the spirit could be called in the names of the planets which presided over his birth, and at the very hour at which the birth took place.

Next the evocant meditated in complete seclusion for a period of up to forty-eight hours. A clear, bright day was chosen. Then, in some place given over to the practice of magic (the magician generally used his own room, or some cave or ruined place of worship), the magical circle was described. Within its six-foot diameter was the tabu space which sheltered the magician, and which no interrupting evil genius could cross. In the circle, often within a concentric ring, the name of God was written, in chalk, on the ground.

In Hebrew and later rituals, this sometimes took the form of a continuous chain of words like: AGLA – ELOHIM – ADONAY or ALPHA – OMEGA – TETRAGRAMMATON.

Inside the circle, too, are kept the instruments of Art. These include oil, a sword with names such as the foregoing inscribed thereon, and a burning brazier for fumigation. The incense is chosen to coincide with the angel of the planet to be invoked. All true magicians were expected to know Words of Power to call the spirits (abracadabras like *Sabaoth*, from the Hebrew, or *Abraxas*, from the Gnostics, and Anrehakatha-sataiu, senentuta-batetsataiu, from ancient Egyptian papyri).

When the magician has taken his place within the circle, and thrown incense on the fire – making sure that he has with him a pentacle or Seal of Solomon as a protection – he would intone the following type of call. This one is taken from a Graeco-Egyptian magical book, translated by Goodwin:

> I call upon thee that didst create the earth and bones, and all flesh and all spirit, that didst establish the sea and that shakest the heavens, that didst divide the light from the darkness, the great regulative

mind, that disposeth everything, eye of the world, spirit of spirits, god of gods, the lord of the spirits, lord of spirits, the immovable AEON, IAOOUEI, hear my voice.

I call upon thee, the ruler of the gods, high-thundering Zeus, Zeus, king, Adonai, lord, Iaoouee. I am he that invokes thee in the Syrian tongue, the great god, Zaalaer, Iphphou, do thou not disregard the Hebrew appellation, Ablanthanalb, Abrasiloa.

For I am Silthakhookh, Lailam, Blasaloth, Iao, Ieo, Nebouth, Sabiothar, Both, Arbathiao, Iaoth, Sabaoth, Patoure, Zagoure, Baroukh Adonai, Eloai, Iabraam, Barbarauo, Nau, Siph.[72]

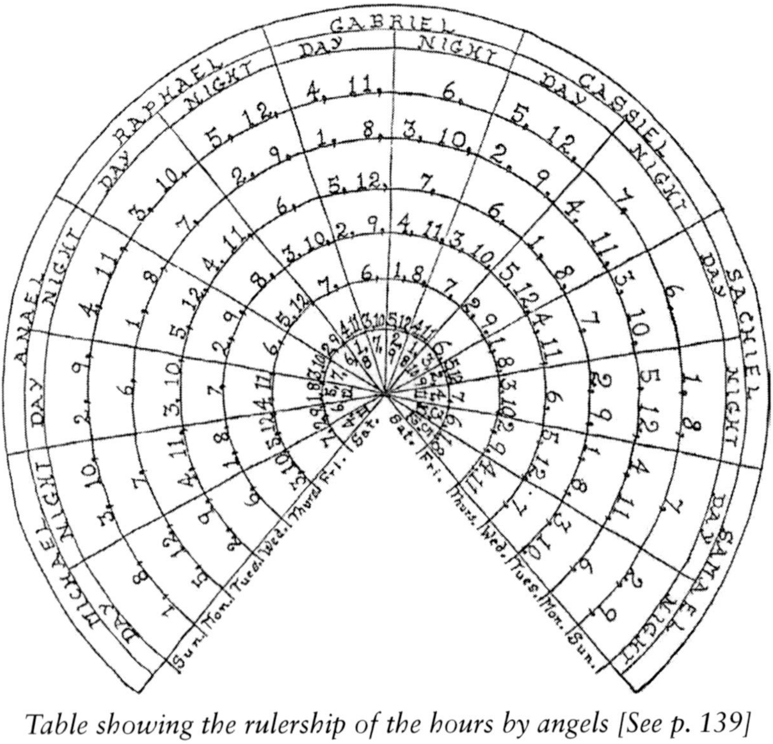

Table showing the rulership of the hours by angels [See p. 139]

The advantage of this spell, we are told, is that it compels the spirit to listen to the instructions of the sorcerer, and to carry out his wishes. Other advantages are that it "chains, blinds, brings dreams, creates favour. It may be used in common for what you will."

This spell is also interesting because of the mixed content of Hebrew, Greek, Syriac and other words.

Another process says that the exorcist should stand within his circle, consecrate it by dedicating the whole experiment in a suitable speech, and then call upon the Good Spirit that he wishes to appear. When he is sure that he is concentrating well, and that no other thought is in his mind, he must address the spirit in a low voice. First he must call his name thrice, and promise that no harm shall befall him. Then, "the spirit should appear".

"Wait for him for the space of a full minute and if the spirit does not appear, repeat the invocation. Pray earnestly during the period of waiting. If the spirit does not materialise within five minutes, strong invocations can be made.

"If the spirit appears, greet him courteously, saying how glad you are to welcome him, and ask him to help you with your problems."

The spirit will then tell the operator the best times to contact him, and may give a "thought-name", which is used to summon him. Some writers say that he must be asked to sign his name in a Book of the Spirits, and to give his sign as well.

"Should you by any ill chance raise an evil spirit, the word 'BAST' will cause him to disappear. This is a word of ancient Egyptian origin, and will make him go without causing any harm."

It is said to be important to ask the spirit to become your guardian angel, and "do not leave the circle for two whole minutes after the spirit's departure. Then say a prayer of thankfulness that he came and went and promised to help you, exactly as you had desired when preparing for his coming. Destroy the circle and the figures, lest a devil or any of his familiars use it against you, which they can do easily. If the circle be not destroyed and an elemental spirit uses it, the former user will never again be able to raise good spirits."

Perhaps the oldest record of the formula for consecrating a circle is the following, taken from the Assyrian *Šurpu*[73] Series of tablets.

Ban! Ban! Barrier that none can pass,
Barrier of the gods, that none may break,
Barrier of heaven and earth that none can change,
Which no god may annul,
Nor god nor man can loose,
A snare without escape, set for evil,
A net whence none can issue forth, spread for evil.
Whether it be evil Spirit, or evil Demon, or evil Ghost,
Or evil Devil, or evil God, or evil Fiend,
Or Hag-demon, or Ghoul, or Robber-sprite,
Or Phantom, or Night-wraith, or Handmaid of the Phantom,
Or evil Plague, or Fever sickness, or unclean Disease,
Which hath attacked the shining waters of Ea,
May the snare of Ea catch it;
Or which hath assailed the meal of Nisaba,
May the net of Nisaba entrap it;
Or which hath broken the barrier,
Let not the barrier of the gods,
The barrier of heaven and earth, let it go free;
Or which reverenceth not the great gods,
May the great gods entrap it,
May the great gods curse it;
Or which attacketh the house,
Into a closed dwelling may they cause it to enter;
Or which circleth round about,

Into a place without escape may they bring it;
Or which is shut in by the house door,
Into a house without exit may they cause it to enter;
Or that which passeth the door and bolt,
With door and bolt, a bar immovable, may they withhold it;
Or which bloweth in at the threshold and hinge,
Or which forceth a way through bar and latch,
Like water may they pour it out,
Like a goblet may they dash it in pieces,
Like a tile may they break it;
Or which passeth over the wall,
Its wing may they cut off;
Or which (lieth) in a chamber,
Its throat may they cut;
Or which looketh in at a side chamber,
Its face may they smite;
Or which muttereth in a... chamber,
Its mouth may they shut;
Or which roameth loose in an upper chamber,
With a bason without opening may they cover it;
Or which at dawn is darkened,
At dawn to a place of sunrise may they take it.[74]

What if no spirit appears, even after repeated concentration? Most books do not envisage the possibility. One of them, however, tells us that the failure means that some mistake or omission has to be remedied. The experiment may be repeated again and again, until successful.

The dynastic (and probably predynastic) Egyptians, the Babylonians and Assyrians believed that the soul could return to earth. Under certain circumstances, too, it could reinhabit the body. Elaborate magical ceremonies were practised, in order that the soul should be happy, and should not need to return, thus becoming an uneasy spirit. These spirits were invoked and it was thought that they could be used in magical rituals.

In a similar way, the spirits of revered but departed witch-doctors are conjured, to give advice to their tribes in times of stress, in many parts of Africa, especially the central portion of the continent. Their bones have been preserved and soaked in the blood of the newly dead, mixed with honey, milk and perfumes. This is supposed to cause the soul to return to the earth. Just as the ceremonies of the spirits were carried out in Egypt in the pyramid burial-places, so elsewhere are grave- and churchyards, or the place where death has taken a violent form, specially revered as sites for this kind of exorcism.

Spirits other than those of the dead may be raised in a similar manner. The following Christianised consecration of a circle is typical of the Chaldaeo-Semitic rites:

After the circle is made, the invocant intones:

> In the name of the holy, blessed and glorious Trinity, proceed we to our work, in these mysteries to accomplish that which we desire: we therefore, in the Names aforesaid, consecrate this piece of ground for our defence, so that no spirit whatsoever shall be able to break these boundaries, neither be able to cause injury nor detriment to any here assembled. [It was usual for magicians to be accompanied by one or more helpers.]
>
> But that they may be compelled to stand before the circle, and answer truly our demands, so far as it pleaseth Him who liveth for ever and ever, and who says, I am Alpha and Omega, the Beginning and the End, which is, and which was, and which is to come, the Almighty. I am the First and the Last, who am living and was dead: and behold I live for ever and ever: and I have the Keys of Death and

> hell. Bless, O Lord! This creature of earth wherein we stand.... [The earth, like all other elements, has its own spirit, referred to as the Creature of Earth.]
>
> Confirm, O God! thy strength in us, so that neither the adversary nor any evil thing may cause us to fail, through the merit of Christ. Amen.

A certain amount of information, however, must be at the disposal of the magician, apart from the invocations and words of power. There are, for a start, the names of the hours. These, as given in one Western magical text, form a strange mixture of Arabic, Semitic and Egyptian names, together with some Greek. They are as follows, and it is probable that they are in fact the names of the spirits of the hours:

Names of the Hours

Day	*Hour*	*Night*
Yain	1	Beron
Janor	2	Barol
Nasina	3	Thami
Salla	4	Athar
Sadedali	5	Methon
Thamur	6	Rana
Ourer	7	Netos
Thamie	8	Tafrae
Neron	9	Sassur
Jayon	10	Agle
Abai	11	Calerva
Natalon	12	Salam

These names are memorised, and the appropriate one is inscribed within the outer concentric circle of evocation, together with words of power, the name of the Season, and the name of the Archangel of the Hour. The names of the Seasons are said to be equivalent to the names of the angels of the seasons: Spring (Caracasa), with Core, Amatiel, Commissoros. Summer comes under Gargatel, Tariel and Gariel. Two angels rule Autumn: Tarquam and Guabarel. Winter completes the cycle with Anabael and the angel Cetarari.

Is evocation to be performed in Spring? If so, the Sign of Spring should be included in the circle and invocations; as well as the name of the earth in Spring, and the names of the Sun and Moon in that season. Four additional sets of information are now needed:

The Name of the Sign of Spring: Spugliguel
The Name of the Earth in Spring: Amadai
The Name of the Sun in Spring: Abraym
The Name of the Moon in Spring: Agusita

	in Summer	*in Autumn*	*in Winter*
Name of the Earth:	Festativi	Rabinnana	Geremiah
Name of the Sun:	Athenay	Abragini	Commutoff
Name of the Moon:	Armatus	Mastasignais	Affaterin

Sign of Autumn: Torquaret
Sign of Summer: Tubiel
Sign of Winter: Attarib

Having mastered these important names, the magician purifies himself with this prayer: "Thou shalt purge me with Hyssop, O Lord, and I shall be clean: thou shalt wash me and I shall be whiter than snow."

The circle is next sprinkled with the correct perfume (which will be described later), and the exorcist drapes himself in a white linen cloak fastened back and front. At the moment of vestment he says:

> "Ansor, Amacon, Amides, Theodonias, Aniton: by the merits of the Angels, O Lord, I will put on the garment of salvation; that this which I desire I may bring to effect, through thee, the most holy Adonai, whose kingdom endureth for ever and ever, Amen."

The Christianised text which we are following, while retaining most of the ritualistic marks of Semitic and other systems, yet has added the warnings that those who desire wealth and power, or any thing material for themselves, will not be able to raise spirits. This is not, however, the established view. "First the heart and mind must be cleansed of desires and if the ability be used at any time towards selfish and personal ends, the power is thereby renounced. Only those with the ability to touch the heights know this."

In necromancy we find the Magic Circle and words of power still in use. The procedure is very much the same in both types of process. When the Asian sorcerer Chiancungi and his witch sister Napala raised evil spirits, they commanded Bokim to appear, and give them his infernal aid. They draped a deep cave in black and then drew the circle, with Seven Thrones and a like number of planets inscribed in it. Even for these notorious sorcerers, it took months before Bokim actually appeared. When he did, he guaranteed them one hundred and fifty-five years of extra life, and many other boons beside. As the "selling of the soul" theory is not so well known in the East, the only penalty that the sorcerers were expected to pay was that they would serve the demon for that period. In their work, as in most invocation spells, they made free use of perfumes and other fumigations.

When the planet involved was Saturn (that is, when the operation was in the hour or day of Saturn), the perfume thrown on the brazier was pepper, with musk and frankincense. When this was burning, spirits in the form of cats or wolves should be seen. Jupiter required offerings of peacock feathers, a swallow, and a piece of lapis-lazuli. Their ashes were then added to the blood of a stork. Spirits of Jupiter had the appearance of kings, accompanied by trumpeters. Under Mars, the fire was fed with aromatic gum, sandalwood and frankincense, myrrh and the blood of a black cat. For the Sun, musk, amber, frankincense, myrrh, saffron, cloves, laurel and cinnamon were mixed with the brain of an eagle and the blood of a white cock,** formed into balls and placed on the flames. Spirits raised under the aegis of Venus demanded spermaceti, roses, coral, aloes, mixed with the brains and blood of a white pigeon. It will be seen that many of the above-named items are familiar in various occult practices.

Mercury called for frankincense, mixed with the brain of a fox. The fires were to be made "far from the habitations of men". Moon spirits were thought to be the most difficult to propitiate. They appeared as ghosts in filmy transparent draperies, with pale and luminous faces. For them the fire needed poppy seed, dried frogs, camphor, frankincense, and the eyes of bulls mixed with blood.

** The sacrifice of the white cock was the opening ceremony of the quarterly gathering of the witches as late as the seventeenth century in Europe. The heart fell to the witch "who could perform the greatest act of sorcery". This organ, it was said, was the open sesame to many experiments. Stuck with pins and roasted, it immunised the witch from discovery and denunciation. Reduced to ashes it sold to witches for as much as two gold pieces. Apart from its use in witch-brews, it was also eaten, we are told, by the cat-familiars of the witch, to preserve the woman from Satan's clutches.

THE METHOD OF CALLING LURIDAN

Magicians are credited with the power to call the spirit Luridan (King of the North) by a method which, though Celtic, seems to have been derived, probably in very early times, from Semitic magic.

Two concentric circles are drawn in chalk on a moonlit night in a lonely valley. The outer circle must be at least eighteen feet in diameter, and the inner one a foot smaller. Two snake skins are worn as a girdle, and two more in the cap: all four must hang down at the back. One side of the circle must have inscribed beside it a fiery mountain "and around the mountain must be written these names: GLAURON + OPOTOK + BALKIN + OPOTOK + ARTHIN + OPOTOK + SNAKNAN + NALAH + OPOTOK."

The mountain must then be consecrated with the words: "OLFRON ANEPHERATON, BARON BARATHON, NAH HALGE TOUR HEELA + + +".

It is supposed that the last three crosses indicate the making of the sign of the cross.

After this has been done the sorcerer should hear awful noises of swords clanking, trumpets sounding, and so on. Then four dwarfs will appear, speaking in Erse, which, however, "they will translate" – presumably if asked.

They are to be asked if they know Luridan, and will reply in the affirmative. Luridan[††] will then appear, in the form of a dwarf.

Now the sorcerer has to "bind" Luridan (get him into his power), by invoking the Great Names that he has already used. He must give the mage a scroll inscribed with mystic

†† "Luridan," we are told in another text, "saith that he is an astral spirit, who dwelt in Jerusalem at the time of King Solomon."

signs, which is a contract to serve the adept for a year and a day.

The sorcerer then dismisses the dwarf-spirit, giving him the famous "Licence to Depart", and the spirit goes away. If the Licence is not pronounced, the apparition was believed to give untold trouble to everyone, and especially to the sorcerer – and a point is generally made of this in magical texts.

It is said that this process will also serve for the invocation of the spirits Rahuniel, Seraphiel, Myniel and Franciel. They are rulers of the North. They will come when called by a magician who is equipped with a parchment bearing the two secret seals of the Earth, if he is wearing a bearskin, with the fur turned inside, next to his own skin.

CHAPTER 11

Iranian Magic

"Destruction of an enemy is wrought by a wax image, seven times melted and congealed... in olden times they believed that its power pursued even beyond the grave."
—Persia: Kitabi Asrari Sihri Qavi, *1526 AH*

"A waxen effigy of a person placed beside a corpse caused evil to befall the cursed person."
—Assyria: Maqlu, *Tablet IV*

PERSIA SHOULD BE the best of all fields for the study of Middle Eastern magic. But the conquests and religious controversies which have affected this buffer country between East and West during the past three thousand years have resulted in much that would have been of great importance being lost. That the Zoroastrians had a body of magical ritual of great antiquity is well known.[‡‡] Some of this is preserved in the secret books of their descendants, the Parsis of contemporary India. The Arab conquest at the beginning of the seventh century swept away many traces of occult practices, and

‡‡ Zoroaster himself is the reputed author of 20,000 magical couplets.

substituted beliefs brought from the Arabian desert. Traces of the Assyrian and Babylonian supernatural beliefs once so rampant in Persia, remain, generally speaking, only in rural areas, preserved in the form of tribal charms and spells.

Works of contemporary magic are of comparatively rare occurrence in Persia, even today: rare, that is, in comparison with such places as Egypt and India, where they are to be bought freely. When, however, one does come across a Persian magical manuscript, it very often bears unmistakable marks of serious occult study and belief: in contradistinction to the Indian and Egyptian efforts, which are most often merely intriguingly titled tracts to lure pennies from the credulous.

On the other hand, the Persians usually take their magic seriously. Evidence of this is contained in a manuscript which I was allowed to examine by a self-styled adept. Containing some four hundred pages, I concluded from its calligraphy and phraseology that it was about two hundred years old. Entitled the *Ocean of Mysteries*, it contained no illustrations, and, unlike many magical scripts, bore marks of a certain amount of research.

The *Ocean of Mysteries* is arranged under thirty headings, seems to have been adapted from some other work of a similar nature, and the copy under consideration had been annotated by some previous owner. Probably to avoid censure by Muslim religious teachers, the Preface contains a warning that "nothing can be done in the way of Magic, without the consent of God; and that consent is only extended to those who fit themselves for virtue by considerable effort of will and body".

The first chapter is designed, apparently, to get the student into a suitable frame of mind for magic. Supernatural practices are referred to as means whereby those with special training may make "one lifetime do the work of two" – an unusual example of time-saving which goes to show, among other things, that the Easterner is not so patient as he may be thought.

No person can become successful in his dealings with the spirits which guard magical secrets, says the *Ocean*, until he has spent thirty days in meditation, eating as little as he can while still maintaining life. As far as possible, the "gaze must be directed towards the ground", and failure to observe five ritual washings of the hands, feet, face, eyes and ears will be punished by complete lack of success as a magician. For the first thirty days' dedication, the invocant must spend some time "alone, and in a room which women are not allowed to enter" in memorising the names of the angels which guard magical secrets. During this time, too, certain amulets must be prepared. The first is a hand holding a crescent moon, made in silver, and wrapped in cotton and silk. The second, which should not be looked upon until the thirty days have elapsed, must be made of clay, and contain three pieces of coloured cotton, each "the length of your small finger". The third amulet is two interlocked squares, inscribed on white paper with a black pen in black ink.

These are the amulets which are supposed to guard the sorcerer from harm. They show a similarity to ancient Chaldean amulets, and the interlocked squares may be connected with the "Seal of Solomon".

A patched cloak, or a cloak made up out of patchwork, must be prepared, in which the predominant colours are saffron, white and blue. Rosewater is employed to give the cloak the requisite odour, and it is put on before any magical ceremony, with the words: "RASHAN, ARSHAH, NARASH" – which, as far as I am aware, are not used in any other important Eastern ritual.

The writer of the *Ocean* tells us that it is essential that the head be covered during all magical rites – though the feet must be bare. "Do not grow your beard beyond the prescribed length." This latter injunction is probably connected with the Islamic teaching current in Persia, that the beard should not be longer than a clenched fist.

"If you wish," continues the sage, "to hasten the illumination which will come to you, make sure that you wear this cloak when you meditate, and also see that you sit on a specially made rug, of skins."

The whole training takes a hundred days: "Thirty of abstinence, thirty of recuperation, and thirty of fasting from dawn to dusk, eating only at night. Then will follow the ten days in which you will feel that the power is coming into you."

During the fasting, the magician must dedicate himself. This means that he must decide what his aims are, and make certain exactly what he wants from his first magical experiment. It is important to note here that "dogs, if allowed to come near the student during the Hundred Days, will so destroy his *barakat* (power) that he will have to commence again, after complete immersion, and start at the New Moon".

Having thus clothed himself, fasted and dressed, the would-be sorcerer must then write (in black, on white paper, etc.) what he wants to do in the way of spells. These are known as the "Kutub" (books), and he must look at them at least once a day – preferably morning and evening.

After preparing himself thus, the magician goes to a spot where he will not be disturbed. This is the place of the first rite – the ritual which will make him a magician. Seven stones are set up "one above the other" on the ground. Around them he circumambulates, repeating the names of the angels to himself.

Three things are to be carried by our hero: fresh clay, mixed with grass; and two small pots, one containing honey, the other goats'wool. They are to be mixed together in the middle of the circle, and the following prayer is intoned, after the eleventh circuit:

"Núlúsh! I do tie thee! I do command thee to come to me, in the great name that was known to Solomon, the son of David, the great magician, in whose name I speak!"

Then the invocant ("without looking for Núlúsh") repeats the formula of exorcism:

"*Ashhadu inna la illaha illa Allah*" (repeated twice) and "*Audu-billahi min ash-Shaitan er-Rajim!*"

This latter formula is to prevent the Devil interrupting the proceedings.

The spirit which is invoked will come, but "will not appear in human form unless you command it to do so". Those, it is to be supposed, who may not be able to face the actual incarnate form of the spirit, can then order it to accomplish whatever is desired – and return home.

But if the spirit is actually materialised, it can be told to come at certain times, to take orders. It can even – reminiscent of the *Arabian Nights* – be induced to enter a bottle, and kept there, by means of the following process:

> Take the tail of a cat, and place it with several drops of indigo-dye in a small metal bottle, that shall not be made of anything but brass. If it is made of brass, dangers will be averted. Remove the cat's tail, but allow the indigo to remain in the bottle.
>
> As soon as you have repeated thirty-three times the words: "In the name of Solomon, son of David, prince of the Magicians, I order the Spirit of Power (name the Spirit) to enter into this bottle," he will appear, and beg that you allow him to go home in peace. Say "Peace be upon you, and know, Spirit, that thy home is now in this bottle, and I am thy

> Master, and all that I say or do shall be thy interest and aim to help." The spirit will then enter the bottle, in the form of a small white cloud.
>
> You must make sure that you have a stopper for this bottle, and this must fit tightly, and be made of lead, and of no other material. This stopper you will then put in the neck of the bottle, so that a space is left. Into this space you will pour boiling pitch, mixed with the sap of the Cedar tree.
>
> When you want to speak to the spirit, call him, and treat him like a friend. You will then see him, through the side of the bottle, and he will have a small face, like a human, but round.

The spirit should be spoken to once a day, and must be "allowed to work small favours, just like your slave, for this is the way to make a slave happy; he likes to know that he is of service to his master". When the spirit sees some harm coming to his master, he will call ("and it will sound like a small shout in front of you") – addressing you as Solomon, son of David. If you can you must also allow him to return home once in twelve years. He will always return to you if you take from him the small, turquoise tablet, which has his name and functions inscribed thereon, "and with which all the Jinni were invested by Solomon, and without which they are not free...."

In order to memorise the entire contents of a book, the genie will be ordered to project it into the magician's mind, and the latter will learn it while asleep. There is a complete catalogue of spells, charms and other processes that can be accomplished – it seems that they can be done with the aid of any genie, unless they contradict his nature. The "nature" of the genii means that some have been given the Dominion of Fire, others that of Air, and so on.

As would be natural in a society where such activities were prevalent, other magicians might try to harm the sorcerer. This will be prevented by the spirit, which will call out when a spell is being woven against his master. He will also tell how this magic can be countered: by making a small clay or wax image and putting this in a boat in a small, artificial pond, which boat is then sunk, and certain imprecations recited over the wreck.

"In matters of the heart," observes the author, "great discretion must be exercised; for there are some things which are possible, and yet reprehensible; and the performance of these tasks will be repugnant to the honour of the spirit, and he might try to escape, rather than carry out instructions which are not allowed to him." Hidden treasures will be brought, we are told, even from the uttermost parts of the earth: "but you will surely not desire them, and you will see that there will be many other things that you will want to do by means of this genie which will contribute towards the wellbeing of mankind, and which will surprise even you, though you had before been a man of exemplary habits and desirous of doing good".

The recreations of a Persian sorcerer, however, are delightful. "To fly: call thrice the name of the spirit, saying, 'I desire to fly to Yemen', and you will be there in a few moments. If you do not secrete upon your person the bottle, you will not be able to return."

It seems that magicians wanted to dwell in beautiful gardens, and the technique for being transported there is the subject of several long passages. There are Indian and Mongolian gardens and those of the garden spirits unknown to the world at large, but existing for the pleasure of the few who find their way there.

Storms can be raised, rich people beggared, poor travellers helped to oases, the ugly made beautiful and vice versa; all the dreams of life can be realised – once you have a spirit in a bottle.

Ordinary magicians, though, cannot maintain their magical powers indefinitely without recharging them. Hence the warning: "The student should always make sure that he has repeated his rites once a year, or the power will become weaker. If he sees that the spirit is not pleased, he must go away to a secluded place, and repeat the magical words, wearing his robes and in the same way in which he did at first; and then he is to return to the spirit, and ask What ails thee?"

Another indispensable requirement is that of secrecy. "Under no circumstances may it be revealed to anyone whatever that you are able to command the spirits. This is not only because such things are frowned upon, but because your power will be lost in this way, and you will not have another chance to develop it until twenty years have passed."

Anyone embarking upon a period of magical training for the attainment of a petty or unworthy end will either become unworthy of the society of men or will become purified. "Do not expect that the exercise of magic will leave you unchanged; your motives and your thoughts, unless brought under restraint, will deepen, and will change. It is not a ritual for those who are weak in heart and courage."

There is a pleasant, almost light-hearted, air about this book which is quite out of keeping with the traditional Eastern writings on the subject. The whole ritual, if such it may be called, is simplified and fairly direct; although there are grave warnings against certain attitudes and practices, they are nothing compared with later tracts and the religio-magical writings of the ancient Semites and Accadians.

Modern writers on occult subjects would call this a "composite ritual", tracing in it characteristics of the

Semites, of India and the Sumerians. Whether it is "bogus" or not naturally depends upon the standpoint of the critic. This much, however, may be said: it is very probably not an entirely original work, and does not represent a transmitted grimoire of sorcery dating from high antiquity. Annotations on the margins indicate that it may have been a text used by a group of independent magicians over a century ago. Although I have never seen – or heard of – another copy, these marginal notes query certain passages, and in one place, for example, the unknown commentator has written "Jasmine is better than goat-hair".

One curious chapter deals with arguments against alchemy, and goes so far as to state that "It should never be attempted, as it is a delusion, and even if not a delusion, is something which was originally intended to be something else, and which is displeasing to spirits and God alike." While the thesis that alchemical writings are allegorical, and refer to the refining of the human soul, is familiar to those versed in Arab philosophy, nevertheless it is unusual to find a magical book actually condemning the art.

Persian magic, as it is known today, contains elements from the rites of the Mongols, Chinese, Hindus and Arabs, in addition to native beliefs and practices. One of the characteristics of a Persian sorcerer of old was his belief in the *Huma* bird, which never alighted on earth, but travelled far and wide, and brought tidings to initiates, of what was happening in every country. The Huma, it appears, does not speak any human tongue. Like Solomon, it is necessary to learn the speech of birds before his messages can be understood.

It is stated that a model of one of these birds was found suspended over the throne of Tipu Sultan in 1799. The Huma flies on the winds, and collects his information partly from the *divs*, or spirits, who are to be found everywhere.

The largest houses in Persia have towers, which catch the wind and cool the rooms underneath in the summer heat. If the day be auspicious, the good *divs* will make the winds blow – unless they are needed by the Huma, during one of his periodical transits across the heavens.

Being such a traveller, and also of uncounted age, the Huma knows the site of the Fountain of Life. Watched over by magicians, and guarded by innumerable jinns and *divs*, the Fountain is believed by many to be situated in the Persian Hills. There is no doubt that throughout the ages people have actually embarked on the search for the Fountain. It is said of those who do not return that they have found it, and either been killed before getting even one precious drop: or that they have drunk it and been transformed into pure beings who do not wish to return to their homes.

Mountains, in Persia as elsewhere, have many magical associations. The *Kohi-Gabr* (Fire-Worshipper's Mountain) rises steeply to a considerable height. On the top there is a ruin, said to be all that is left of an ancient fire-temple. Here the concentrated essence of magic lingers, and a host of specially endowed jinns dwell. The "power", it is claimed, causes people who approach to recoil. There is something almost physical about it. Tales are told of those who have climbed the Koh and returned mad, or lame, or wasting away. It is possible that these legends are a survival of pre-Islamic times, when Zoroastrians probably circulated such rumours, to enable themselves to practise their arts there unobserved.

Not everyone, however, who approaches the dread ruin will suffer danger or destruction. Young brides consider it the ultimate token of love if their husbands climb the heights and bring back a stone from the ruins.

Not far from this famous place are other hills equally endowed with magical beliefs. Here the fire-worshipping magicians used to place offerings of fruit, to propitiate certain spirits, and to lure them into captivity, to do their bidding. Those who had a desire to fulfil used to have it written and placed in a bowl of fruit, for the Magians to take to these heights. On the top of one of these hills grew the Tobo tree, the tree of eternal happiness. This is said to be like the one in Paradise, which grows at Allah's right hand. Great griefs and fears are carried by good fairies to this spot, where they are cleansed and the sufferers set free from unhappiness.

CHAPTER 12

Magical Rites of the Atharva Veda

> *"A curse with a thousand eyes comes, wheelborne: and it seeks him that curses me: like a wolf seeks the dwelling of the owner of sheep... strike he that curses me, O Curse!... Him do I cast to his death!"*
>
> —*Veda IV, 6:37*

THAT THE ATHARVA Veda of the Brahmins – the "Secret Work" – is a textbook of magic will be obvious from the extracts presented here.[§§]

What is more important to realise is that it is not regarded as a work of witchcraft or sorcery. Among the spells included are several which actually curse magicians: and others which seek to arm the Brahmin priest with effective counters to the magic-working of others. Thus, from the Brahmin point of view, the Veda is White, or legitimate, Magic. While the usual

[§§] Originally memorised by Brahmin priests, and supposed to be used only after purification and dedication rites, the spells of the largely magical Atharva Veda are believed to be efficacious by millions of Hindus. Originally called the "Brahma Veda" (Book for Brahmins), its status, according to Hindu theology, is lower than the Three Vedas; hence the title of Fourth Veda sometimes applied to it.

difference between the two is taken to be the degree to which actual evil is encouraged, the Atharva Veda strikes at the root of the magical problem. Where a spell can cause either good or evil, depending upon the purpose for which it is used, is it Black or White magic?¶¶

According to the beliefs of the compilers of the Veda, magic is not only true, but lawful when applied by those pure in heart. This is the main reason why for centuries the Atharva Veda was only read to select initiates.

These extracts form an interesting study of the scope and purpose of magical practice among the Vedic Brahmins.

SPELL FOR EVERLASTING LIFE

Immortality be upon this one! He is a sharer of the Sun's everlasting life. Indra and Agni have blessed him, and have taken him into immortality. Bhaga and Soma are with him, carrying him high, to prolong his days.

> There will now be no danger of death:
>
> This world will keep you, forever, rise up!
> The Sun, the Wind, the Rain, are all with thee!
>
> Thy body shall be strong and unaffected by any disease.
> Life will be thine, I promise it; enter this ascending
> Never-perishing, age-old chariot....

¶¶ The theory that "Black" Magic is connected with Satan-worship is a later, Christian opinion, which was at its height during the Inquisition and the reign of such monarchs as James I of England.

Top, left: Sudanese sorcerer in magical regalia, about to conduct an initiation ceremony (Ch. 6)

Centre, left: Indian cave-temple at Ajanta, considered the ideal place of Atharvic rites (Ch. 13)

Bottom, left: Pre-Islamic cave-shrine at Petra (Ch. 8). "Still the haunt of Solomon's Djinns"

Top, right: Unique picture of the shrine where the cloak of the Prophet Muhammad reposes, in Kandahar (Ch. 8)

Bottom, right: Ritual magical dance at Kordofan, Sudan (Ch. 6). Note magical axes and state of exaltation of the performers.

Top: Tiksay Lamasery, reputed home of an "abominable snowman".

Bottom, left: Chung-Khwei, the Chinese demon-destroying spirit, accompanied by a bat

Centre: Chinese ritual sword of exorcism, made of brass coins strung with red cotton on a magnetized rod. All coins must be of the same dynasty (Ch. 17)

Bottom, right: Shoki: Japanese counterpart of Chung-Khwei. Belt, sword and robes are similar and considered necessary

Bottom, centre: Ancient Buddhist Stupa, where the Bonist demon, Yama, is invoked. Unique photograph.

> Thy heart will be strong, thou shalt be apart from others.
> Forget those who have died, they are no longer for thee.
>
> The twin many-coloured dogs of Yama, guards of the road,
> Shall not follow thee (to take thy life).
>
> Follow the path where the fire will guide thee, the purifying flame, and it will not harm thee, this celestial burning!
>
> Savitar, the Saver, will guard thee, taking into converse
> The great Vayu, of the living, Indra; and strength and
> Breath shall be with thee: the spirit of life will
> Ever remain. No illness shall touch thee; all Powers are on
> Thy side.
>
> By a variety of efforts I have rescued thee: henceforth
> There will not be any danger, nor death, nor disease.

This spell, like the others in the Veda, is chanted by the Brahmin before the man who desires everlasting life. The next charm is used if the operator himself wishes his days prolonged.[74]

> Take hold of this charm that subjects to immortality, may thy life unto old age not be cut off! I bring to thee anew breath and life: go not to mist and darkness, do not waste away!
>
> Come hither to the light of the living; I rescue thee unto a life of a hundred autumns! Loosing the bands of death and imprecation, I bestow upon thee long life extended very far.
>
> From the Wind thy breath I have obtained, from the sun thine eye; thy soul I hold fast in thee: be together with thy limbs, speak articulating with thy tongue!

> With the breath of two-footed and four-footed creatures I blow upon thee, as on Agni when he is born. I have paid reverence, O Death, to thine eyes, reverence to thy breath.
>
> This person shall live and shall not die. We rouse him to life! I make for him a remedy. O Death, slay not this man!
>
> The plant "quickening", forsooth-no-harm, a victorious, mighty saviour-plant do I invoke, that he may be exempt from injury.
>
> Befriend him, do not seize him, let him go; though he be thy very own, let him stay here with unimpaired strength. O Bhava and Sarva, take pity, grant protection; misfortune drive away and life bestow!
>
> Befriend him, Death, pity him; let him rise unaided. Through old age over a hundred years, let him be well.

HEALTH CHARMS AND INVOCATIONS

As with other magical systems, the Atharva Veda holds that while certain plants and trees possess healing and other supernatural powers, these functions can only be exercised subject to certain conditions. Knowing the kind of herb to employ for each spell is not enough. The plant must be exorcised, invocations made to the spirit residing within it, and the usual requirements of ritual purity and prayer observed.

In treating disease, much depends upon the diagnosis. Specific complaints – coughs, lameness, blindness – have their known cures. Diseases caused by demons, however, must be combated in accordance with the formulas laid down in the Veda for this purpose.

If the cause of the illness is not known, recourse is made to universal panaceas. Those who are apparently healthy call to their aid either elixirs of life or charms to produce complete immunity from all disease.

In all cases, however, the magical plants and remedies must be addressed in suitable terms. This is the first step, undertaken by all Hindu magicians working according to the discipline of the Atharva Veda:

Invocation to the Plants

> We invoke and address the magical plants: plants that are red, those that are white, and the brown and black herbs: all these do we invoke! Verily the spirits are in control of the infirmities. Herbs, rooted in the seas, mothered by the land, fathered by the sky!
>
> Plants and herbs of the Heavens! Illness and maladies coming from sinfulness do you exorcise!
>
> I call upon the creepers, upon those plants that bear luxurious foliage. These are herbs that give us life: they multiply by division (of their stems), they are vigorous, they have strong shoots.
>
> O plants and herbs! You have the power to rescue this sufferer! I call upon you and adjure you to make the remedy that I shall prepare powerful and effective.

Certain plants are then gathered. Very often their family is not so important as their appearance. Ailments which cause swellings are believed to be alleviated by herbs with bulbous roots. Those who have the jaundice can be cured by invocations to yellow leaves – and so on.

When the requisite number of leaves and roots have been collected, they may be addressed: as in this instance of a panacea for all ills:

Panacea for all ills

> It is these plants, these highly endowed ones, which shall liberate the sufferer! Verily I acknowledge, O Herbs, that your lord is Soma, and that you are made by none other than Brihaspati! The shadow that is over us, that threatens us, shall be overcome!
>
> We demand release from ills. From curses and the snares of Varuna we claim freedom. From the shackles of Yama, and from the consequences of our sins against the spirits!
>
> We have committed sins of thought, or of speech, against the Gods: let these be expunged from us, let us be free of ills!

The Talisman of Force

Considered one of the most potent of all charms is that made from the wood of the Sraktya tree – the *clerodendrum phlomoides*. A piece of the wood is cut, then shaped into something representing the object of one's desire. For victory in battle the supplicant fashions a sword or spear from the wood. In many cases, however, a simple disc is made, bearing radiating lines to indicate the Chakra – an ancient Indian sun-sign.

Theoretically the wood of this tree is credited with a wide variety of virtues, embracing almost every sphere of human ambition. In the secret writings, however, its use is generally limited to protection, fecundity, virility, prosperity and defence against witchcraft. When completed, the charm is tied on the right arm. The hymn addressed to the charm itself varies with the effect wanted, though the very possession of such a charm is believed to grant many of the powers associated with its traditional virtues. This is the "protection-spell" used in conjunction with the talisman:

Protection Spell of the Sraktya Charm

Bound upon the owner this charm is all-powerful. It makes the possessor strong and brave, kills enemies, brings fortune to him who has it. It is potent, too, against all magic. This is the charm used by Indra to kill Vritra. He smashed the Asuras, and became master of heaven and earth, and with its aid he overcame the four spheres of space. Yes, this talisman is an attacking and victorious one. It will destroy the enemy, and will protect us from him.

This is what Agni and Soma have said, Indra, Brihaspati and Savitar, all concur in this. Those who attack me will be repelled, and the same force as they use shall rebound upon them: by the force of this talisman!

Heaven, Earth, the Sun, the Sages, all shall stand between me and the enemy. Their force shall rebound upon them: by the force of this talisman!

This talisman is to me and other users as is an all-powerful armour. It ascends the spheres like the Sun rising into Heaven, destroys all magic against me. It is a potent force, and the Rashas will fall before it!

Indra, Vishnu, Savitar, Rudra, Agni, Prajapati, Parameshthin, Viraj, Vaysvanara, all of them, the powerful spirits, shall stand behind the amulet, which is affixed to the wearer, as a powerful armour.

O most potent tree, potent like a leader amongst beasts, thou art my guardian and my help, such did I need, such have I found. And I, wearing this charm am like a tiger, like a bull, like unto a lion: nothing can touch me, wearer of this charm. He who wears it can command all, and be their ruler.

Produced and made by Kassyapa, worn by Indra in his battles, surely he is a vanquisher. It is the power of the spirits that makes this amulet one of power multiplied a thousandfold. O Indra, with a whip of a hundred lightning-flashes, strike him who would seek to strike me, by virtue of this charm!

And this great and powerful talisman does strike to victory wherever it is used. It produces children, fecundity, security, fortunes!

Those who are against us in the north, in the south, in the west, in the east, uproot them, O Indra!

My protection, like an armour, is the sun, the day and night, the heavens and the earth. My protection is Indra, and Agni. Dhatar will give me that protection! Every spirit that there is cannot pierce the defences of Indra and Agni: this is the strength that I have between me and the enemy. O spirits! Let me become old and not be cut off in my youth!

Nothing can happen to the wearer of this amulet. It is the very talisman of invulnerability!

If the talisman is being given to someone by a sorcerer, the master will end his recital with the words: "This is the all-potent talisman! O Indra, giver of prosperity, killer of Vritra, overlord of enemies, the conqueror, safeguard against all peril, protect this man and grant him thy help, by day and night!"

Sometimes an offering of butter is made. If it is desired to use the amulet in war, a fire of broken arrows is kindled before it to symbolise the destruction of the foe.[***]

OCCULT MEDICINE OF THE VEDA

According to the Atharva Veda, most diseases can be rapidly cured by spells.

Spell against Sores

> The sores upon the neck (or wherever the sore may be) will disappear. These are the fifty-five sores, and the seventy-seven sores, and the ninety-nine sores: they shall all disappear!

While the repetition continues – and it should be said seventy times – fifty-five leaves of the parasu plant are lighted with some burning pieces of wood. The oozing sap of the leaves is then collected, as far as may be possible, into a cup, and applied to the sores. Then a balm composed of the saliva of a dog, ground seashells and "stings from insects" is rubbed into the affected place.

*** This ritual is closely paralleled in Semitic Magic. The Babylonians, too, made ceremonial destruction of war symbols their victory rite – even to the offering of butter; invoking Ishtar, Shamash and Nergal (Zimmern, *Ritualtafeln*, 173).

But perhaps more attractive to the general spell-minded public is one, designed to combat all evil, to banish disease of whatever origin:

Spell against all Evil

> Release me, evil power; please release me, the unfortunate victim of your malice! Let me escape this evil thing, and be happy again!
>
> If you do not release me, then I will abandon you at the next crossroads: and you will follow and possess another!
>
> Go, follow another: join the man who is my enemy, strike him!

The manufacture of this spell is complicated by the ritual which supplements its recitations. These are repeated at night, while dried corn is sieved, then discarded. The following day the invocant throws three small offerings of food into running water, as a sacrifice to the Spirit of a Thousand Eyes.

Repairing to a crossroads, he then scatters three portions of cooked rice there as "bait" for the evil to enter, prior to its taking up a new abode in the body of the enemy to whom it will be consigned.

Spell against Poison

Poison, says the Veda, can be combated by this ritual. First the spell is recited, in a low voice, while bowing to an idol representing the Serpent-god Takshaka. During this, the patient drinks a small quantity of water, while water is also sprinkled upon him. This water has been specially prepared by soaking in it a piece of the Krimuka tree. Next, an old garment is heated and plunged into another vessel of water which the patient has to drink also. Some mix the two drinks with clarified butter, and stir the whole with the shafts of poisoned arrows. It is perhaps not surprising that the patient is expected to become sick after these ceremonies. This is the spell to be recited:

> Brahmana, drinking of the sacred Soma, he of the ten heads and ten mouths, rendered all poison without power. I have announced, throughout the breadth of the heavens and earth, throughout all space, the power of this charm.
>
> Garutamant, the eagle, drank of the poison: but it was powerless against him. In a like manner I have deflected the power of the poison, as an arrow is deflected.
>
> O arrow, thy point and thy venom have no power: equally, all those concerned in the making and use of this poison, those too have I rendered impotent. Even the crags upon which the plants of poison grow have become powerless before me. Everything of this poison is negatived. Poison, thy power is gone!

CHARMS AGAINST DISEASE AND DEMONS

The Atharvan magician has to guard against disease and demons: the former on behalf of his clients – often the ancient kings and their families – the latter because they might affect the power of his magic adversely. The following charm is said to be effective against both types of menace, and against illness caused by malignant spirits as well. It represents a formidable challenge to hostile forces. A charm is first made, from the Gangida tree, and over it this spell is intoned:

> The seers, while speaking the name of Indra, gave to man the Gangida. It had been made a remedy by the gods from the beginning, and a destroyer of the Vishkandha.
>
> Protect us, Gangida, for we look after his treasures, verily the gods and the Brahmanas made him a protection that nullifies evil forces!
>
> I have approached the evil eye of the inimical; O thousand-eyed one, destroy all these! Gangida, thou art our refuge.
>
> The Gangida will protect me from the heavens, from the earth, from plants, from the air; and from the past, and from the future. I am to be protected in every direction!
>
> May the all-powerful, protective Gangida render all the magic of gods and men weak and powerless!

This quotation, apart from its interest as typical of the protective type of Hindu spell, tells us that such is the power of the Gangida tree, that even spells cast by gods cannot have effect against it. Here we note the merging of magic into a power almost of its own, a power that seems to exist apart from that merely "borrowed" from gods and men. This is a point which, I think, has been insufficiently noted by many commentators on magical practice. It has often been remarked that the typical sorcerer will first appeal to gods, then repudiate them or threaten them if the spell does not succeed. This occurs, too, in the conjurations of the Jews. Surely it is an extension of this idea that the god or being which is addressed is not the ultimate power invoked? In later codices where Christian formulae have been substituted for earlier ones, this is made clear enough. Equally, then, it could be maintained that the pagan gods or spirits called upon to serve the sorcerer are merely acting as intermediaries or agents for the power by whose mandate magic is exercised. What is this greater power? It may or may not refer to the subconscious unitarian yearning in man. This raises theological issues, but it could prove a fertile field of study: if only occultists and even anthropologists would venture off the beaten track; that is to say, if they would cease to be content with merely cataloguing the observations of others.

In the final analysis, it should be noted that charms and spells are not always of themselves certain to effect a cure. This explains why several charms for achieving the same result are prescribed in the magical writings.

If, then, a charm does not work, is another tried, and so on, until a cure is found? I asked this question of the Brahmin priest who was my guide to the magical codices of Hinduism. He replied that this was a Western, empirical and cart-before-the-horse method. According to the established view, a cure is not only possible, but certain. It may be, however, that certain planetary influences are suitable for one type of incantation and not another. Or, it may be that one kind of demon causes one disease, and one another. These facts should be known to every practitioner of occult medicine.

Hence the variety of charms and amulets employed in various circumstances. This practitioner then quoted the following alternative exorcism of disease:

VARANA-TREE EXORCISM

> This disease shall be cut off by the divine force of the Varana tree; so, too, will the gods shut off this disease!

> I am shutting off this disease, by command of Indra, by command of Mitra, and by Varuna, and all the gods.
>
> Just as Vritra held fast these everflowing waters, thus do I shut off disease from this person, with the power of Agni Vaisvanara.

Certain plants, as well as water and barley, are important adjuncts to the power of incantations and amulets. In order to bring out the latent power in these objects, they have to be consecrated and "sensitised".

The very fact that the magician has such magical elements in his home will cause the occult power to be attracted, and to build up in intensity day by day. This is the general oration made over fresh water and barley:

> This barley was ploughed with force, and there were used yokes of eight and of six. Ailments will be driven off with it. As the wind blows, downwards, the sun shines downwards, downwards comes the milk from the cow; thus let the ailments (that can be healed by this) pass away! Water is healing; water drives off illness; waters cure all ills; these waters will make a cure for thee!

HYMN TO THE PLANTS

When magical plants are gathered fresh for curative purposes, this hymn is chanted over them:

> We invoke, brown, white, speckled, coloured and black plants; they are to protect this person from ills sent by the gods: their father is the sky, mother

> the earth, root the ocean. Heavenly plants drive forth sinful disease.
>
> The plants that spread forth, plants that are bushy, some with a single sheath, and those that are creepers; these I do invoke. I call the plants that have shoots, plants that have stalks, those that cause their limbs to be divided, those that have been made by the gods, strong ones that give life to man.
>
> With the might that is yours, ye mighty ones, with the power and the force that is yours, with that do ye, O Plants, rescue this man from his ill-health! I am now making the remedy.
>
> The plants givala, naghrisha, givanti, and the plant arundhati, which takes away (ills) is flowering, and I call upon them to help him.
>
> The wise plants are to come here, they understand what I am saying, and we may come together to bring this man safely to good health.
>
> They are the food of the fire, the children of the water, they grow and regrow, strong, healing plants, with a thousand names, brought all together here.
>
> Prickly plants, thrust aside evil. Plants that act against witchcraft, shall come here, plants which have been bought, which protect animals and men, they shall come.
>
> The tops, the ends, the middles of all these plants are steeped in honey, and they shall all, even unto thousands, aid against death and suffering.
>
> The talisman made of plants is like a tiger; it will protect against hostility, it will drive off all disease.
>
> Diseases will flow away along the rivers....

These invocations continue for several lines. Invoking all manner of gods and powers, speaking of classical instances in Indian mythology, wherein great victories were won and lost, the thundering voice of the magician relentlessly carries on his struggle to bring together all the powers that he can invoke.

As he sways backwards and forwards on his haunches, the Brahmin must nod his head with the rhythm of the recitation, and he should feel the power derived from the plants perceptibly growing inside his body. It has been described to me as a real physical feeling.

CHAPTER 13

India: Rites of the Priest-Magicians

"I am dedicated to achieving power and knowledge in this world, and promotion in the other world...."

—Rite of Invocation to the Asuvata Tree

WHILE LITTLE COMPARATIVE research into the fundamentals of Eastern and Western occult lore has been carried out by dispassionate scholars, certain principles important to this study have been established. Perhaps the most startling of them is the strange similarity between the ancient Greek school, the rites of the Jewish Cabbalists, and the arcane disciplines of Vedic India.

Stemming from a mystical approach to wonder-working attained through magic, all these schools embraced in common purification rites, ceremonial dress, incantation and asceticism. The sanctity of a divine name, whose very utterance was reserved for special occasions, and three degrees of initiation form another cornerstone of their occult practice.

What are the Indian schools of magic, and how do they achieve their aims? In the first place India, like any other country, abounds with charlatans whose main object in life is the extraction of a mere livelihood through sleight-of-hand or confidence tricks: some of them ingenious in the extreme. But a very large section of the population subscribes in some degree to belief in, if not actual practice of, magic. Those whose whole-time occupation is the study and attempted use of occult science – such as the Sadhus and Fakirs – prepare themselves by one of the strictest and most austere disciplines recorded in human history.

In the same way, their "miracles" – which I have myself seen and attempted to test as scientifically as possible – seem to exceed in scope almost anything else.

Briefly, Hindu occult science rests upon the belief that power over anything and everything on earth may be obtained by means of benign spirits. As with the Chinese, such beings may be souls of the departed, or simply disembodied entities under whose supervision come the laws of nature. Should, for example, it be desired to interfere with the law of gravity, the spirit guarding that law must be invoked, and beseeched for help. This type of experiment is considered among the most elementary; so startling are the results obtained by these Sadhus, that I am almost driven to the conclusion that there may be some natural law which is as yet undiscovered in the West, which enables seeming miracles to be performed by those who have attuned their minds to it.

Here is a case: I induced a Hindu magician of considerable importance to demonstrate certain tricks to me. He came one evening to my bungalow, dressed in a small loincloth and carrying nothing but a small, seven-ringed stick – the badge or wand of Hindu occultists. I made several tests. First, having made sure that there was no confederate or apparatus present, I asked him if he would make a chair rise from the ground, and hover in space. Knitting his brows in deep concentration, he closed his eyes and extended both hands towards the largest chair on the verandah. In ten seconds – timed with a stopwatch – the chair seemed to rise into the air, and, turning slightly, actually hover in space, about five feet up. I approached it and pulled on the legs. It descended to the floor; but as soon as I let go it sailed upwards again. I asked the man if I could myself be carried up with the chair. He nodded his head. Pulling it down again – the thing seemed to have a life of its own by now – I sat upon the seat and *rose into the air on it.* Convinced that some sort of hypnosis was behind this, I got him to make all the furniture in the place rise. Then I asked him to bring flowers from a nearby garden – which all appeared.

I had no flashlight camera, or this would have been an opportunity to test the matter once and for all. Yet I could not believe that hypnosis as we know it was behind the affair. In the first place the induction of the hypnotic state must have been amazingly rapid; secondly, even while the phenomena were being produced, I could not bring myself to believe that they were genuine. I seemed in no way *en rapport* with the magician – for I was easily able to refer to my prearranged list of phenomena, and ask him to produce them for me. But what finally disposed of my suspicion that hypnosis as we know it might have been used was this: I asked the Hindu to describe to me the contents of the next two letters that I should receive – and he did so correctly. Next, I asked him to bring me immediately a rifle that I knew belonged to a neighbour, and to be in the next house about five miles away. And the gun appeared. The following morning, while I was having breakfast, the owner of the rifle came to collect it. At the time I was almost too confused to think. He claimed that he had dreamed the previous night that I had borrowed it. Two years later, in England – by which time the hypnosis must surely have worn off – we again compared notes, and my friend agreed that this event had actually taken place. What was I to think? The magician never asked for any payment or reward, and I never gave him any. He came, as he said, "to demonstrate the powers that come to a man who genuinely follows the path of virtue". If this *is* hypnosis it surely is of a very high order, incorporating some sort of hypnosis at a distance, telepathy, inducing dreams, hypnosis in ten seconds of a stranger – and some foreknowledge of what will be contained in a letter.[†††]

This experience is representative of a large number of experiments which I and various other students of Indian occult lore conducted during a period of some three months. Certain broad outlines of magical practice among the Sadhus emerged from this study.

In the first place it seems possible – if not probable – that a number of Hindu magicians can in actual fact induce phenomena which could be classed as supernatural. What is the nature of their power, what is its source? In common with several Western investigators, I have been forced to the conclusion that we must conceive of the existence of some principle, whose harnessing becomes a possibility through the disciplines of the Indian priest-magicians. Occult it may be – since anything which is not understood may be termed

[†††] The reader will notice that there seem here to be three types of "magical" phenomena operating. It is possible that there was a form of snap-hypnosis, and that this could be induced for a matter of seconds or minutes, at the operator's will. In between times (that is, when released by the magician) one would feel quite normal, as I did. Secondly, the prevision as to the content of the letters. This is difficult to account for, but it is not an unknown faculty – just, I suspect, an unrecognised one. Then there is the "projection of matter" problem: when the rifle was apparently conveyed over a distance under mysterious circumstances, and by an unknown power. It is of additional interest that the owner of the rifle seemed to be under the impression that I had borrowed it. Further instances of Indian magic are given in: Notes, No. 75.

occult: it is much more likely that there are forces – perhaps akin to magnetism or electricity, or forms of these – whose functions we do not as yet understand. After all we know very little of the *nature* of electricity or magnetism, even today. We know how to *use* these forces, and we know what they can do. Yet they were known for centuries before they were harnessed. What places this "occult force" in a slightly different category is the apparent fact of its use through mind control.

On the other hand, it may well be that one day machines will be developed which can control this strange power or force. From personal observation of the trance-like condition of the practitioners, my own feeling is that the greatest barrier preventing the objective study of this power is the lack of scientists prepared to undergo the rigorous training necessary to become adepts.

It is true that the Sadhus claim that their power comes exclusively from spirits; that they within themselves possess no special abilities except that of concentration. At the same time a man might believe fire to be a spirit, and still be able to use it as he wished. This seems to point to the actual possibility of some principle or force, whose nature is not fully understood, being employed by Hindu magicians.

Whatever may be the truth underlying these phenomena, the following dissertation gives details of the initiation and discipline of the Brahmin priesthood according to the magical treatise *Agrusadapariksay*.

RITES AND INVOCATIONS OF THE MAGICIAN, ACCORDING TO THE AGRUSADAPARIKSAY

The first part of this secret work of Hindu occult science treats of the rites to be observed by the parents of a child from birth, until it is old enough to receive the initial degree of novitiateship. The actual training in magical power does not, however, come until the third part of the work, the study of which commences at the age of about twenty years, when the young Brahmin leaves his Guru (master), and launches into what might be termed individual study.

Carrying now the title of *Grihasta*, the young magician commences a severe life of rituals and taboos, of invocations and fasting, of prayer and self-denial. Fortunately for him, every detail of his future life is planned meticulously by the book: for any omission of even the smallest observance carries the inexorable penalty of delaying his spiritual development.

Sleeping on the floor, on a simple mat, he must rise before dawn. As soon as he stands up he must speak the name of Vishnu, calling upon that deity for aid and blessing. Then follows the Supreme Formula, in a low voice:

> *Brahma, Vishnu, Siva, you, and the*
> *Spirit of the Spirits of the Seven*
> *Orbs: I call upon you all, asking*
> *that the day should dawn.*

This is followed by the invocation of Brahma: "Brahma, come into me, enter within me, O Brahma, tranquillity and blessings are to me. Brahma is within me, I am at ease."

CONJURATION OF VISHNU

This is said immediately after the prayer to Brahma:

"Lord, greatest of all, basis of all, and power behind all, Lord of the Universe, initiator of all life: Thou hast instructed me, thou hast commanded me, to rise and make my way in this, my everyday life."

Then follows the period of contemplation. This is an hour devoted to thinking exclusively of good; and the planning of kindness and pious acts to be achieved on that day. When the mind is thus settled and calm, "Say then the name of Vishnu, one thousand times."

This brings the magician to his ritual ablutions, which are made with a copper or brass vessel, while the mind is concentrated upon the spirit of Vishnu.

The washing over, he turns round nine times slowly, repeating the names: Brahma, Siva, Vishnu, then nine times and again three times.

The next part of the ritual is the invocation to the Sun:

INVOCATION TO THE SUN

"Thou art the Sun! Thou art the Eye of Brahma, the Eye of Vishnu, the Eye of Siva: in the morning, at noon and at night. More precious than anything else, thou art a Jewel of Jewels, priceless watcher over all, hanging in the sky. This is thy power: fertiliser of life, yardstick of Time itself – of days, nights, weeks, years, seasons – all Time.

"Of the planets thou art the leader, the most high. Destroyer of darkness, power extending over uncounted millions of miles, golden chariot of the universe, accept my adoration!"

RITE OF THE TREE

The rites continue with a daily invocation to the tree. This is generally the type known as Asvattha, and the magician sits in its shade, repeating the following words:

"O thou, Asvattha, King of jungles, representation of the spirits! In thy roots I see Brahma, thy trunk is Vishnu, thy branches are dedicated to Siva. This means that thou art within thyself the Trinity of the Gods!

"I am dedicated to achieving power and knowledge in this world, and promotion in the other world. All who honour thee by circumambulations around thee will achieve these aims!"

Starting with the sacred number seven, the magician then revolves round the sacred fig tree in circumambulation in multiples of seven. He must do this at least eighty-four times.

This concludes the Tree Ceremony, and is followed by the donning of clean garments, a further period of meditation and dedication to the sacrifice which the operator is about to perform.

SACRIFICIAL RITES OF THE MAGICIAN

The room which has been specially set aside for the rite – or specially cleaned preparatory to it – is then darkened. A pitcher of water and a small bowl containing cooked rice are placed on a table, which acts as an altar. Above this hang a lamp burning incense, and a small quantity of yellow pigment – generally saffron or sandalwood.

The operator then claps his hands or snaps his fingers before the doors and windows, "sealing" them against evil spirits. An imaginary circle is also drawn before the door.

Two small images – one of the magician, the other to house the sacrificial spirits on their appearance – are then made from mud and water, and held momentarily over a flame. They thus comprise the elements of Fire, Earth, Water and Air.

EVOCATION OF THE SPIRIT

The magician seats himself on the floor in front of the altar where he has placed the figures. Crossing his legs, he spends a few minutes in reflection. With his right thumb he closes his right nostril. The magic word "YOOM" is spoken aloud sixteen times. At each repetition of the word, the invocant must concentrate upon the spirit of the Pitris. He must take strong inhalations through his left nostril, also imagining that his body is disintegrating, and that he is being left as a pure and disembodied spirit.

When the sixteen or more repetitions of the word are completed, he closes both nostrils with the thumb and index finger of his right hand. Holding his breath as long as possible, he intones the magical syllable "ROOM" six times. Theoretically he should have reached the stage when it is not necessary for him to breathe at all. In fact, I have been told by self-styled magicians that "the spirits appear even if one is compelled to breathe".

The next step is the pronouncing of the all-powerful word "LOOM" – thirty-two times. "Your soul will then leave the body. It will mingle with the Pitri-spirit, and after a short space will return to the body. When you are again fully conscious, you will find that the invoked spirit has appeared, and taken up its temporary abode in the clay figure prepared for it."

Taking care to make no mistake in the ritual the magician comes out of his trance, repeating "OOM" thrice and "YOOM" nine times. Looking into the smoke of the incense, the student invokes the spirit:

"O mighty spirit of the Pitris! O Great and noble One! I have invoked thee, and thou hast appeared! I have provided a body for thee – a body formed from my very own body. Art thou here? Come, manifest thyself in this smoke; partake of that which I have offered as a sacrifice for thee!"

The book goes on to tell how the shape of the spirit will appear in the smoke, and will take some of the rice offering. It will then bring any spirit that is desired, including those of ancestors. They will give advice and answer any questions put to them.

When "suitable replies on natural and supernatural things" have been received, the magician puts out the light. The spirits, continues the book, will stay for a while, speaking to one another, and much wisdom may be gleaned from their conversation. When they have gone, the operator can relight his lamp and stand up.

He will then remove the coverings from the doors and windows, and inform the evil spirits (who have been compelled to remain within the magical circles) that they are free again. Only after this may he eat.

After finishing his meal, the sage washes his hands, gargles twelve or more times, and eats nine leaves of garden-basil. It is necessary to perform after this some pious action. This usually takes the form of giving charity to the poor.

The Guru, or master, among the Hindu Sadhus is supposed to have – through such observances as these – amazing and supreme powers. "To him there is no god at all: for all the gods or spirits are under him. He gets his power from the One Superior Being. He can, by means of his voice alone, change the course of rivers, turn mountain ranges into gorges, produce hail, fire, rain and storms. His power is in his stick: the stick with seven rings (or knots). Into a magical circle he commands all the evil spirits of the world, by means of this stick. Even the stars are at his behest."

The magical circle of the Guru – which may be drawn on the sand, or merely described in the air with his wand – is a double circle. Between the two are a succession of linked triangles.

The strange and unfamiliar Hindu doctrine of *Akasa – life-spirit* or *spirit-power* – lies at the basis of all occult phenomena described or attempted by the Hindu school.

Briefly – if it is possible to be brief about such a matter – Akasa means that force of which all spirits are a part. It is also the source of all power. There is, or so the Yogis state, only one substance or power from which everything else derives. Natural laws, such as gravity, or the life-process of man or plant, are obedient to certain laws. These laws are not distinct and different phenomena: they are simply phases of the Akasa. A Hindu magician would contend that matter and energy are the same thing: just different aspects of Akasa, which is the principle of which they are both composed. Recent research has confirmed that belief.

Akasa, in one state, causes animal life. In another it determines the movement of the planets. One form or state of it can be transformed into another. Thus to nullify the force of gravity is simply a matter of charging the object with a lighter form of Akasa. If you want to lift a load of ten tons, it is necessary to change the type of Akasa which is present in the load. If the ten tons is steel, you will have to divert the "steel Akasa" somewhere else.

Modern science with the atomic theory admits that all *matter* is composed of the same prime material – electricity. But where this oriental theory differs with Western science is when the Hindus claim that this prime material – Akasa – can be changed by means of the mind: not by mechanical methods. Very similar, incidentally, is the Arab philosophical argument about the transmutation of metals. Gold, held the Arab alchemists, is made only by the concentration of a suitably ripe mystical intellect. It could be made of anything, but making one metal out of another was simpler than making, say, gold out of wood.

CHAPTER 14

Indian Alchemy Today

"Gold! Which the Sun has given wondrous hue; which those before you, with plentiful progeny, did ever seek: may this gold surround you with its brilliance! He who wears gold will live for ever!"[75][76]

ONE OF THE most flourishing industries of modern India is the teaching of alchemy. Whereas traditional manuscripts require concentrated study to absorb their teachings, mixed with a good deal of ritual, contemporary goldmakers – at least those who aim at a quick turnover – have developed their teachings along pseudo-modern scientific lines.

I recently transcribed one document issued by a Hindu alchemist and sold to an acquaintance for the staggering sum of £150! Though I may seem to be cutting the sod (or the market) under the alchemist's feet, this is in reality not the case. For I was able to trace the author of the process, and to promise him that, if and when I succeeded in making gold, I would send him half a ton, free of all charge, in exchange for the right to publish the recipes given herewith. He was, it is true, reluctant to agree to publication: but when, in front of witnesses, I argued that he was really losing nothing (since he could make all the gold he wanted at very low cost by means of the formulae) and because he himself said that he was in no need of money (for the same reason) it was only right that his discovery should be made known to the world. I am still not quite sure whether he really believed that he had made gold. (I am not responsible for the quality of his English!)

FORMULA FOR THE MANUFACTURE OF GOLD

Introduction

It must first be realised that gold cannot be made except by those that are pure in spirit and in body. Therefore, make sure that every time that you are trying these experiments, you are in a state of complete purity. Next, you must be sure that the moon is full, and that the *Soma*[‡‡‡] plant that you gather is fresh, and plucked when the moon is riding high, and the moonlight must be shining directly upon the plant. On no account must the invocation to the *soma* be left out; and you will also see to it that the juice of the *soma* is kept in due cleanliness in sterilised test-tubes.

What must be guarded against in the making of gold is oxidation. The various processes that I shall give after this are adapted to avoid loss of metal and injury to the gold from this cause. The most common one is to cover the metals with carbon, which not only excludes air admitted to the furnace, but tends to absorb oxygen liberated from metals during fusion. Union between the components of these golds is secured by stirring the contents with a carbon rod which

‡‡‡ *Asclepias Acida* or *Cynanchum Viminale.*

promotes chemical admixture without the introduction of any substance likely to contaminate the chemical compound and modify its properties.

In making experimental tests, a small furnace, such as that used in a metallurgical laboratory, a strong pair of hand rolls, and an anvil, would be very useful adjuncts to everyone contemplating to adopt this Art!

It is interesting here to see the abrupt switch from the supernatural aspects of the ritual and the Soma plant, to the metallurgical phraseology of the alchemist. This Soma has a very wide use in Indian Vedic magic, and figures, too, in the ritualistic texts of the Iranians. It is believed to be the *Asclepias Acida*, or the *Sacrostremma Viminale*, which is identified with the moon-god. But to return to the alchemist:

> The successful preparation of these golds depends upon one more condition that the metals should be of the purest quality and entirely free from iron. If this is not the case, then the compounds would indeed show the requisite colour, but will be too hard, and so brittle that they cannot be drawn out into thin sheets or fine wires. The metals used in preparing these golds must, therefore, be tested beforehand for the presence of iron, and any which contain the slightest trace of it excluded.

Then follows Formula No. 1 (see table below).

> Take a large smelting-pot and set it on a good red-hot furnace, in the bottom of which place A about the size of a small finger; upon this sprinkle B;

> cover these with a little of C; and then force the fire so that B may fuse: then throw in D and then a like quantity of E; and then the same quantity of F as that of B. Then let this mixture boil, but take the greatest care not to inhale any of the gases rising from E. Then pour it into another smelting-pot that must be perfectly clean, and by the aid of G and H the Gold will settle down at the bottom in the form of black particles which should be collected and placed in another crucible and remelted. This metal is fit for use, when cooled down.

The requisite items for this recipe are given in a concise Index:

A.	Colophony (black resin) (*Kala ral*)[1]	8 parts
B.	Pure iron filings (*Lobe ka burida*[††††] *ya ret*)	2 ”
C.	Red sulphur (*Lal gandak*)[††††]	2 ”
D.	Borax (*Suhaga*)[††††]	2 ”
E.	Red arsenic (Realgar) (*Lal Sankhiya*[††††] *Mainsil, Mendal*)[††††]	2 ”
F.	Silver (*Chandi*)[††††]	2 ”
G.	Soma juice, correctly collected	1 teaspoonful

This is the whole process: words in *italics* are the original Indian words used in the formula. There may be, however, some that cannot produce gold from this recipe. For them the thoughtful alchemist has produced another type of experiment. “It is possible,” he told me, “that supernatural influences may clash with the experimenter’s personality. He should then try Experiment Number Two.”

[††††] Indian words, Hindi and Urdu.

Here it is:

Process of Formula No. 2

> Melt A in a plumbago crucible over a gas or oil fire (these being the best fuels to use). Then A should be covered with charcoal to prevent oxidation and the absorption of gases as much as possible. After A has been melted, B should be dropped into the pot through the charcoal. As soon as B goes into the pot the first action will be a cooling one, caused by the temperature of the added B. As soon as B is heated to the melting temperature it combines with A. Now add C; and when C has been combined with the mass, concentrate upon the fact that it will be gold, add the *Soma* juice from five plants, remove the crucible from the fire and skim the charcoal from its surface. The contents, which are now gold, should be poured into moulds of convenient sizes. The liquid should be stirred as much as possible until poured. This metal is then fit for use. Before adding C to the mass, care must be taken first to melt C separately in another crucible.

Perhaps you want 22-carat gold, of a reddish hue? In that case, it will be better to try Formula No. 3. Meanwhile herewith the list of ingredients for Formula No. 2:

A.	Copper (100% pure) *tanba*	70 parts
B.	Aluminium (100% pure) *ek safed si halki dhat*	5 "
C.	Pure gold (*sona*)	25 "
D.	Carbon (*ek kism ka koila*)	30 "
E.	Charcoal (*koela*)	30 "

Formula No. 3 seems upon superficial inspection to be one for making a copper-platinum alloy:

Ingredients for Formula No. 3

A.	Copper, 100% pure (*Tanba*)	800 parts
B.	Platinum, 100% pure (*Ek safed sab se bhari dhat*)	28 "
C.	Tungstic acid (*Ek kism ka dawa*)	20 "
D.	Pure gold (*Sona*)	170 "
E.	Flux (*Dhat piglane vali chiz*)	
F.	Alkaline water (*Sajjikhar ki pani*)	
G.	Juice of the *Soma* plant	

Method of making gold from the above ingredients:

> Melt in a crucible under a flux A, B and C, and then granulate this by pouring it into alkaline water when in a molten state. Remelt, at the same time adding a cupful of the juice of the *Soma*, and then add D. After being cooled down, this metal is ready for use.

It is very probable that these processes originate in the gold-type alloys that are used in the West to make tarnish-resisting jewellery. As to the function of the *Soma*, the reader may be left to judge for himself; but there is at least one modern Japanese metallurgical patent which describes the making of acid-resistant alloys with molybdenum and tungsten.

Indian Alchemical Formula No. 4

The following metals and other ingredients are prescribed:

A.	Copper, 100% pure	100 parts
B.	Antimony metal	8 "
C.	Pure gold	5 "
D.	Charcoal ashes	15 "
E.	Magnesium metal	15 "
F.	Lime-spar	15 "

Process of the Formula No. 4

> Melt A in a crucible during the last three days of the full moon. As soon as it has reached a certain degree of heat, add B. When B has likewise melted and fused with A, add three or four drops of fresh *Soma* juice. Then add some of the D, E and F. Stir constantly with a carbon rod, then cover this mass with carbon, and allow it to fuse for 35 minutes. When this compound has been completely combined with all these ingredients, add C, and when C has likewise entered into intimate union with the mass, it is finally covered with carbon, the cover is placed over the crucible, and all is kept in fusion for five minutes more. Then this metal is fit for use, as gold. Care must be taken to see that C is melted separately before adding it to the mass.

Two further processes are given. The first, which is known as Formula Number Five, is to be used in winter, during the hours of darkness. The second (Formula Number Six) is operative in the case of people who have failed to make gold: providing that they are unmarried, and dedicate their operations to the god Hanuman, and keep his statue (part-man, part-monkey) in "a prominent place overlooking the scene of operations".

Ingredients for Formula No. 5

A.	Copper	100 parts
B.	Zinc	17 "
	Tin	17 "
C.	Pure gold	25 "
D.	Magnesia	8 "
E.	Sal-ammoniac	60 "
F.	Limestone	20 "
G.	Cream of tartar	10 "
H.	Jasmine flowers	5 "

Method of making Gold from Formula 5

> First A is melted with 1 fluid ounce of *Soma* juice, then D, E, F, and G are each added, separately and in powder form. They must be gradually added while stirring, while battle-songs (*sic*) of the Purohitas are sung.

It should, perhaps, be explained here that the Purohitas – royal priests and advisers of the ancient Hindu kings – used battle-hymns that are today to be found in the pages of the magical Atharva Veda.[§§§]

[§§§] The Atharva Veda is divided into two parts: the Holy or legitimate magic, so acknowledged by the Brahmins, and Sorcery. It is held that these two divisions are derived from two perhaps mythical authors: Bishag Atharvana and Ghora Angirasa. Followers of the Atharva Veda contend that this book should properly be called the Brahma Veda, and that the orthodox Brahmin (high caste) priesthood is required to know and practise its rites. But there has always been a dispute on this point: others claiming that all three Vedas should be known and practised by Brahmins. It is, however,

But to return to Process Number Five:

> The whole mass is stirred for a quarter of an hour. B (Zinc and Tin) are dropped in then, piece by piece, the stirring being maintained until they melt, and the mass is covered by carbon for thirty-five minutes or so. Finally, the item C is added, and when it has likewise fused with the whole it is covered at the top, and after five minutes is fit for use. Care must be taken to see that C is melted separately before adding it to the mass.

The simplest process of all is Formula Number Six, of the same manuscript. Nothing is said here about Soma, jasmine or rites of purification. The process is apparently simple, and fewer ingredients are employed. Upon inspection, however, the whole thing seems to be little more than a fairly straightforward alloy, capable of deceiving only such goldsmiths as might not be expecting its existence in such a country as India.

Formula Number Six

> Take the following ingredients: twenty parts of platinum, the same amount of silver, plus 240 parts of brass, and obtain also 120 parts of nickel.
>
> Melt these items separately in different crucibles. They are then combined together when in the molten condition. This alloy is then poured into moulds to cool. Then use the metal.

certain that the *Atharva Veda* was an important source of the magic used by former Purohitas.

THE ALCHEMIST

It is interesting to see how traditional alchemy in the East has been harnessed with modern ways to produce the kind of twentieth-century alchemical teaching that I have described. Equally fascinating is the tale of one who was less anxious to sell his wares, and who operated in the old style. The following notes are transcribed from the experiences of Mme Morag Murray Abdullah (with her permission). She is a Scotswoman, married to an Afghan, and has lived in the East for over thirty years.

> Aquil Khan was an alchemist. It is strange, at first sight, that a man who is thought to be able to make all the gold he wants should live in a cave. The explanation, like the sugar cake the child saves at a party, comes last.
>
> At first, with a Western mentality of judging by externals, one does not feel like placing too much reliance on Aquil. Tall, of that wiry Pathan race so well known in the Khyber, he was thin, bearded, turbaned, and the colour of mahogany. Clad in a pair of not-so-near-white tight-fitting trousers and an old army tunic, he is a man of few words.
>
> Our mutual friend Ahmed explained that he had brought a very important friend from England to visit Aquil Khan, and to learn his wisdom of the making of gold. Neither of these pieces of information had the power to unfreeze the immobility of Aquil – or even, it seemed, to interest him.
>
> He shrugged his shoulders, pursed his lips: "please yourself". The first requisite was to have a bath and change into clean clothes. The other

requirement, if Aquil's example was any indication, was silence.

Ahmed and I stood outside the cave until Aquil appeared. In silence he handed an empty ordinary pint bottle to each of us and strode off. We brought up the rear. It was a hot day, and we were thankful when he struck off into the shade of the jungle. We had tramped for a couple of miles, crossed a fence and the railway lines, and plunged once more into the trees. Aquil halted after another two miles.

Here were a few plants like tall dandelions. We watched the alchemist break the stems and collect the few drops of milky juice from each into his bottle. It was a slow business, and we soon understood that he expected us to do the same. For the next two hours we wandered about collecting the thickening juice, hands sticky and mouths parched.

The two of us had collected by this time about a quarter of a pint of the juice. Aquil approached, took our bottles, and added their contents to his. Then we started back.

Nothing was said about thirst. When we washed in the spring near his cave, I tried to take a sip of water. Aquil shook his head violently. Clearly he was a man of the most spartan habits. This seemed, however, a part of the ritual. As we were not being told anything, it behoved us – we who were going to buy London before long – to observe, and learn this thing.

After sitting for a few minutes, apparently in contemplation, Aquil signed to us to go home. Ahmed told me that he had heard that alchemists do not speak during their work, because the spirits which guard gold must not know that there is goldmaking afoot. The next day we went at dawn to the cave. He was waiting, and led us off in the opposite direction from that which we had previously taken. Three hours of walking in the jungle brought us to a clearing. Through this ran a small stream of icy water. The ground on either side was moist and the colour of mustard. Aquil proceeded to collect mud, just below the surface – where it was a creamy yellow. We took about two pounds each, and the whole was amalgamated into one large round ball, and carried back in a knotted cloth. During all this time, there had been no word from Aquil, and no audible sign of any magical utterances on his part.

Back in the cave we watched Aquil make two deep bowls from the yellow clay, each one about six inches in diameter. These were put on a ledge to dry, and we were again dismissed.

The next day there was a long hike to collect wood, although there were quantities quite near the cave. I noticed that it was all hard, dark-brown wood, though of different types of tree.

The next day we had to visit a stone quarry, and find a number of stones. These had to be grey, almost square and the size of a cricket ball.

Another day came. Aquil signed to us to build a fire outside his cave. We made a semicircular wall, scraped out a hollow and laid the fire: first paper with squares written on it, then the special wood, then charcoal: and finally the dried blood of a white goat.

The blood had to be powdered and mixed with powdered nutmeg, cinnamon and Hindu incense.

For once Aquil spoke. The fire, he said, was to be kept burning for four days without cease. If it went out, the whole performance would have to be repeated. Even the fire itself could not be kindled until the first night of the new moon. Certain things must not happen. One was a jackal's cry; another an owl's hoot. We took turns to sit up all night and stoke the fire.

Our horoscopes had to be cast, to make sure that there was no inauspicious conjunction which might interfere. Aquil laboured long over these. It seemed, however, that all was well. Then the two bowls were taken and placed on a piece of linen about two yards square. This was laid on the ground. Now fifty yards of new cotton were taken and cut into strips one inch wide, and laid on the linen.

What remained of the clay was mixed with spring water (carried five miles in a new jar), to the consistency of thick cream. A piece of stone the size of a large apricot was placed in one bowl, with a piece of silver the size of a sugar-lump. Over these was spread two table-spoonfuls of the "milk" sap we had gathered. All the time the goldmaker kept looking at the stars – restlessly, like a man consulting his watch. He now placed the other bowl on the one containing the stone, silver and juice, and formed a kind of circle of the two.

The whole thing was then carefully wound round with the long strips of cotton, dipped in clay which stuck like glue.

This was continued until all the cotton was used up, and the mass was greatly enlarged. Lastly more of the clay (ordinary clay) was moulded round the package, and the whole was put into the heart of the glowing fire. Hot charcoal was spread over this, and the vigil began.

The "bowl" had to remain at white heat for seven days and seven nights. Fortunately it was not necessary to sit over the fire all the time: but we had to keep a constant shared watch over it. This was because "Satan cannot make gold, and if this gold in the making were left unwatched, he would come and steal it in its present form, and learn the secret." Even Ahmed and I – the uninitiated – had by this time formed the habit of looking anxiously at the stars. Excitement ran high in my mind. Aquil crushed that: every experiment of this nature must be treated as a matter of course: no talk, no laughing, no optimism, no doubt. No eating or drinking on duty!

The weary days and nights passed. Aquil removed the red ball from the fire, and laid it aside in a pile of sand to cool. It took twelve hours to cool sufficiently. Not all the cotton, we noticed, had burned, due to the presence of the clay, as Aquil unwrapped it.

At long last the bowls were prised apart, and within lay a piece of yellow metal. Aquil handed it to me: "Take it to a jeweller and see if it is gold."

When I hesitated, thinking that there must be some trickery, he went into the back of the cave, and brought out a large cotton bag. Out of this he turned about fifty other nuggets, just like the one which lay in my hand. "These are some, there are many more.

"I would have doubted, once, as you doubt. It took me thirty years to learn this. Thirty years... of water and nuts, berries and starvation, contemplation

> and experiment. I had to learn to read the heavens, tame animals, know signs. All I had when I started was a formula which was garbled, and I had to put it right. As to the finding of the places where the right ingredients are... that took years."
>
> I asked him what he wanted to do now. "Now? It is five years since I perfected the system. I have been making gold ever since. I cannot do anything else. And I do not want to. But what is the use of it all? I set at naught all my old Master warned me against. It becomes an obsession. The very fact that I can do what none other can (except a few) is my joy, and I do not want anything else.
>
> "What is the good of gold? Can it restore life? I am its slave. I cannot get away from it. There, my friend, is my story. The fascination has me in its grip. I cannot, will not, give the gold away, sell it or let anyone else have it. I do not know why this is, either."
>
> I took the gold to the jeweller. He offered to buy it. It was not mine. I took it back to Aquil. He threw it like a piece of coal into the back of the cave. "Go back to London," he said. I have no way of knowing to this day what the answer to all this is.

This is the strange story told me by Morag Murray. She got nothing out of either the gold or the story, which she gave me, free, to use as I would. So I give it here.

CHAPTER 15

A New Thought-Force?

AKASA AND MAGNETISM

THE SUPPOSED CONNECTION between hypnosis and magnetism is again under review. It is possible that traditional contentions made by Far Eastern wonder-workers that there is a "life-force" by which such a phenomenon as gravitational force is nullified, may have some substance in fact. This, of course, does not support that magical practices might receive scientific support: rather that some of the subjects formerly thought magical could come within the ken of better understood natural laws.

It appears that the following phenomena are related to magnetism and electricity:

1. Akasa (Hindu theory of "life-force")¶¶¶ which can defy gravity.
2. Healing by touch.
3. Hypnotic phenomena.

¶¶¶ Parallel concepts echoing the *akasa* idea are to be found in several other systems of thought. The Polynesian *mana* idea is almost identical.

M. J. Roucous has spent several years in France examining the characteristics of human electricity under scientific conditions. Briefly he claims that the human body is a type of electricity-producing and storage plant. The presence of negative electricity, it is held, accounts for certain marked phenomena of hypnosis and "healing".

Taking a number of "faith-healers" of established reputation, Roucous discovered that their finger-tips seemed to repel small articles charged with negative electricity. In electricity, it will be recalled, like repels like.

Accumulated under the skin, he says – in his recent work *Les Maladies et le Magnetism* – this electricity is discharged into the body of the patient by the "healer". In this way a supposed deficiency of subcutaneous electricity (the so-called protective electrical shield) is removed:

"The human body is like a wonderful electrical generator; producer, accumulator, receiver and transmitter, of which the centre is the brain. Through the nervous system the positive fluid is discharged, causing the entire system to function...."

How does a person become a natural healer? Roucous holds that "natural" healers seem to be those who have abnormally dry skins, which encourage the accumulation of subcutaneous electricity, a negative charge. In normal persons, this charge is constantly being given off; surplus electricity not needed for running the nervous system simply "leaks" away.

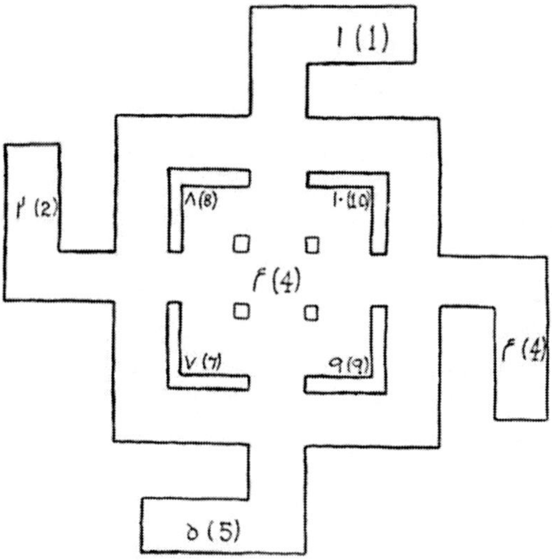

Solar Swastika charm, "to be written 120,000 times and thrown into running water". Said to grant any wish
—From Inder Jail

Readers will at once see here a reflection of the Akasa thesis of the Yogis, who claim that a vital fluid has to be stored up in the body and mind, and discharged into an object in order to influence it. Roucous' experiments, claimed to have been held under scientifically controlled conditions, seem to parallel the Akasa activities of the Fakirs.

In order, however, to establish such a phenomenon as within scientific bounds, it is essential that easily controlled experiments be devised: and that they be capable of repetition with invariable results.

Here is one, according to supporters of Roucous: it may not prove that a negative electrical charge is emitted by the human body. But it is claimed to prove that *something* apparently physical does interact between human bodies:

The subject sits on a chair, while five or six others place their hands, one over the other, above his head. The object is to charge the subject with a negative electricity through the "leakage" of human electricity provided by the other "human batteries". After several minutes, the effect of gravity can be proved to have been reduced. Two of the experimenters, using only two fingers, are able to lift the subject, chair and all.

But the effect does not last long under these conditions. The static leaks into the earth. Thus the lifting must take place at once.

The parallel with levitation is interesting. Why do the Fakirs specialise in stopping certain bodily functions, such as respiration? This theory claims that in this way electricity is saved and a hoard built up: either to produce supernormal effects or, more generally, to "step up" cerebration to a higher pitch than the normal.

Hypnotists, too, are familiar with certain phenomena which remain unexplained. Among them is the following: a test for hypnotic susceptibility:

The subject stands facing North, with his back to the hypnotist. The operator holds his hands, palms parallel, to the back of the subject without, of course, touching him. The subject cannot see what is going on. Slowly the palms of the hypnotist's hands are drawn with a "wiping" motion, downwards parallel to the subject's backbone, and about an inch away from it. Easily affected subjects invariably sway backwards during this process.

It is important to note here that, while most hypnotists accompany this operation with verbal suggestions of sleep and falling backwards, these are not necessary, as I have myself ascertained: words merely enhance the effect.

Roucous claims that this phenomenon follows from the "static electricity" postulate, and that the "aura" said to surround sensitive mediums and others, is merely the constant discharge of static from the skin.

The hypnotic trance, then, concentrates the brain, charging it with the bodily electricity, and can cut off the supply from the nerve-complex which serves the limbs and organs.

Recent researches by Professor J. B. Rhine[77] of Duke University, relating to the supposed effect of the mind over inanimate objects, might fit in with the above theory. Dice, among other things, were used in thousands of controlled experiments, and attempts were made to influence their fall merely by an effort of will. In terms of the Roucous theory, Dr Rhine trained his subjects to project their cerebral electricity towards interrupting gravitational force.

In his latest published researches, Professor Rhine – whose integrity as a scientific investigator is unchallenged – shows that such influencing of material objects by apparently mental means is a possibility that cannot be ruled out.

A whole new field of research is now open: how to establish the nature of this force and its scope, how to harness it, having regard to its presence in that most difficult of all media, the human brain?

The first step is foreshadowed by current work being undertaken by Roucous at Paris: the construction of an electro-static machine to measure the nature and extent of human electricity, and particularly the means of its engendering and discharge.

The main obstacle to this type of research is that the vast majority of occultists fall into two groups: the converted, who believe things because they want to – as a sort of wish-fulfilment – and the over-enthusiastic, who let their enthusiasm run away with them. It is the latter who too often find themselves called upon to explain their "discoveries" to audiences so pitifully anxious to hear wonders that they are almost disappointed if they are not rewarded by exaggerated claims.

To illustrate: Louis de Wohl speaks briefly of this problem in a recent book on astrology. "Draw up a chart, make a few hasty calculations, and say your say in a dark, slow voice. And they will do what they are told. You will direct their lives, you. With a spoonful of knowledge and two spoonsful of acting."[78]

What is the remedy? There is, so far as I can see, none. No more than there is a remedy against the spread of indiscriminate education without culture and the development of common sense.

The only avenue open to students of the occult in their strivings is to operate strictly on a basis of science. And modern science, which often struggles against occult studies (when it troubles to take any notice at all), should not be regarded, surely, as an enemy? The very fact of the existence of unparalleled reservoirs of knowledge accumulated by modern science itself means that there is material enough for serious occult students to draw upon for their investigations.

How does all this fit in with Akasa, magnetism and the rest? Take one example. In the 1930s, a strange series of experiments took place at Harvard, in the United States. The Faculties of Economics and Astronomy discovered that there seemed to be a positive correlation between certain terrestrial and solar phenomena. More precisely, the Harvard Committee on Research in Social Sciences financed a study which claimed to show that sunspots were associated with trade cycles. By means of statistics, graphs showed that sunspot activity affected world trade. Economic conditions seemed to react according to the amount of ultra-violet rays that penetrated the stratospheric barrier.

As far as I know, this concluded the investigation. Astrologers immediately claimed that this fact "proved astrology".[79] What it may have proved was that the sun affects things on earth in ways that man had not generally realised. How or why was not known, and is difficult of further investigation. As far as theories like Akasa are concerned, this indicates that there are still forces which we do not entirely understand. Who is to carry the research further? Occultists and astrologers, because – with few exceptions – orthodox scientists are not deeply interested at the moment. How many astrologers, however, *are* concerned with this and similar problems? It is probably safe to say that not many of them bother. I am certainly not against astrology as such: in fact I write on it myself quite a lot. But I do feel that many astrologers want things both ways. While their subject is very much on a similar empirical basis as other sciences were in the Middle Ages, they still strive for recognition among sciences which are more developed, and capable of greater materialistic proof. Now, either astrology and kindred semi-occult studies *are* to be on the same footing as, say, chemistry, or they are not. If they are, they should either be similarly organised in their thinking and practice, or at least should be less empirical. If they are not, are astrologers barking up the wrong tree?

It seems to me likely that the semi-occult arts may find their own level on a slightly different basis from that of materialistic science. It may well be that it is the very ultra-sensitiveness of astrologers and others which makes them such attractive targets for attack by their opponents. As anyone who has been to school knows, there is no fun in teasing people who are unaffected by it. Even if you call it bullying, the mechanism is the same.

Whatever may be the correct attitude, the fact remains that phenomena like *akasa*, or sunspots – or anything else which seems to point towards forces which are not fully understood – will bear closer examination. The people who want to believe that there may be a vast potential use and meaning in these phenomena are those from among whom serious students and investigators should emerge.

CHAPTER 16

Love-Magic

One of the most popular branches of wizardry in India is that of venereal magic. This term (known as Strikarmani) covers every known form of association with the opposite sex. Men go to the practitioner to obtain the love of women whom they intend to marry; women seeking children buy a charm for this purpose; those who are already married invoke the spirits to allay discord or to ensure reconciliation.

Rite to arouse passionate love in a woman

This spell is recited, as many times as possible, during the waxing of the moon, and is believed to be universally successful:

> With the all-powerful arrow of Love do I pierce thy heart, O woman! Love, love that causes unease, that will overcome thee, love for me!
>
> That arrow, flying true and straight, will cause in thee burning desire. It has the point of my love, its shaft is my determination to possess thee!
>
> Yea, thy heart is pierced. The arrow has struck home.
>
> I have overcome by these arts thy reluctance, thou art changed! Come to me, submissive, without

> pride, as I have no pride, but only longing! Thy mother will be powerless to prevent thy coming, neither shall thy father be able to prevent thee! Thou art completely in my power.
>
> O Mitra, O Varuna, strip her of willpower! I, I alone, wield power over the heart and mind of my beloved!

This spell is accompanied by the manufacture and waving of an arrow which is the physical counterpart of the imaginary arrow of love referred to in the text. As with other spells of this kind, the rite may be performed either by the lover or by a sorcerer employed by him.

Spell for arousing the passion of a man

There are a very large number of these charms. In general, they follow a pattern similar to those employed by the opposite sex. The main difference seems to lie in the fact that they have to be practised at least seven times, and women are always enjoined, for some reason, never to confide their magical activities to other women.

> I am possessed by burning love for this man: and this love comes to me from Apsaras, who is ever victorious.
>
> Let the man yearn for me, desire me, let his desire burn for me! Let this love come forth from the spirit, and enter him.
>
> Let him desire me as nothing has been desired before! I love him, want him: he must feel this same desire for me!

> O Maruts, let him become filled with love; O Spirit of the Air, fill him with love; O Agni, let him burn with love for me!

The following charm is also frequently used:

> By the power and Laws of Varuna I invoke the burning force of love, in thee, for thee. The desire, the potent love-spirit which all the gods have created in the waters, this I invoke, this I employ, to secure thy love for me!
>
> Indrani has magnetised the waters with this love-force. And it is that, by Varuna's Laws, that I cause to burn! (repeated twice)
>
> Thou wilt love me, with a burning desire!

Estrangement also brings many opportunities for the exercise of magic. In the case of a wife deserting her husband, or of a woman preferring some other man, this spell is repeated, at least forty-nine times, in the evenings, until "such time as she returns":

Method to Secure the Return of a Woman

> I have commanded the Heavens, the Earth, all creation, to stand still. I invoke through this power the spirit which has the power to make all things stand still. Through Agni, by every means and ways of return, do thou cause (so-and-so) to return to me! This powerful charm cannot be denied. In a hundred and a thousand ways, thou shalt return to me!

As with most other peoples, the preoccupation of many single individuals in India is to obtain a spouse. According to the Atharva Veda, this is simplicity itself:

Spell to obtain a Wife

Taking a bamboo stick or wand with seven knots in it, the magician attaches to the end a metal hook – symbolically representing the Hook of Indra. The "client" sits on the ground in front of the master, without uttering a word. The following spell is then pronounced by the sorcerer:

> I take upon myself strength, strength of a hundred men. I take up this power in the name of the spirit that comes here, that is coming, that has come. O Indra, give me that strength!
>
> As the Asvins took Surya, the child of Savitar, to be a bride, so has destiny said that here shall come a wife for this man! Indra, with that hook of gold, of power, bring here a wife for him that desires a wife!

Though the uninitiated are not supposed to practise these rites, a large number of more or less correct versions of the printed Vedas are now in circulation. Many of them are incomplete, but all contain the love-magic spells actually used by thousands of laymen.

A favourite one of women to procure a husband is this:

Spell to procure a Husband

> I seek a husband. Sitting here, my hair flowing loose, I am like one positioned before a giant procession,

> searching for a husband for this woman without a spouse.
>
> O Aryamanl! This woman cannot longer bear to attend the marriages of other women. Now, having performed this rite, other women will come to the wedding-feast of hers!
>
> The Creator holds up the Earth, the planets, the Heavens. O Dhatar (Creator), produce for me a suitor, a husband!

Charms against Rivals

There are a very large number of these spells. They follow, in general, the established pattern of identifying the invocant with some supposedly supernatural power. After reciting the statement that he (or she) is thus super-endowed with magical force, the spirit is called upon to exercise its good offices in favour of the operator. Some charms involve the digging up of a plant with suitable incantations. This spell is used by a woman against a rival, to ensure that she does not get married:

> This woman's power, her good fortune, her advantages, have all come to me. She no longer has them. She will, like the mountains, sit in her parents' house (i.e., she will not be married).
>
> O Yama, great King, this woman will be for thee, and for none other. She will have to remain in the household of her mother, her father, or her brother!
>
> She will keep the house for none other than thee, King Yama: to thee I have presented her! She will remain with her family until she has no hair left!

> O woman, thy fortune is covered, concealed by me, as within a deep box. This is done in the names of Asita, and of Kasyapa, and of Gaya. It shall remain hidden!

In the case of a woman fearing that she might be replaced in her husband's or suitor's affections by another, this charm is used: digging up a plant with erect leaves, the woman recites the following formula over it:

Charm against a Rival

> Verily I do dig up this plant, this powerful plant, for a certain purpose. This herb is possessed of a power; the power to overthrow women who are my rival; the power to obtain or keep a husband.
>
> O plant, thou with leaves so erect, so full of beauty, let this man be for me alone. Let my rival be put to flight; use thou the power which thou hast, and that of the gods (spirits) also!
>
> I am greater than the other woman, more important, powerful. Together do we banish her, far away, farther than any other distance, in her hopes.
>
> I am full of power. Thou, O plant, are also all-powerful in this respect. Together we shall easily overcome this woman!
>
> O man! I have enchanted thee by the virtue of this plant. Nothing is stronger than the force which I have invoked and placed upon thee. Thy thoughts will never stray henceforth from me; but will follow me, as water follows its predetermined way, as the calf follows its mother!

Having obtained a husband or wife, presumably, the next logical step according to Vedic magic is this spell to ensure the birth of a son:

> Lo, the seed hath blended, and this is the way to the birth of a son; This has been ordained by Pragapati. Pragapati, Anumati, Sinivali, they have made him. Pragapati will cause the birth of a female child to others – to us will he make a son!

Spell to prevent Miscarriage

> Just in a like manner as the Earth does produce created beings, so shall a child be successfully produced! Thy embryo, like that of the mountains, shall be guarded, and a child shall be born safely!

Under the same heading come prescriptions for hate-magic:

Spell to make a woman Sterile

In a society where plural marriages are not at all uncommon, the birth of a child to one wife inevitably places her in a stronger position than the childless women of the household. Consequently, loss of seniority or affection causes many women to hope that they will be the only child-bearers among the wives.

If the husband has brought home another wife, her rivals in the harem will repeat this spell:

> O Gatavedas, prevent those who are on the way from being born! Thy womb (O woman) I have by

> these magic arts enchanted, and it is reversed, and will not produce offspring! Thou art sterile, this stone I take and it represents thy sterility!

At the same time, the woman who knows of the jealousy of another will fortify her cause thus:

Spell against Jealousy

> This jealousy that you feel for me, that strong feeling do I hereby destroy. The fire of it I cause to fly away, as does the wind the fire. As sure as death, and as sure as dead is dead, so is that hatred dead! I have squeezed the jealousy from your heart, as air is squeezed from a bladder!

The magician – who is often being paid according to how many spells he casts – will urge his client to make assurance doubly sure by using several different charms for the same purpose. A woman whose husband is losing interest in her will weave one spell for his love to return, and perhaps another to increase her own beauty.

Charm to increase Beauty

> The Arati, that Demon which is causing my ugliness, thee do I cast out. All the lack of grace that I have will be removed by the powerful Varuna and Mitra. Aryaman, make my hands beautiful, let me be happy. Happiness is the purpose for which woman was created!

> By the spirit Savitar, let all uncomeliness be banished! All unwelcome things of mind, or body or look, these will disappear.
>
> All blemishes, all lack of beauty, they have been driven away!

Hymns for Virility

Virility seems to be considered so important that special practitioners devote their lives to a study of its production. Elaborate hymns are chanted during the preparation of the spells to ensure this end. It is probable that the psychological element plays quite a significant part here.

Two plants are used: *mucuna pruritus* and the root of *feronia elephantum*. They are dug up with the following words: "O herb, thou has been uprooted by bulls" – a characteristic piece of symbolism, which can be traced in many Indian magical rituals – "thou art a bull, abounding in lusty strength: and it is for a bull of that kind that thou are being excavated by me today!"

An iron ploughshare is used to uproot the plant – which may be either of those already mentioned. Often they are both collected at about the same time. After being bruised and steeped in water, infusions from them are mixed with a little milk. Sitting upon a pestle or stake, the patient drinks the mixture, repeating this Virility Charm:

> Thou art the plant which Varuna had dug up for him by Gandharva, thou potent and lusty herb, which we have uprooted.
>
> Ushas, Surya, Pragapati, all are with me; all will give me the potent force I seek! O Indra, give this

> material power; it has heat like that of the fire. Like the he-antelope, O Herb, thou hast all the force there is, as the brother of the great Soma.

This hymn ends with a graphic and appealing invocation of all the powers of Indra, likened to the “lusty force of animals”.

CHAPTER 17

The Occult Art in China

"It is sublime to be Master of the World..."
—Emperor K'ien Lung (AD 1764)

CHINA, WITH THE oldest living civilisation, claims a magical system and ritual dating back to the highest antiquity.**** Three things characterise Chinese occultism: the widespread belief by all classes in the efficacy of occult practices, the belief that most phenomena are dominated by specific spirits, and the mysticism of Lao Tze.

The present magical framework of China – and of the Chinese communities stretching throughout South-East Asia – can be traced from the Mongolian origins of primitive Chinese religion (Shintoist cults), through esoteric forms

**** Two main types of sorcerers are to be found in Chinese history: the "Official Wu" (magicians), and the "Free-lances", or those who retained their power through popular, as opposed to official, support. Magicians were for centuries employed by the State. Their hostility to independent practitioners was traditional and intense.

It was in the Han Dynasty that court magicians reached their greatest power. From the 17th to the 3rd centuries BC, both male and female *Wu* wielded considerable authority with the Emperors. Cf.: *Shu-King*, Ku Yen-Wu's *Jih Chi Luh*, etc.

of Taoism, to the current form: which, in turn, has deeply affected the occultism of the West.

The shamanism and witch-doctor practices of the tribes of Mongolia, and those of their related communities, the Eskimos, show traces of being the parent of Chinese Shinto. In its turn, Shinto travelled to Japan, and there are strangely comparable phenomena well known in Europe as well: among these are mediumship, "spirit-writing" and the forms of certain charms.

Shinto seems to have become established in China about three thousand years ago, and is an adaptation, made in the Chow Dynasty, of the magical practices of Mongolian northerners.

It is from this that both the Chinese and Japanese systems have derived their conception of spirits. These are carefully organised: first comes the One Supreme Intelligence; under it are the Angelic (Celestial) Intelligences; below them come the Spirits of the Planets. Next are the spirits of the dead who may be worshipped. They are invoked in magical rites, and are thought to co-operate with the higher Intelligences, or gods.

Confucius appeared upon the scene when the people of China were feeling that this form of religion – animism – was somehow in need of readjustment. His tenets were almost entirely speculative and philosophical, and he was Lao Tze's contemporary, though his senior in age.

Lao Tze, on the other hand, worked for the reconstruction of Chinese philosophy through mysticism rather than logic. As an Imperial librarian, he had access to books of "ancient philosophy", which seem to have exerted a great influence on him, and he often quotes from them. His followers seem to have pursued this link with the past back to a point where magical rites and thaumaturgy were an important part of the "ancient" (Shinto) system.

There are four main influences in Chinese philosophy. Shinto, with its pantheon and unashamedly magical rites, battled with the negativity of Buddhism, imported from India. There was no decisive victory for either. Confucius, like Plato and Aristotle, was a superb political and ethical thinker – but his precepts did not exercise a sufficiently powerful influence to overcome the older cults. Lao Tze's system, to some extent rooted in Shinto, and containing all the apparatus for development into a magical cult, ceased to be a reformation, and served as the vehicle through which the magical operations of tradition were passed down from a now defunct Shinto. Thus it is today.

In his book on the Tao, Lao Tze frequently refers to the "Power of the Tao", and the "Secrets in it", and similar obscure phrases have given adequate scope for the development of occult practices.

While Confucius and Lao Tze met, and are reported to have liked one another, subsequent rivalry between the two schools grew until it reached the proportions of almost open hostility which are evident today.

Confucians will have nothing to do with the teachings and practices of Taoism. They repudiate the mystical doctrines and occult rites alike. Buddhists, on the other hand, have their own mystical and magical systems, which do not differ radically from those of the Tao – at least in externals.

These pages are mainly concerned with the occult phenomena practised and guarded by the Chinese of the Taoist persuasion.

Remarkable in the study of magical practices there is no disguising the fact that many of the operations found in European "Black Books", and known to be undertaken by Western sorcerers, are paralleled in Chinese magic.

In the case of Hindu magic, for example, relatively few links with European sorcery can be found. Yet a Chinese wizard of the Middle Ages and his Western counterpart might well have understood each other's motives, and even certain rituals.

Willow-wands and water-divining, spells cast through wax images, superstitions connected with builders, and a whole host of other points immediately spring to the mind. There may be some Semitic connection here: for most of the European magical rites are derived from such books as the *Key of Solomon*, the *Sword of Moses*, or the two Alberts – well known to be rooted in the Jewish-Assyrian-Chaldean systems.

Character for "felicity" written as a charm, with 100 variations

It is possible that some of the rites may have entered Europe through the Arab impact in Spain and Italy. Certainly English and other sorcerers went to the reputed "Occult Universities" of Spain, to study the Arabian system. And the early contact of the Arabs with China is well known. Even today, certain superstitions about not destroying paper (an item brought to Europe by the Arabs) are shared by Chinese and Arabs alike – but by no other peoples.

MAGIC MIRRORS

Magic mirrors are among the most important instruments of the Art in China. Ko Hung, one of the highest authorities on this, regarded them as essential in the constant battle against demons: and it must be remembered that these spectres are at the bottom of almost everything. Protection against evil, death and disease, can only be secured through combating the demons which control these phenomena. Success, riches and victory – the so-called Positive Advantages – can likewise be attained through the co-operation of the spectres within whose domain these subjects fall.

The use of magical mirrors was twofold: reflected within them was to be seen the true shape of the demon,[††††] which only revealed under compulsion. Once he had thus been seen, his powers were severely curtailed, and his attacks on the possessor of the mirror ceased. Celestial happiness also attended the owner of one of these priceless objects: one man actually became Emperor through its aid, as we are told in the *Si-King Tsah-ki.*

Wang Tu, of the Sui Dynasty, published a rare booklet in which the virtues and importance of the Magic Mirror are exhaustively described, and illustrated by his own mirror, which he received from the great Heu Sheng himself.

†††† Cf. Magic Crystal: Its manufacture and use, as given in Francis Barrett: *The Magus or Celestial Intelligencer*, London, 1801.

"Whenever you bear it in your hand," declared this savant, "hundreds of demons will flee." Decorated with a unicorn, animals of the four quarters of the Universe, and other mystical symbols, it contained a representation of the Order of the World according to the Taoists, inscribed thereon. "Whenever the sun shines on this mirror, the ink of those inscriptions permeates the images which it reflects, so that they cannot possibly show any false shapes."

It was in the second year of the Ta-Yeh period (AD 606) that Wang Tu started out for the Chang-ngan country to test this amazing object's virtues.

The author claims that his chance came soon. Staying at a wayside inn, he learned that a mysterious girl lived there, and the innkeeper wanted to know something about her. Fetching his mirror he saw a spectre reflected therein – none other than the mystery girl. Coming to him, she begged him not to kill her by means of the magical mirror. Confessing that she was a thousand years old, she admitted to having been cast out by a demon who owned her, and after various adventures found herself there.[‡‡‡‡]

Deciding that she wanted to die, she drank some wine, changed into her true form of a vixen, and expired on the spot.

How is a magical mirror made? No Chinese book of any antiquity gives the recipe. But Shi Chen gives a clue. Any mirror which is sufficiently antique, he says, and large enough, when hung in the house, is capable of detecting spirits. It should be kept covered until needed, and not used for any other purpose.

An immense number of stories are told of the virtues of these mirrors in China.

‡‡‡‡ Such *Succubi* and their habits in Europe are described and discussed in Refs 80 and 81, Notes *infra*.

CHARMS AND SPELLS

Charms are probably more widely used in China than anywhere else. One of the "guarded books" of charm-writers is the classic of Koh Hung, who wrote his *Pao Poh-Tsze* in the fourth century. Written charms, he says in the seventeenth section, are especially efficacious for travellers, particularly in the mountains – where spirits frequently reside. Peachwood, with its magical properties, is the material used in the magical pen for inscribing the characters:[§§§§] while red cinnibar paint is the pigment. So powerful are such amulets that they defeat not only all ghosts and spectres, but hostile animals and men as well. Some of these protective spells took the form of five arrows – which were also used in a similar way by the Moors of Spain during the Arab period.

Charms are written in a strange form of script known as Thunder Writing, or Celestial Calligraphy.[¶¶¶¶] While many of the characters resemble conventional Chinese ones, some of it cannot be interpreted by the usual methods, and may be meaningless. It is interesting to note here that the Chinese method of indicating the stars and planets in vogue among charm-writers are found in a number of the Books of Sorcerers published in Europe during the Middle Ages.[*****] If these have been copied from Chinese originals, the intermediate links are missing.

§§§§ For the Western use of magical rods (witch-hazel, walnut wood, etc.) see Scot: Discoverie 1665, and *The Grand Grimoire*; for the "Manufacture of the Pen of the Art", see B.M. MSS. 36674.

¶¶¶¶ Cf. for Western and Cabbalistic magical alphabets, the *Fourth Book of Occult Philosophy* (attributed to Cornelius Agrippa) and the *Heptameron* of Peter of Abano, 1665.

***** Ibid.

Women in China greatly favour a triangle of gold or silver, with two swords suspended from the outer angles. This is considered to contain within it all the fortune which any woman needs or desires.

Charms, when written, are always inscribed on red or yellow paper. "Sometimes a picture of an idol is printed or written upon this paper, with red or black ink. It is then pasted up over a door or on a bed-curtain, or it is worn in the hair, or put in a red bag and suspended from the button-hole."[82]. Or it may be burned, and the ashes mixed with tea or water and drunk, so that its influence permeates the body. Many houses have eight or ten of them, suspended in the eaves and other places where evil influences are thought to reside.

This habit of drinking the water in which a charm has been steeped is also widespread in the Middle East.

Bells are regarded as a powerful charm, being also used in the rituals of magic as practised by Chinese wizards. This belief in the power of bells is thought to have come from India: certainly it was widespread in Arabia when Muhammad prohibited the superstitious ringing of bells, which had been imported into the Hejaz from Byzantium, and is still known among the Yezidi devil-worshippers of Kurdistan.

Raising thunder by means of charms is considered an important part of the Taoist system of magic. Such spells must contain in written form the representation of the characters "Thunder" and "Lightning". The intention here may be to smite spirits which are causing trouble, or merely to raise thunder and storms to punish someone meriting it. An example of the versatility of the thunder-charm is contained in a story of Shun-yu Chi, in the fourth century AD, as given in the *Standard History of the Tsin Dynasty*:

> Kao Ping is a place in Shensi where Liu Jeu, while asleep one night, was bitten on the middle finger of his left hand by a rat. He consulted Shun-yu Chi, who said: "This beast wanted to kill you, but could not succeed: I shall now kill it in retaliation."
>
> And, having drawn around his pulse a red line, and three inches from it the character EI3, one inch and two-tenths square [this character is a component of the Chinese figures expressing thunder and lightning], he ordered him to leave his hand uncovered while asleep. Next morning, a big rat lay dead close by.

This character is a modification of the sign denoting the roll and flash of thunder and lightning; and occurs in very many Chinese charms.

The whole system of writing charms and their combination is extremely simple: only unfamiliarity with the meanings of the Chinese characters themselves makes them appear inexplicable. An understanding of the fundamental characters, and a list of the forms of "Celestial Calligraphy", covers most of the forms encountered in the usual charms. Exceptions to this are those written in fragmentary script, and those which have been copied from archaic versions.

The curving line wriggling downwards from such charms is the magician's version of the normal character for a bow, symbolically used to smite the spirit or other object of wrath.

The signs for happiness and felicity are used to counter the supposed evils which are being combated. Those for long life, peace and prosperity are likewise employed against spirits and powers which bring illness, adversity and poverty to bear upon their victims. It is natural, from this, to expect the signs for "murder" and "slaying with a sword" to appear in talismans whose arcane power is believed to act in this manner against evil forces.

Thus a combination of some of these ideographs will, when interpreted, read sometimes like this: "Murder, death with a sword (like) lightning, against this spectre; (let) happiness, prosperity and order (come)."

The "all-powerful" seal of Lao-Tze, used in Taoist magic – "bringer of good fortune". Worn by psychic mediums [See below]

In addition to these, the inclusion of planets – such as the sun and moon – ensure that the effect is deepened: for both the sun and moon are reputedly powerful in charms.

Light and Fire are two further potent powers which ensure the complete victory of the spell against anything. For this reason these characters are widely used. The sign for "East", when repeated many times, invokes all the power of the purifying sun which rises from the east, multiplying by its repetition the force of the rays.

These powers are not seen simply as abstract forces. In the Taoist System, each sign stands for a particular god. Pre-eminent among these is said to be Chang Tao Ling, the founder of the cult. Hence his surname – Chang – is often found upon the reputedly most potent charms. Chieftainship of the Taoist magical sect is vested in Chang's lineal descendant, who lives in the Kwang-sin department of Kiangsi Province, being greatly revered, and carrying the mandate of Chang himself.

His charm is perhaps the most potent of all, and serves for any purpose: its action depends upon the desires of the possessor. For this reason two people with the same charm may believe that it will bring them, respectively, wealth and relief from disease. A third may use it to ensure abundant crops, or a woman may carry it for the purpose of bearing a male child.

Another form of spell consists of sentences written on strips of paper, commemorating some event connected with the result desired by the magician. Thus we find "Let General Li Kwang shoot his arrows here"; the general was a redoubtable warrior of the second century AD, whose victorious campaigns against the Huns have passed into legend. By association of ideas (and hence the supposed association of forces), this charm is considered to be immensely powerful.

Charms not containing the names of gods are fewer; but they do exist. In all cases such talismans must contain the characters Shen or Ling. The theory behind this is that of "concourse". It is believed that the crowding together of many people produces a certain power of its own. This concentrated power is stronger than that of either single people or spectres. While it is not always possible for the wizard to collect a number of people to concentrate upon a desired effect, he can achieve a similar result by putting this desire into writing. Hence the use of the character Hiao or Wao, which signifies "shouting by many mouths".

In addition to being inscribed with a peachwood pen on paper of imperial yellow, certain other requirements must be observed in the making of charms. Foremost among these is the uttering of powerful spells.

At the same time, the magician concentrates upon a particularly powerful god, generally a thunder-deity. One spell considered most effective if repeated seven times when making the charm is this:

"Heart of Heaven, eyes of Heaven, core of Heavenly light, defeat the spiritually powerful light of the earth, sun and moon, produce your light; quick, quick, let the Law and the command of the Five Emperors be obeyed."

Following this, the talisman is vigorously blown upon: in exactly the same manner as the pre-Islamic Arabs blew upon the knots in which they "tied" forces for their form of the death spell.

A number of other miscellaneous requirements must be fulfilled to make a charm effective. The pen or brush must be new, the ink "complete in purity" – and also never before used. Really powerful magicians can weave spells merely by describing the characters in the air with the forefinger.

Historical and legendary instances of Chinese miracle-workers are many. One of the most famous was the great Ming Ch'ung-yen, the sorcerer of the T'ang Dynasty. It is related that he was tested by the Emperor Kao Tsung, in the following way:

"The Emperor, in order to test his powers, caused a cave to be dug, and put some servants therein, to make music. Calling Ch'ung-yen, he asked what good or evil this music portended, and whether he could stop it for him.

"Ch'ung-yen then wrote two charms on peachwood, fixed them in the ground over the cave, and immediately the music stopped.

"The musicians declared that they had seen a strange dragon, which had frightened them so much that they could not continue."

One of the most famous wizards of China was Kiai Siang, who was asked to give a demonstration of his power before the king of Wu, and some of whose feats are reported in the works of Koh Hung.

The monarch having expressed a desire to eat fish, the magician dug a small pit, filled it with water, and an excellent sea-fish was caught. While it was being cooked, His Majesty complained that there was none of the famous ginger of Szchewan to eat with it.

Immediately, continues the chronicler, Kiai Siang wrote a charm, which he enclosed in a green bamboo stick, and handed to one of the king's couriers. Then he was instructed to close his eyes and ride away. As soon as he did so, the messenger "found that he was in that distant land; bought the ginger, and closed his eyes once more". In a flash he was back at the court, just as the fish was ready.[83]

It is hardly surprising that, backed with a huge number of such tales – which are in most places implicitly believed – tens of thousands of charms are in active use among the Chinese.

SPIRITISM

In the nineteenth century the strange resemblance between Chinese and Western mediumistic phenomena was first described.[84] Confined to the intellectual classes, these practices were mainly devoted to discovering facts about the future, particularly in relation to whether a certain course of action should be taken.

Where "automatic writing" was the method of communication, a peachwood pencil was used.††††† It had to be made from a twig which, when on the tree, faced eastward; before cutting, a magical formula was pronounced, composed

†††††Willow-wood is also very often employed.

of four lines, each of four syllables: "Magical pencil, powerful one, each day bearer of subtle power, I cut thee, to tell all."

The word signifying "spirit of the clouds" is cut in the tree's bark, on the side opposite to the twig. Following this, the characters for "Wondrous Revelation of the Heavenly Mysteries" are cut below the first hieroglyphics. The chosen twig has to be so curved as to form a hook at one end. After being fitted into a small piece of wood – some six inches in length – it is placed in the hands of the man or woman chosen as the medium.

All the participants in the ceremony must be in a state of ritual purity, wearing clean clothes, and having observed a fast. Two long tables are placed side by side in the hall which forms the scene of operations. One of these holds the "altar", bearing wine, fruit and sweetmeats; while the other is sprinkled with powdery red sand, rolled smooth to ensure the legibility of the characters which the "spirit pen" will trace upon it.

Completing all these operations before nightfall, the officiating magician then writes on a card his prayer to the Great Royal Bodhisattwa, stating that the sacrifices are ready, and asking that spirits be sent. The exact location of the house, together with the name of the enquirer, are meticulously added, in order that the spectre may be able to make his way there without undue difficulty.

This card, and a quantity of gold paper, is then carried to a shrine dedicated to this deity, and burnt before his altar. After returning home, the owner must write his name and address clearly on another card, which is fixed to one of the door-posts.

When evening falls, several of the supplicants make their way to the door, burn gold paper, and make a number of bows, to welcome the spirit to the house with due ceremony.

A short pantomime is then enacted. The invisible spirit is conducted into the hall, candles and incense are lighted in his honour, and a chair is pulled up to one of the tables for his use.

While this ceremonial is being observed, the medium approaches the sand-strewn table. The handle of the twig rests on both hands, while the end touches the surface of the sand. The supplication to the spirit follows, in some such form as this: "Great Spirit, if you have arrived, please write 'arrived' in the sand on this table."

Immediately after the medium has finished speaking, the pencil traces the requisite character in the sand. The whole company then asks the spirit to be seated; and the Deity, who is thought to have brought him, is offered another chair. Everyone now bows before the empty chairs, offering a little wine and gold paper.

The ritual proper always begins in the same way. The medium invokes the spirit with the words: "Great Spirit, what was your august surname, what your honourable name, what offices did you hold, and under which dynasty did you live on earth?"

The "magic pencil" traces the answers in the sand at once: and the séance has begun. The session is now open for individual questions. These are put by writing them on a piece of paper, and burning them together with a slip of gold paper. As each piece is burned, the answers appear in the sand-tracing. The end of the reply is indicated by the character "I have finished"; frequently the replies are in poetic form. If a message cannot be understood, the pencil again traces its writing upon the table-top, until it has been deciphered. When someone has correctly read the message aloud, the pencil writes "that is right". After each reply, the sand is smoothed in preparation for the next.

Medical charm, revealed at a Chinese séance
[See pp. 232–8]

During this proceeding, the strictest rules of decorum are observed. If anyone shows any sign, however small, of irreverence or uneasiness, the pencil rapidly writes a rebuke on the sand.

As the medium balances the pencil between his two upturned palms, and appears not to exert any control over it, an explanation for this phenomenon by means of ordinary reasoning seems difficult. All the Western observers who have been present at such séances seem at a loss to understand how the pencil writes: particularly because the method of holding it would make it extremely difficult for the medium to manipulate the stick.

It is considered most important that, while the table is being prepared for the next question and the sand smoothed, the entire company should humbly thank the spirit for his kindness and help. His poetical ability is also praised. With true modesty, the pencil replies to these compliments by writing the words "absurd", and similar self-effacing formulae.

After midnight, the spirit begins to write phrases asking for permission to depart. He is invariably asked to stay "just a little longer". His reply is that he "must go at once". He also thanks the company for their kindness and hospitality.

When it is apparent that he will not stay, the assembled company chorus: "If there was any want of respect or attention, great Spirit, we entreat thee to forgive us this sin." He is then "conducted" to the door, accompanied by more burning of gold paper, and seen off the premises with bows and prostrations.

The most excellent form of *Ki* – "magical pencil" – is said to be one cut from the east or south-eastern part of the tree. The twig should be commanded to give clear and accurate information. It is sometimes forked, like a water-diviner's rod, painted red, and about a foot and a half in length. Variations of the ritual allow the red sand to be replaced by incense ashes or bran. Other methods of holding the fork include that in which the medium himself grips one arm of the twig, while any other member of the company holds the other. The writing-instrument, when not in use, is kept with great honour in silk or other good material – always red in colour. Many finely carved examples exist. An instrument capable of passing on information from the respected spirits of the other world, it is felt, should be treated with the dignity which must obviously be its due.

The remarkable "life" which is felt in the pencil, once the spirit has appeared to get control of it, can only be compared to the twitching of the willow or hazel wand in an accomplished water-diviner's hands.

The reason for ascertaining the spirit's true name and offices is because an undesirable spectre or demon may well get hold of the fork, and write misleading messages: but he is unable to "impersonate" a good spirit, and can thus be detected by his signature.

When such attempted deception does take place, it is seldom for more than a few moments, and the true spirit expels the demon of his own accord.

Many strange happenings are reported from such séances. In some cases a mighty deity may arrive and declare his presence, indicating that he is in need of certain sacrifices before his altar. Great men of the past apparently here communicated by this method, and their signatures and messages have been obtained by means of red ink on the brush passing over a sheet of paper. Even an ordinary brush has been used for this purpose, when the "power" of the visiting spirit has been felt to be strong.

If it is desired to consult any specific god, his image is brought into the house where the session is to be held, and honoured with offerings for a few days before the date fixed for the interrogation. It is considered much more difficult to conjure gods into the pen than the spirits of those who have already passed away, and who are people more connected with the earth.

Mediums of the *Ki* in China do not form a distinct class. Often a person is chosen at random to hold the magic stick. But the interpreters of the writings upon the sand or paper are highly esteemed.

Due to the difficult nature of Chinese calligraphy, relatively few people can interpret with certainty some of the hurried scrawls of the pencil. This art is thought to date back to a very early era, and a great many predictions by this means are on record.

One is contained in a small book of the T'ang epoch, by Li Siun.[85]

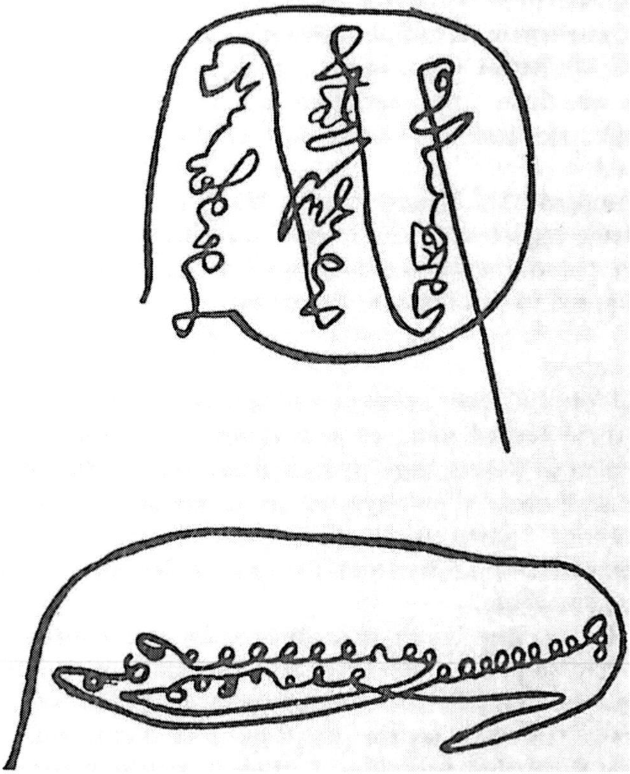

Charm against plague "revealed by spirits"

Its title – *On Strange Matters Collected and Written Down* – is amply vindicated by this extract:

> When the high Minister of State and feudal prince of Wei was only a secondary officer in Ping-cheu, before he had been on duty there for ten months, suddenly a man from the country, named Wang, politely applied at the gate of his mansion for an interview.
>
> The prince told him to sit down, and he said that he was a man who could find out things from the

> unseen world. As the prince did not show much interest, the visitor bade him place a table in the principal inner room, with some paper, a writing-pencil, incense and water. Then he told him to lower the mat which hung over the door, and silently pay attention to what would happen.
>
> After a while Wang said "Now let us go and see", and they found eight large characters on the paper, with an explanation in ordinary square writing, reading thus: "Your dignity will be that of the very highest Minister; you will live to your sixty-fourth year."
>
> Wang now hastily asked permission to go home, and it was never ascertained whither he went. In the Hwuichang Period (AD 841–847), the prince was three times registered as a grandee of the very highest official rank. He died in Hai-nan just at the age which Wang had ascertained.

The Emperor Shi Tsung of the Ming Dynasty, reigning from 1522 to 1567, regulated most of the Court affairs by means of spirit-writing, in spite of the fact that in general the rulers of that House were greatly opposed to this form of divination.

DEVIL-DANCING

Several forms of "possession by evil spirits" are recognised in China. Most of these accord more or less closely with the possession by spirits familiar in Semitic and Medieval occultism. Phenomena of the type now attributed to "poltergeists" are common, both in recent fact and in historical references. Devil-dancing, however, is interesting in that it has several characteristics foreign to demoniac possession as understood elsewhere.

Devil-dancers may be either voluntary or involuntary. That is to say, they may be persons driven to ecstatic frenzy by a hostile spirit, or they may be professionals or amateurs who deliberately induce in themselves a state of frenzy for the purpose of divination.

The actual dancing resembles the state which is induced by *Obeah* workers in the West Indies, or the Nilotic Nyam-Nyams of the South Sudan. If a Chinese family feels that some problem demands supernatural aid or information for its solution, professional devil-dancers are called in.

Like all other observances in China, the correct ritual must be followed. A great feast is prepared, which the dancers first consume, while incense is burned, and all present compose themselves in a state of mind conducive to concentration upon the question which will be asked.

During the meal the host gives the chief dancer all facts relevant to the case. It may be that he is uncertain as to whether to seek a certain person as the husband of his daughter, or he may want to know where treasure is buried. In other cases, there may be a haunting which charms have failed to remedy.

Accompanying the dancers there will be a troupe of musicians, equipped with drums, bells, cymbals and other instruments. These they begin to play, at first very slowly. Within minutes the pace quickens; as the tempo increases, so the whirling of the dancers becomes more rapid. Intricate steps and revolutions are described and more incense is lit. The contortions of the performers come to a sudden and dramatic end with the head dancer falling heavily upon the floor.

During this time – which may last from twenty to fifty minutes – no word is spoken by the audience. As in the case of the "whirling dervishes" of the Mevlevi Order, the dancer picks himself up after a few minutes of rapt silence. He is now receptive to questions. These are put to him one by one. As the replies are sometimes extremely rapid, it is usual to have a scribe on hand to record the answers – particularly when these refer to remedies for sickness, in which the list of medicines can be long and detailed.

Different troupes of dancers have their own special methods of inducing the trance-state. Some demand certain food, like a whole pig, eaten hot out of the cauldron while the dancer is held by each hand by two small children. Others have such a flourishing practice that they do not visit homes, but must be met at their houses, and propitiated with expensive gifts. Their ways and rites vary from one province to another.

The devil-dancers of Manchuria, men and women, are particularly feared and yet revered. "In seeking their aid," says one authority, "the suppliant takes with him presents of incense and paper money to worship the demons, besides valuable presents of bread, red cloth and red silks. These neither dance, beat drums nor ring bells, but sit and commence a slow shaking as from ague. Then they fall into a fit. They tell the suppliant to return home and place a cup on the window outside, and the right medicine will be put into it by the spirit. The suppliant is at the same time made to vow that he will contribute to the worship of the particular demon whose power and intervention they now invoke, and that he will also contribute towards some temple in the neighbourhood."

The initiation and practices of the Taoist magical priesthood are based upon degrees of specialisation. That is to say, the Wu (magicians) are divided into those concentrating upon soothsaying, exorcism, theurgy or sacrifice. Both men and women are admitted into this priesthood, though it is usual for the office to be hereditary. Few advertise their powers: the clientele comes, as it were, by recommendation, and they are styled "honourable sir", or "Wuist Master", or some such honorific title.

The overwhelming majority of candidates for admission to the priest-magician order have been for years associated with their parents in occult practices, so that the time for final ordination finds them already possessed of considerable knowledge. Only the initiation remains to be done, and this is entrusted to any respected magician other than a relative.

For seven days preceding the rite, the candidate must isolate himself in a cell, abstaining from fish, meat, onions, leek, garlic and alcohol. During this time, he remains in a state of ritual purity and cleanliness, and repeats conjurations and incantations. The entire process is minutely described in one of the books of the *Li Ki*.

> The superior man, when he desires to sacrifice at the seasons of the year, observes a vigil. Vigil means collection or concentration (of the vital qualities of his spirit and intelligence). It is a concentration of what is not yet concentrated, and must thus be effected. The superior man does not undertake a vigil unless he has to perform some important act, or worship. Without the vigil, no precaution need be taken against material things, nor desires or lusts restrained. But he who is going to undergo it must protect himself from things that are objectionable, and check his desires and lusts. His ears may not listen to music. The saying in the Record, to the effect that man while observing the vigil "has no music", means that he does not venture to divert his attention in more than one direction.
>
> He has no vain thoughts in his mind, but strictly adheres to the principles of the Tao. His hands and feet make no disorderly movements. They

> move strictly according to the ritual rescripts. Such is the vigil of the superior man, purporting the development of the highest faculties of the vital spirit, and of his intellect. The vigil is rigorous for three days, and less vigorous for the rest of the seven days. The fixation of these attributes into the desired concentration means the perfecting of the vital spirit, after which he can enter into communion with the gods.

On the last day of the vigil is celebrated the ceremony of initiation. For three days offerings have been made at the Taoist altar, in honour of the idols therein. At a set time the initiate enters the precincts of the shrine, clad in his sacerdotal garb, with bare feet and an emblem of the sun on his head. His journey from the place of retreat to the temple, if it is not the same place, is performed without his feet touching the ground. This is generally effected by someone carrying him on his back. Should he touch the earth, the power which has been concentrated by the vigil will pass away into the ground and nullify all.

Once within the temple proper, the chief priest, sprinkling rice, written charms and water upon the ground, interrogates him, in order to ascertain whether he has attained a due degree of abstraction from the material world. He must answer each question in the affirmative. Having passed this test, he begins to ascend the spirit-ladder of swords accompanied by the music of cymbals, drums and the wailing notes of a buffalo-horn. Upon his descent from this ordeal (though the swords are not sharp) he is considered to be initiated, and is now a fully-fledged priest of the order.

The ceremony is completed by the neophyte approaching the altar, ringing a hand-bell, and informing the gods that he is now a Wu-magician.

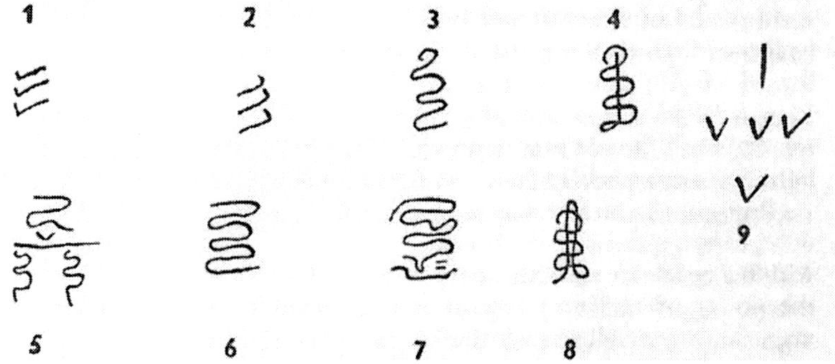

Characters used in Chinese Magical Invocations
(Celestial calligraphy)

(1) "Go away"
(2) "Come"
(3) "Dragon"
(4) "Rise in the air"
(5) "Spirit"
(6) "Clouds"
(7) "Thunder"
(8) "Descend"
(9) The Five Elements

[See p. 225]

RITUALS AND INSTRUMENTS OF CHINESE MAGIC

Before examining the robes and methods of the sorcerers, it is important to note the immense faith in the magical efficacy of swords which is common to almost all forms of magic. In China, the main use of the sword is in the exorcism of evil spirits: as in other systems, however, magical swords must be subjected to special treatment, and may also perform a variety of functions in the ritual.

Daggers of peachwood and the two-edged *kien* are considered among the most valuable of demon-destroying weapons. A sword once owned by a famous warrior or general is also thought to be most effective. Failing this, the iron or peachwood blade is consecrated in the name of the renowned sword which it is supposed to represent. Frequently red cloth is wrapped round the hilt. When not in use, it is carefully preserved, with appropriate ceremony, in silken cloth. A small model of a sword, cut from willow wood, is often worn as a badge-amulet – recalling the Arab use of a model of the marvellous Sword of Ali, worn by the Sayeds (descendants of Muhammad) in Yemen. When willow is used, it must be cut in the fifth day of the fifth month, when the sun is at its apogee. Trees which have been struck by lightning are especially favoured for all magical purposes.

Protection from evil may be ensured, by hanging such swords at the door, carrying them on the breast or at the girdle, and decorating them with red tassels or nets. Mulberry wood is also used; and in Chehkiang the power of mulberry swords is considered so great that an evil magician is generally struck dead by it, when directed against him.

Swords made of coins are most potent for all magical purposes. There has been a certain amount of speculation as to the reason for this – insofar as any reason for some magical practices can be ascertained. The circular Chinese coin, with a square hole in the centre, is said to resemble the guard of a sword. Hence a collection of such guards, made up in sword-form, might be expected to exert great protective power.

The coins (preferably all of the same reign) are fixed on an iron rod, ending in a conventional handle and guard. These twenty to twenty-five coins are threaded upon the bar, each overlapping the other. Two rows are used, to form two "blade faces". The hilt may be composed of a pile of coins, as sometimes, too, may be the guard and knob. The coins are held in place by means of red silk cord. Tassels, threads and nets (the latter to entrap demons) may decorate the sword. Such is the potency attributed to these weapons that their mere brandishing is enough to cause any effect desired.

As might be expected, sword-lore has many variations. Some swords have inscribed upon the blades powerful spells, which enhance their force, such as the following:

"I wield the large sword of Heaven to cut down spectres in their five shapes; one stroke of this divine blade disperses a myriad of these beings."

This formula is the one reputedly used by Fuh Hi, the first legendary sovereign of the five who established human order. Another spell, written on the willow blade of sword or dagger, is: "Power over all spirits; power to make all things come to pass; the greatest power of all."

Some swords can operate by themselves. One Taoist sage was reputed to own one such for the purpose of destroying demons. "Whenever he desired to practise it, he placed his sword in an empty room, spurted water upon it from his mouth, and in threatening tones ordered it to cut down the spectres. He then kept the room closed to everybody, not opening it until the next day, and – flowing blood then stained the floor everywhere."

The author of this book[86] professes not to have been taken in by this trick. He claims that no demon can have blood. Therefore, he says, it was the water which turned into blood. This metamorphosis, he believes, is relatively simple, and not of the order of things which include killing devils.

Besides the officially initiated Wu, a huge class of self-appointed magicians also exist. Having attained their powers through private study, they are often no less respected by the people at large, though bitterly opposed by the established Taoist element. The Taoists, in their turn, are condemned by the Confucians as heretics, animists and devil-worshippers of the deepest dye. Though they themselves do not always claim powers of invisibility and invulnerability, the Confucians hold that their devil-expelling works are merely bluff – while black magic and the use of occult powers for illicit ends are attributed to them.

CEREMONIAL GARB OF THE WU MAGICIANS

The "Red Garment" (Kang-i) is the principal robe worn for the accomplishment of any important magical work. It is a square sheet of silken cloth, with a slit cut in one side to form the front opening, and a round hole in the centre for the wearer's head. It is sleeveless, and generally embroidered with symbolic representations of trees, mountains, dragons, and the spirals of rolling thunder. A wider border of blue silk is sewn round the Kang. Stitched to the neck portion is usually a broad silken ribbon, whose ends hang down in front. This is identical with the "Gown of the Universe", whose name, however, is also given to a second magical vestment. This is the dress of assistant priests, or magicians officiating at lesser rites.

Made of silk or sometimes another cloth, it has wide sleeves, being closed in front by hanging tapes. Embroidered upon it are the mystical dragons, octagons and tortoises traditionally associated with Taoist magic.

All magicians of the Tao persuasion wear the same type of head-decoration. When officiating, the hair is piled on the top of the head (in commemoration of the style common before the pigtail was made obligatory), surmounted by a round cap. Over this is fixed a metal representation of the sun's rays – the "Golden Apex" to the black cap. There are many variations in the priestly garb in use: but the orthodox claim that only the traditionally accepted garments are powerful enough to concentrate true magical power in favour of the genuine Wu.

RITES AND PRACTICES OF FEMALE MAGICIANS

As with their masculine counterparts, women Wu (known as Wu Ladies, Female Wu, etc.) may be either amateur or professional workers. Common to both types is a strange degree of concentration upon their rites, and implicit belief in their powers.

As mediums, women are often in demand. Going into a trance, the witch may either speak with spirit voices, or merely mumble unintelligible words which have to be interpreted by experts – much in the same manner as the messages traced by the magical pencil need special translation for mortal understanding.

As with mediumistic phenomena in the West, specific spirits are believed to enter into communication with the medium in the trance state. At the same time, it is more usual for the communicating spirit to be a certain well-known lady (Lady Tzse), who has been consulted in China for many centuries. Women mediums generally work among members of their own sex; and even children are reported to become rapid adepts at calling up Lady Tzse. That this spirit also sometimes materialises is evidenced by a report from Ch'en Kwah:[87]

> It is an old custom on the night of the first full moon of the year, to receive the spirit of Tzse-ku. This practice is not, strictly speaking, confined to the first month. She may be conjured at any time. When I was young, I saw children in their leisure hours call her for mere amusement.
>
> Among my own kinsmen it has come to pass that after being called she refused to go away; and as this occurred more than once, they would not call her again.

In the King yiu Period (1034–1038), the family of Wang Lun, doctor in the Court of Sacrificial Worship, was inviting Tzse-ku, when a spirit descended into one of the girls of the female apartments, and itself said that it was a secondary consort to the Supreme Emperor (of Heaven). That girl thereupon was able to write literary compositions of exquisite beauty, which even now are circulating in the world under the title of Collection of the Female Immortal.

She wrote in several different styles, and manifested the greatest artistic skill in the use of the pencil. But never did she write the seal characters or square characters which are used in this world. Wang Lun being an old friend of my father, I was conversant with his sons and younger brothers, and thus I saw her handwriting myself.

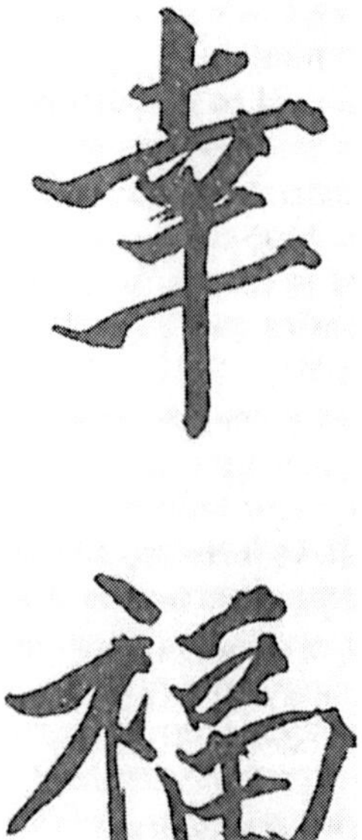

Talisman of Fortune *[See p. 228]*

> In that house the spirit occasionally showed her shape, and then it was perceived that above the loins it was like an attractive woman; but below the loins it was always veiled as by a cloud. She could play beautifully on the lute; and when her voice chimed in, it was so sweet and pleasant that all who listened forgot his cares. Once someone asked her whether she could travel with her on a cloud. She answered that she could: and suddenly, in the courtyard a white cloud whirled up like vapour. She mounted it, but it would not bear her. Then the spirit said: "There is some mud on your shoes – put them off and mount." She now mounted in her stockings, and it seemed that her shoes slowly stepped towards the room. On her descent she said: "You can go now, we will wait for another day." Afterwards the girl was married, but the spirit did not come to her in her new home. Nothing specially good or bad resulted from the spirit's visits. All the written traditions concerning the latter give many details; and what I have seen myself is no more than roughly sketched here.

It is said that the calling of the spirit of the Lady Tzse is gaining in popularity. The most usual attribute which she bestows is the ability to write magnificent literature. But the spirit also "understands the medical art and divination, and can play at draughts as well as the best hand in the realm".

How is the spirit called up? She may, according to traditional custom, either come through a medium, or be conjured into a small doll, and made to answer questions.

This latter operation is said to be performed as follows:

On the 15th day of the first month – sometimes any other day when it is desired to consult the oracle – the women take a straining-ladle, used for food, and also a door-charm. This is pasted upon the ladle; after which a human face is drawn on it. Willow branches are then taken, to form the doll's arms and legs. The effigy is then dressed in clothes.

All the women – or only one if there is a single invocant – call upon Lady Tzse to come, placing a small offering of food and incense before the figure. Within a few minutes, in most cases, it is said that the puppet is found to have become heavy: the spirit has entered into it. Questions are now put to the Lady, who is believed to answer them. This custom is paralleled in many parts of China, under different names, when brooms, trays and all sorts of different articles are consulted for guidance through a spirit conjured into them.

Those who desire to project their spirit into the land of the dead, attempt to do so by repeating an incantation: "Sister San-ku, Lady Sze-ku, please do guide me to the land of the region of Yin. What do I want there, in the region of the Yin? I want to search there for a near relation. When I have found him, I want to speak a few words with him: then pray lead me quickly back, to the region of the Yang."

The incessant repetition of this formula is believed to ensure that the invocant is carried to the land of the passed away, where she can find her relation, and is safely brought back.[88]

IMAGE-SPIRIT OF THE AMOY WITCHES

In Amoy, a special kind of image is manufactured by women magicians, for the purpose of housing a spirit which is conjured in to it, to be used for any purpose desired by the practitioner.

A small doll is made of peachwood – the wood containing the vital shen-magic. Before making the doll, the wood is collected under cover of darkness, or in some other way which will avoid suspicion of witchcraft falling upon the women. The carving of the doll is made after treatment. The latter consists of concealing the wood somewhere in or near the house of a pregnant woman. There it stays until the child is born: but the mother must not know of its existence.

As soon as the infant is born, the wood is removed and carved by the witch, who at the same time utters spells calling upon a spirit to come and inhabit it. The doll is made as far as possible in the shape of the new-born child, and must be of the same sex. It must then be hidden behind a Taoist altar, so that spells pronounced over the latter will have effect upon it. Alternatively, the witch herself calls upon a spirit, through her own altar, behind which she has placed the peachwood effigy.

This is considered to be an operation of the Black Art: for, as the spirit enters the doll, it may well leave the body of the child in whose image it is made. Alternatively, the infant may become maimed or mentally affected. For this reason such practices are hated by most Confucians, and by many other people.

Called the "Operation for Drawing Out Life", or the "Means of Compelling a Spirit", the dangers of detection seem only to add to the value of the rite. It is implicitly believed that after it has been completed, the familiar will remain in the doll, and answer any question. Another method of using an image is this:

> The image is first exposed to the dew for forty-nine nights, when after the performance of certain ceremonies it is believed to have the power of speaking. It is laid upon the stomach of the woman to whom it belongs, and she by means of it pretends

to be the medium of communication with the dead. She sometimes sends the image into the world of spirits to find the person about whom intelligence is sought. It then changes into an elf or sprite, and ostensibly departs on its errand. The spirit of the person enters the image, and gives the information sought after by the surviving relatives.

The woman is supposed not to utter a word, the message seeming to proceed from the image. The questions are addressed to the medium, the replies appearing to come from her stomach; there is probably a kind of ventriloquism employed, and the fact that the voice appears to proceed from the stomach undoubtedly assists the delusion. Anyway, there are scores and scores of these mediums implicitly believed in, and widows who desire to communicate with their deceased husbands, or people who desire any information about a future state, invariably resort to their aid.

DEATH SPELL

A common form of the death spell as used in China may be quoted here as typical. Most houses and all villages have a tablet consecrated to the name of the local deity. Upon it is placed a piece of paper, containing the name of the person it is intended to kill, with an intimation that they "are already dead". The spirit will then think that the person has already died; and he will prepare for the soul's arrival in Heaven. Such will be the force of this belief among the spirits connected with receiving departed souls, that their concentration will attract the soul out of the body of the person named, and he will thus die.

Of course, if the doomed man were to know that his name had thus been placed before the spirit, in a number of cases he would expire from pure fear. This is an interesting parallel to sympathetic magic and the curse-mechanism throughout the world.

RAINMAKING

It is believed that rain can be caused to fall by burning an image of a deformed or otherwise pathetic person. The idea behind this is that Heaven will feel pity, and will pour down water to relieve his plight.

ETERNAL LIFE

Like all other peoples, the Chinese have always been highly interested in the possibility of securing eternal life. Many believe that the following method will secure it, but that it does not always function satisfactorily:

A silver-coloured insect – the "silver-fish" – (*Lepisma Saccharina*) is captured, and made to eat a piece of paper upon which the characters *Shen-Hsien* have been inscribed. This formula, signifying "immortal-spirited", will, it is thought, cause the creature's body to take on multicolour hues. Anyone eating the prepared silver-fish will then be protected from death for ever. The magicians recommending this process warn that it "may take months of experiment before a suitable fish be found, whose body will react correctly, and will display several colours".

CHAPTER 18

Wonder-Workers of Tibet

TIBET, MORE THAN any other part of the world, has suffered from a spate of misrepresentations, distortions and downright invention in Western literature which is almost unparalleled at any time. Reading the supposed travels of armchair authors, the strange tales of magic, mystery and spiritual wonders that are supposed to make up Tibetan life, one is reminded of the fanciful maps of ancient geographers. When they were uncertain of the features of some place or other, they would fill the space with such legends as "Here be Dragones".

Tibet, it is true, is one of the last countries where Buddhism flourishes without much interference from outsiders. Its Buddhist history, however, shows that in cultural development it is far behind such places as Bamiyan in Afghanistan, where (before Islam replaced it) much of the extra-Indian development of Buddhist art and theology took place. Again, Tibet is certainly not impenetrable. It is far easier to enter and gain the confidence of the Lamas than it is to get into Mecca – as I know from experience – or to take photographs of the Mahdi's Tomb in the Sudan.

Dozens of non-Buddhist Westerners have travelled in Tibet: not one non-Muslim has been allowed into Mecca.

The second thing to remember about Tibet is its size. Those Westerners who have been there have, in almost every case, spent most of their time in Lhasa or within what a Tibetan would call "easy reach" of it. They have travelled from India,

Bhutan, Nepal and China. Some have gone in by the Kashmir route. Very few – if any at all – have been through the eastern and north-eastern areas, to Eastern Turkestan and Mongolia. Yet it is in those very parts that the most important aspects of Lamaist and Bonist magic prevail.

Buddhism is a relatively recent import into Tibet. There are, it is true, vast and richly endowed monasteries, millions of devotees. In the western parts of the country, one person in eight is said to be a monk, nun or acolyte of the Jewel in the Lotus. This part of the population have been deeply affected by religious ideas through Buddhist propaganda during the fifteen hundred-odd years since the religion came from India, and since their numbers were increased by the migrations of Afghan monks during and after the Muslim conquest of Afghanistan.

Yet, though Tibet is called the "Most Religious Country in the World", this, too, is in a way a misnomer. The country, from the purely anthropological point of view, is far from being a unity. There is, in the first place, the constant struggle between three elements within the Buddhist fold: the "Pure Buddhists", who constitute the established priesthood, the lay public, and the Tantrics, which latter have been gaining in power for the past thirty years.

The established church of Buddhism, here as in all countries professing that faith, has little time for magic and supernatural thaumaturgy. Life is given over to contemplation and the perfection of the soul as a prerequisite to reincarnation. There are no short cuts to *Nirvana*, and the ambitions of this world are not for the devout orthodox Buddhist. Why, therefore, should he indulge in magic? On the contrary, magic in all its forms is not only frowned upon in Tibet among the established clergy, but is distinctly forbidden. And the true Buddhist takes his religion very seriously. This is why you must steadfastly discount any alleged stories of the wonders of the Lamaseries of the Buddhist faith in Tibet.

The laity, on the other hand, is still permeated to some extent by beliefs which are partly derived from the primitive, pre-Buddhist animism of the country (Bonism), and partly by the tantric form of Lamaism – an offshoot of the orthodox rite. Lamas, of whatever persuasion, tend rather to look down upon the uninitiated: leaving them to follow the magical practices which are contained in the few books at their disposal. Access to books of higher learning and esoteric meaning is restricted – not only by their scarcity but by the obtuseness of their meanings.

Probably by far the greatest part of the country is under the "spiritual" ministry of unorthodox Lamaism and particularly Bonism. Bonism may be said to resemble closely the Taoist and shamanistic religion which has been treated in this book under China. Believing in the possibility of raising demons, in the powers of darkness and good, in the importance of words of power and the supernatural powers of its priests, Bonism is perhaps the world's best organised magical cult. Like the Buddhists against whom they wage physical and psychological warfare, Bonists have their own Grand Lamas, their armies and their temples.

Many of their places of worship, their monasteries and palaces are embellished with a luxuriance that would make even a Dalai Lama's palace seem ordinary. Unlike the Buddhists, they repeat the creed (*Om Mani padme hum!*) backwards: *Muh-em-pad-mi-mo!* Again, unlike their neighbours, they believe in taking life, and have from time immemorial practised this and human sacrifice in their propitiation rites. Their priesthood issue talismans against disease and demons, even to make the crops grow or wither, to cause and annul love, to make the wearer invincible and rich. These, like those of the savage peoples of High Asia, are often consecrated pieces of ordinary bone, hair, teeth and metal. Divination and the taking of auguries is widely practised, both by the initiates and the laity. There is a strange resemblance between their rites of propitiation of the Spirit of Hades (Yama) and dragon-worship, and the rites of the Black Mass in European witchcraft.

At a typical ritual of the Bon magician-priests, the chief sits in a lonely clearing, surrounded by his lesser associates. In the middle of the place, surrounded by small bowls of burning incense, the altar is raised, offering meat, wool and a yak-skin to the Spirit that it is intended to conjure. Three blasts are given on the bone horn. The congregation chants the invocation to the demon and his fellows, following the lead of the High Priest: *Yamantaka!* – thrice repeated, then thrice again. Everyone is supposed to concentrate upon the image of the deity, which is generally to be seen in huge and frightening effigy in Bon temples: a bull-headed monster, with fangs and horns, trampling human bodies underfoot, with skulls and human heads as ornaments, and surrounded by licking flames.

Charm to attract wealth to the wearer

It is believed by Bonists that the deity will appear and partake of the nourishment, which is a sign that their homage is accepted. The Chief then addresses a prayer to the spirit, telling him of the desires of the people, and these will be fulfilled. Those who do not exert their utmost to contribute their own particular share of the spirit-force to the gathering will suffer terrible pains, and may even lose their sight or some other faculty.

Bonism, like Lamaism and Buddhism in general, does not seek to make converts. If one is not of the initiated, one does not matter in the least. There is an interesting account of one Bon gathering preserved from the sixth century of the Christian era, which is typical of those dark rites: "The (Tibetan) officers assemble once a year for the lesser oath of fealty. They sacrifice sheep, dogs and monkeys, first breaking their legs, and then killing them.... Sorcerers having been summoned, they call the gods of heaven and earth, mountains and rivers, Sun, Moon, stars and the planets...."[89]

With the enormous pressure of this kind of devil-propitiation current throughout much of the country, ordinary, devout Buddhism of the Lhasa variety finds itself surrounded by the tantric and magical rites. There have been several attempts to combat this menace, which was started – it is said – by Asanga, during the sixth century, and embodied in the widely read work *Yogachara Bhumi Sastra*. Devils and lesser gods of the lower heavens are invoked and adapted from orthodox Buddhism to serve as genii of the tantrics. Reincarnation, as understood by the devout but unlettered laymen of Buddhist Tibet, is very often far from the ideal which their followers in the West imagine. You will frequently come across some person in the process of performing a hostile (hence forbidden) act against another, amply reassured by the belief that he would not have had such an uncharitable thought, even, had not the other individual done him an injury in a former life.

The orthodox Buddhist contribution towards oriental magic insofar as it affects our study is far more philosophical than the familiar rites of magical thought elsewhere in the East – with the exception of Sufism. Dedication, for a start, is held in common by Tibetan Buddhism and occultists as essential for attaining the thought-concentration which all desire. Like other supernatural thinkers, the Tibetans emphasise mental (though not so much physical) hygiene. [‡‡‡‡‡]

The mind must be purified until it can receive impressions which will enable it to become ever more suitable for eventual absorption into Nirvana, or annihilation into the Spirit of All. Whence does this power come? Partly from inside, that small entrapped piece of the psychic force of the mysterious "wireless station" in some far mountains, to which all spirits must return, and from which they are destined to re-emanate, in the form of incarnate beings, until the purification process is complete, and perpetual Nirvana is the reward.

These vibrations, which are to guide the anchorite, are perceptible all over the world. They guide the initiate, while leaving the ignorant in his ignorance. It is no real part of the dedicated man's function to spread this doctrine, or even to enforce it, unless his station in life be such as to make this necessary.

Those who attain near-perfection are presented with a ring by Lamas of high degree – Doctors of Buddhism. They must not think, however, that they will reach perfection itself in one lifetime: that happened only in the case of the Gautama

[‡‡‡‡‡]The seeker must always purify himself before undertaking any magical operation. Sometimes he has to ensure that this step has been taken even by his servants. At times it is for nine days, which includes the tabu on contact with women, and abstinence from fish or venison (Ref. 90).

himself. At this stage it is possible to apply for release from the monastic life, in order to wander far and wide, to acquire merit which will outweigh sin.

He is generally warned, however, before he leaves the Lamasery, that he is sure to return broken and distressed, to relearn much that he has lost through contact with ordinary mortals. Here, the esoteric philosophy of Lamaism differs radically from Sufism: although superficial orientalists delight in asserting a close identity of thought between the two systems.

Charm used in cursing an enemy

At the time of "returning from a life of perfection to the life of imperfection", two stones are removed from the ring by his mentor. The first to signify the loss that he will undergo, as already stated, the second because he is supposed to have "doubted the advice given" to remain in the Lamasery. When the lessons are learned, and the monk returns to the fold, the stones are replaced, and then never leave the finger – "even in the fire of cremation".

If, however, the Lama rises to such perfection that he is embalmed and gilded, and placed behind a lattice screen for all time, the ring is placed above him. Then "all who gaze at the glorious remains, and especially at the ring, have shamefacedly to hang their heads in humiliation, before such power and such greatness, and utter a prayer that turns the prayer wheel that the soul may continue to hold that which it had so painstakingly and slowly attained in this most scourging of all worlds, compared to which the first twelve years of monastic study were light as a feather".

There is more than a hint of the elusive idea of a secret worldwide priesthood in the explanation of the Path of the Great Masters, which was transcribed by Mme Morag Murray Abdullah from a Tibetan original in one nunnery which she visited, and which she has kindly allowed me to quote here:[91]

> The masters of mystical powers, who choose to remain away from the world, are able to assist through contemplation the affairs of other peoples, far away. While those who have returned as missionaries and failed, for any reason, and so returned to the source of all earthly knowledge, are often debarred from assisting further in the world. It is but forgetfulness for them. And they are content, must become content, with the inconsistencies of the world. Having successfully trod the Path of Forgetfulness, which may take many years, the traveller is able to see all the world laid out below him. He will be able to see what will develop into earthquakes, wars, famines, and he can start in advance to mitigate by his thoughts the human suffering engendered thereby....

Part of the training for this sort of spiritual diagnosis of the patient's ills, is to stay out on a hillside, day and night, for a week – an exposed hillside, and during winter. Thrice a day the trainee is obliged to steep a sheet in icy water and wrap it around himself. It is then allowed to dry, by the "inward heat generated by his concentration". If the cloth does not dry, or the Lama feels the cold, his concentration has been at fault, and the process has to be repeated. The rigours of this training are not such as would appeal to our more impatient magicians or even philosophers of more westerly cults. Where such patience and endurance reign there is, conversely, little room for the briefer rituals which are directed towards producing power rapidly. The training does result in a gentle and very dissimilar creature from the ferocious Bonist who may be lurking not very many miles away.

"True Lamas of Tibet count among their number some of the last true followers of their master's teachings." One would expect them to be sceptical of foreigners and, shut away in their mountain fastnesses, unresponsive to friendly gestures. Instead I found them like friendly children, trusting and willing to hear all that I had to say about the world beyond. At first, coming from the West, where diplomacy is not confined to the diplomatic service, one doubted their sincerity; they seemed altogether too confiding, as though they kept politeness on the surface to hide something less tractable underneath. That, of course, was a personal feeling, until I found that inside as well as out they seemed to have no ungracious thought concerning anyone. In this I refer to monks of a decade's standing. If they heard of the wonders which they will never see, in our world, they showed no signs of jealousy, or even disbelief: although I was to learn that they had very definite ideas about the West. In my experience, they would no more think of breaking a promise than they would of being inhospitable – which latter is carried out almost like a religion, as among the Afghans and Arabs.

"Tibetan lamas are convinced that they can, by the mere power of prayer, overcome any invasion, whether spiritual or otherwise: it is the power of the magical words *OM MANI PADME HUM*." When I spoke to them of war, they said that only those with unhappy spirits go to war, and that hence they deserve it, and it is something which is decreed for them to undergo: "If we who have so little can accomplish the little we do, surely you people beyond the seas, who have everything material, as you say, can create beauty."

One of the most absorbing things about Tibetan wonder-working, from the magical point of view, is undoubtedly the fire-walking rite. The apparent ability to walk across glowing coals is demonstrated in India, Polynesia and other parts of the Far East. But since my personal experience of a demonstration is confined to Tibetans, I will comment only on this, and refer readers for corroborative material to others who have reported their own experiences in full.

Both the Bonist (animist and devil-propitiating) and Lamaist priesthoods regard fire-walking as an important part of their rites. Why does this activity figure in Buddhist circles, where magic is not encouraged? Because it purports to show the heights of self-discipline that the initiate can reach. A man who can so overcome his natural disadvantages as to be able to tread glowing coals is clearly one who has established the rule of mind over matter. The Bonist theory – if not practice – is very different. Fire-walking is a propitiation ceremony, first and foremost. It is done because the fire-god demands homage. And, in return for this homage, he gives the power to endure the heat to those who believe in him.

In both instances it is probable that some sort of mental dissociation akin to hypnosis is induced: though there seems to be some other factor; for while a person hypnotised in the normal way would, perhaps, be able to endure the pain of the fire, there is the question of actual physical hurt to be considered. Not one Lama or Bonist priest who indulged in fire-walking while I watched seemed to suffer any pain or wound. This leaves only the possibility of mass-hypnosis: of which one has heard a lot, but can prove little – as in the case of the Indian rope-trick.

At one Bonist ritual, in addition to the priests passing through the flames, a number of candidates for "holy orders" were led through the fire. None of these laymen was harmed; it may be that there is some trick by which the whole thing is accomplished. In common with parallel rites elsewhere, this amounts to a testing of applicants for ordination: a form of the ordeal thesis.

Another small fact that may be of interest here is that it is reported that in many cases fire-walkers are seen to have scorched hands and faces, frizzled hair, and so on – but no marks on the soles of their feet.

The experiment that I saw was performed in a large clearing: the actual site of the fire being a trench three feet deep by thirty feet long and about ten feet wide. After rounded, smooth stones had been placed in the trench, a vast quantity of wood and branches were piled on the top, set alight, and kept burning for about six hours. Then the charcoal was scraped off, and the surface swept flat.

There was a crowd of about two hundred people watching the display. A wizened Bonist priest, hung with amulets and characterised chiefly by the raggedness and apparent filth of his face, hands and sheepskin cloak. Under the skins, which he peeled off, there was a loincloth wrapped round the body and between the legs. In his hand he carried a wand: a stick about fifteen inches long, which ended in a clump of small feathers. He walked about the fire, first three times clockwise, then five times in the reverse direction, at the same time raising and lowering his hands towards the blaze – which was still very hot. Muttering prayers or incantations, he began to strike his legs, first one, then the other, with the wand.

At the signal of a bone horn, ten men walked slowly through the crowd, and lined up in front of the magician. As each one bowed, he was tapped first on one shoulder, then the other, with the stick. Not a sound was to be heard. There almost seemed to be something uncanny in the air. The heat from the fire and the sun above was overwhelming. Several people in the audience, overcome by the heat or emotion, fell where they stood. Nobody took more than passing notice of this, and all eyes lingered on the sinister figure of the priest.

In single file, while the sorcerer kept up a high nasal chant, the men crossed the white-hot mass, stepping off through a small bowl of water as they reached the end of the course.

Now the old sorcerer followed, and performed a dance in the centre of the trench. He then called for people – not being initiates – who would like to take part in the rite, telling all and sundry of the great powers that were conferred by the Sun God for this act of devotion.

Three men and two women only accepted the challenge: one of each sex being clearly of an Indian, rather than Mongolian, cast of feature.

The same performance of running round the fire, the same salutations and raising of hands, the incantations, and this time the first ten added their singing to the sorcerer's voice. Led by the two women, who were almost pushed ahead by the sorcerer, the five negotiated the fire without mishap. I noticed that their faces were covered with sweat, and they seemed deadly afraid. As they stepped off the track, I examined their feet: I could hardly escape doing so, for they were showing them to all and sundry, and such was their relief that it was almost touching.

Talisman of victory

There was no sign of burning, either on their feet or on any part of their cotton or yak-skin garments.

I was unable to get any further information about how this was accomplished. Another person, who saw the rite performed in a similar way in an Indian State, where four Britishers took part, wrote:

> The quartette of Britishers – a Scot, two Irish and an Englishman... were showing their feet to the other guests for days afterwards.
>
> They begged the ancient to tell them the secret, and I joined in their request. He would not even accept £500 for the knowledge, but said if the four cared to attach themselves to his temple he would teach them everything... none of the

> four was able to accept. The only thing that the old man would confide was that only those with developed psychic power would be able to do the experiment unharmed by themselves. This power was something that "you" would one day accept as natural, "though you hope in your heart not to be obliged to do so". This power was practically unknown in most places (especially "materialist India", as he called it) owing to a lack of real faith, as opposed to hypocrisy.
>
> Talismans and charms, he said, could be given to those who had no power, and these would enable them to fire-walk and do many other things: but why should they have them, if they did not benefit the soul?

Evidently this particular priest belonged to the established Buddhist cult of Tibet.

With these talismans "the ignorant, being then able to concentrate their lower minds on something tangible, because they could not get really absorbed in spiritual things, could derive power from the symbols and secrets (in the talismans) because there were some sort of spirits which should help them".

When questioned about the "real" power which made talismans unnecessary, this authority says: "Concentration and meditation were able, in time, to achieve all that was needed. The mind must first be taught to think of nothing. This is another way of saying that there must be no conscious thought at all. This is the most difficult part. When it was achieved, help came to the student. Many people at this stage got mental impressions, which were nothing more than phantasies of their minds, trying to re-establish the thinking process. If these were not identified for what they were, and 'thought away', then they would remain for life with the person, and kill his spirit. They would also seem to give messages, and that these might even be from evil demons." When asked how one knew when one had become enlightened, he replied that one saw and felt it, and that hence the invisible world became something which was in fact reality, only a different reality from the one in which the laity lived: but it had a substance and a host of analogies.

Contrary to the idea widely current in some circles in the West, there is no parallel among the Tibetans to the practice of "spiritualism". There is, it is true, a form of Shamanism (witch-doctoring) among the Bons, or animistic demon-propitiators of whom I have already spoken. Their "séances" are in some ways similar to the Taoist ones, and do purport to conjure spirits. But the content of the spirit revelations are entirely different, in general, from those which are produced in the West. There is far less of the materialisation of the dead, and more contact with what are called "spirit entities", which have not, apparently, had an incarnate form. Again, communication with the spirits is used for different purposes: for the encouragement of crops and casting out demons of disease, such as plague; for the realisation of worldly ambitions, and for advice as to what to do in one's career. There is never a suggestion of the kind of well-meaning and generally insignificant greetings which are exchanged between relatives in the West and those that have "passed on". One reason for this is that the belief in reincarnation and transmigration is so universal that it is assumed that dead relatives are already in all probability in process of another life on earth, and out of contact by spiritualist (spiritist) means.

CHAPTER 19

Magic Art of Japan

As in many other countries, Japanese occult practices take two main forms: in the first, which consist of highly ritualised observances stemming from the national cult of Shinto, specialists hold undisputed sway. In "low magic" (*majinai*), spells, curses and sympathetic charms are in wide current use among the general public. Apart from the national cult of Shinto, certain secret sects indulging in magic are known to exist among the Buddhist element. In all three cases there are both similarities to Western magic, and copious borrowings from the arcane beliefs of the Chinese.

The main source of Shinto magic is undoubtedly the *Norito* – the manuscript collections made in the tenth century, which bear marks of far earlier origins. Like many of the repetitive Indian and Babylonian rites, these involved ceremonials are not as appealing to Western students as they might be. On the other hand, the codices contain valuable material for study.

Several remarkable coincidences of practice are apparent even from the most cursory survey. As in Western, Chinese and Jewish magic, swords play an important part. Rice is used to ward off evil spirits: which is the origin of its use in European weddings today. Jewels and talismans take the place of the Solomonic pentacle – but their uses are very similar. The reputed powers inherent in gems are considered and described.

The Semitic thesis that magic (particularly that part of it called Black) equates with worship of the Devil is, as in many other communities, unknown to the Japanese. Magic is described as "Good" or "Evil", depending mainly upon the intentions of the practitioner. It is certainly not believed that the Devil seeks to rob man of his soul in return for a compact, whereby some satanic power is granted to that man. Spirits there are, it is true, and even demons. But these spirits (*kami*) bear a closer relationship with the Indian "life-spirit" theory than with the organised demonology of, say, Christianity.

This does not mean that there is no such thing as witchcraft. Sorcery, and the doing of evil to others, is both recognised and condemned by Imperial decree. At the same time, there is the significant belief that he who practises bewitchment may very well die of it: and this parallels the anxiety displayed by Western wizards of old, and their preoccupation with methods of preventing demons from harming the magician himself.

One of the standard procedures of Japanese magical texts contains an interesting example of what might be called "emotion-concentration". A hungry dog (dogs are believed to have some special occult significance) is tied up within sight of food. The emotion of hunger is brought to a fine pitch by changing the meal for one more appetising. When this feeling has been thus "concentrated", the animal's head is chopped off. It is then thought to contain the essence of concentration. It is interesting to reflect two things: first, that for thousands of years man has practised fasting as a means to clear and sharpen the mind.

Chinese talisman to attract money ("silver")

Those who have fasted regularly – whatever their motive – have invariably claimed that a sense of concentration of power does in fact result. This may be a reason for this particular rite. Alternatively, excluding the possibility that the process is merely sadistic, it does seem to reflect the theory (in India, among other places) that there is a force connected with the brain which is capable of being concentrated. Some people attempt its cultivation by prayer or incantation. Perhaps the Japanese think that it may be engendered and preserved by this method, combined with the severing of the animal's head.

Where else does this mysterious concentrated power occur? According to Japanese sources, in trees. Every tree has its spirit: which is a part of the life of that tree. What form the spirit or force takes, no one can tell. It is, however, implicitly believed that if a tree-spirit is disturbed by hammering a nail into his abode, he will seek revenge. When the actual sap has been reached by the nail, out comes the spirit. This is the magician's opportunity. Dressed in white, he repeats a request to the spirit to "pursue and annoy so-and-so" – or whatever spell he happens to be exercising at the time. It has been said that the reason for dressing in white may be traced to a symbolic identification of the operator with the spirit's own kind. While this is quite possible, it may alternatively indicate a state of dedication on the magician's part, and the ritual purity which is supposed to be the state of all invocants, if they desire communion with the spirit world.

What are the main objects of Japanese magic? No different from those which we encounter in almost every magical ritual, wherever it may be. There are rites to propitiate hostile demons, to overcome the works of rival sorcerers (whether on one's own behalf or that of clients), charms and spells to excite love and hatred, to cure disease and procure children, to make fields fertile, to secure riches, revenge, invisibility and power.

Many of the processes can be placed in the category of "sympathetic magic". Typical of these is this one, for the restoration of virility:

A drawing is made on paper, portraying certain organs. Then the following are mixed together: vinegar, *sake* (rice-spirit), soya bean, oil, mixture for blackening the teeth, water and pith. The seven ingredients are boiled, and the picture added to them. When the whole lot has been boiling for some time, the desired result will be obtained. This charm is recommended for use by women who want their husbands to become more constant. Many other charms are in use, whereby the aid of Shoki – the demon-devouring spectre – is sought. Shoki, the Japanese version of the Chinese Chung-Khwei – intervenes in cases of demoniacal possession, as well as to help people whom demons have rendered indifferent to their spouses.

The most powerful of all Japanese love charms is made from newts, burned and cindered. The cinders are powdered very finely, and divided into two portions. One is carried by the magician (generally a lovelorn swain) and the other may be secreted among the personal possessions of the beloved, or sprinkled in her hair.

The use of reptilian remains in love and hate magic is very widespread. In Central Europe, there was once a common belief that powdered and incinerated frogs' bones would act in a very similar manner. Whether the bones are used for love or hate, say the Arab sorcerers – whom we will allow to complete the picture here – depends upon whether they sink or swim when cast into water. If they sink, they are potent for hatred: if they float, they are used in love charms.

The currency of another type of love charm shows that the Japanese are not content with loving or being loved from afar. The object of one's affection may be drawn inexorably to one's presence: and for this a special poem, "Waiting on Matsuo's Shore", is used.

The invocant may proceed in various ways. He may write half of the ode on a piece of paper, fixing it on the northern side of something. Why the northern side? This may be connected with the Hindu and other mana-akasa theses, which contend that the north is magnetically powerful, and that magnetism is not simply a physical phenomenon, but one manifestation of the mana, or thought-force by which all magic works.

To return to our lover: within three days of fixing the half-poem towards the north, the person desired is bound to come and seek him out. The spell is completed (and the beloved presumably "bound") by writing the rest of the poem after her arrival. The lines are as follow:

> Waiting on Matsuo's Shore
> This quiet Evening....
> For you who do not come,
> I burn with longing:
> Fierce as the fire of the salt-pans.

But there does seem to be a division of opinion upon the certainty of the beloved's arrival. This is best illustrated by the following variation, which not only invokes the lady (or gentleman, as the case may be) but informs the operator of his chances.

The verse is recited three times in succession, and in one breath. There are certain other requirements, too. The man or woman should go into a room which is not generally used, in the very early hours of the morning. The supplicant's sandals are removed and placed upside down in the room, and the door closed.[92] Then the operator goes on to the veranda, placing his hand on his bosom. Closing his eyes, he repeats the words of the poem three times.

According to some writers, a voice will then be heard, telling him whether the desired one will come or not.

One notices here a reflection of several interesting beliefs which exist in Egypt and elsewhere, connected with the inverted slipper. It is believed that if a woman's slippers are placed soles upwards in a room, she will quarrel with her husband.

The shoes may be pointing in any direction except the side of the house facing Mecca.

What is the significance of the slipper rite? There are two main possibilities. Both Arabs and Mongolians believe that footprints and feet in general have a special magical *rapport* with the individual. If this be so, then it would suggest that disturbing the Egyptian woman's slippers would upset her inner ("magical") personality. In the case of the Japanese form, the invocant indicates his or her disturbed state of mind by the symbolism of the shoes.

General Description: Charms in Chinese Calligraphy
Individual Descriptions

(A) Charm to ensure safety
(B) Charm to secure happiness
(C) Talisman for long life
(D) Talisman of success

The other explanation? It was given to me by a Chinese friend, to whom the slipper charm was also known: "According to established magic workers, there are two forms of magic: (1) That wrought by magical properties of things and words discovered by man; (2) That brought about by rites which have been revealed to man by spirits and gods. The slipper is a true object embodying magical power, and this is the 'official' view. Magicians are always careful to distinguish between the two sources, because the margin of possible error in relation to man-made magic is higher, and they do not want to lose their reputations."

The dog-charm is another potent object. Geishas and others particularly favour this method, and it is found throughout the islands in what might be called household use.

Two pieces of very thin paper are rolled into a stringlike form, and a figure very approximately resembling a dog is made from this by twisting and knotting. There is no standard shape, and much depends upon the skill or otherwise of the maker as to whether the finished article really looks like a dog or not. The result very often seems something like the rabbits that people in the West make out of handkerchiefs to amuse children.

There are, however, two artistic (or magical) conventions in the styling: one paw is beckoning, and the tail is long.

This model, after being placed on a special small shelf (the *Kami-dana*) devoted to supernatural usage, is pierced with a needle through one of its hind legs. As soon as this has been done, the woman addresses the dog, promising it that it will be released from its "torture" if the lover comes. In addition, food and (rice) wine will be given it.

Needless to say, if the spell succeeds, the promises have to be kept.

There is another use for the dog-image, by which it becomes an ally in relation to guests. The guest is left in the next room. The girl (the hostess) goes next door, where the dog is sitting, and asks if the person is planning to stay long or not. "A guest who is thinking of taking his departure goes away forthwith, while one who wishes to stay immediately expresses his intention."[93]

Hate magic – so often bound up with the magic of love, where love for one can mean hatred of another – has an interesting manifestation in Japan in the buried charm. If a person passes over a buried spell, it will affect him. This, briefly, is the theory, which is probably linked with the belief that the foot and footprint which touch the ground where the charm is hidden are especially sensitive to magical forces.

> Someone who intended to kill you by means of sorcery has buried here a magic object, thinking that you would pass over it.

Such was the deduction of an authority called in to investigate, in old Japan.[94]

It has been said that the magical object (which is a spellbound symbolical mixture of items which will be detailed later) is buried in order that the victim, passing over it, would "sensitise" it with part of his being. The object then had a special relationship – a link – with the victim. As a result of this, the magician would retrieve it by night, and submit it to torture, which would then be felt by the victim himself.

This, however, is not the standard method, if the term can be used at all in magic. It is more probable that there has been a confusion here with the "waxen image" type of spell. If there is a connection between the two, it is possible that the buried-spell method is derived from the image-curse. We read that after the presence of a buried curse was suspected,

> Michinaga caused the ground to be dug up, and two pieces of earthenware were found, crosswise bound together, and wrapped up with yellow paper twisted into a string.

There is an actual description of how to cast this spell in one Japanese text:

> Take a clean bit of earthenware. Inscribe it with the name of the person (victim) and the Chinese character for "stop".[§§§§§] Put it up in yellow paper, tie it crosswise, and bury it in the ground three feet deep at the place by which the person usually approaches.

In making up spells, Japanese sorcerers generally specify that *Chinese* ideographs should be used, and not the Japanese. In the present work, most of the illustrations of Chinese characters are used by both the Chinese and Japanese for their charms and spells. In the case of a written spell for happiness or money, the Japanese follow the Chinese custom of using yellow paper.

[§§§§§] N.B.: the character "stop" is used here merely to stop a visit. Hate spells involving harm or death demand the requisite Chinese word – compare ideograph illustrations in this chapter, and s.v. Chinese magic. Source: *vide* No. 95 of my Notes.

Bibliography

THE WRITTEN SOURCES OF ORIENTAL MAGIC AND COMMENTARIES

Grimoire References

Chaldea

The following "Black Books" of the sorcerers have traces of Chaldean magical rituals or processes attributed to Chaldean origin:

Sefer Raziel (The Book of Raziel). B.M. Slo. 3826.

The Grimoire of (attributed to) Pope Honorius II. Paris: 1760 and 1800.

Solomon

Grimoires and commentaries containing so-called Solomonic Magic are the following:

The Key (Clavicle) of Solomon (tr. Mathers, London, 1888)

Ars Notoria, by Robert Turner (MS., B.M. Slo. 3648)

De Novem Candariis Salomonis

True Black Magic

Lemegeton (The Lesser Key), B.M. MS. Slo. 2731 (1676)

The Grimoire of Honorius (Rome, 1760)

Kitab-el-Uhud (Arabic MSS.)

Speculum Salomonis

Semphoras

Septem Sigilla Planetarum
Anelli Negromantici del Salomone
Verum Chaldaicum Vinculum
Beschwerungen der Olympischen Geister
Salomonie Trismosini
De Tribus Figuris Spirituum
Liber Pentaculorum
Officiis Spirituum
Hygnomantia ad Filium Roboam

Many of these works are mainly composed of extracts from *The Key*: some are almost certainly forgeries. In any case, there is frequent confusion as to whether the Solomon referred to is the king or one of the several rabbinical writers of that name.

These books, however, in many versions, and those grimoires which follow, have all at one time or another been used as the authoritative books of the sorcerers. The mere possession of MSS. such as these meant death at the time of the Spanish and other Inquisitions.

EGYPT

As in the case of Chaldean magic, Egyptian rituals seem greatly to have influenced magic throughout the West and the Middle East. At the same time there are very few works extant which even claim direct Egyptian inspiration in their entirety. Works by the Egyptologists Wallis Budge and Flinders Petrie contain the references for magico-religious papyri and inscriptions.

The following three formerly well-known and much-used grimoires either contain Egyptian traces, or themselves claim Egyptian originals:

The Sage of the Pyramids
The (Sworn) Book of Honorius
The Arbatel of Magic

HEBREW

European and Arabic sources abound with books containing real or attributed Hebrew inspiration. In some of these – as in several of the foregoing grimoires – Chaldean, Salomonic and other magicians are cited as authorities. For this reason there must of necessity be some duplication in any bibliography.

It is generally agreed that the grimoires most used in Europe have contents which mark them as of very probably Jewish authorship or derivation. Those with Gnostic, Egyptian, Chaldean and Arabian inspiration very possibly filtered through Arab Spain to the more western parts of Europe; where they were generally first known in their Latin form.

The following list completes the major works of black and white magic known collectively as the Books of the Sorcerers. One or more of these volumes formed an essential part of all witches' and wizards' repertoires. They are almost all clandestine works. Those copies which are known are mostly to be found represented in such libraries as the British Museum, the Bibliothèque Nationale, and the Bibliothèque de l'Arsenal in Paris.

The few reprints and French editions are extraordinarily hard to come by, and command high prices.

The Arbatel of Magic
The Enchiridion of Pope Leo III
The Pauline Art
The Almadel

The Book of Sacred Magic of Abramelin the Mage (tr. Mathers, London, 1898)
The Grimorium Verum (tr. Plaingière, Paris, "1517")
The Grand Grimoire (The Red Dragon), Paris, 1822
The Heptameron of Peter de Abano
The Fourth Book of Occult Philosophy (attributed to Cornelius Agrippa), London, 1783

Bibliographical material concerning other occult works and commentaries, with particular reference to the oriental traditions and rites, is given in the body of the text of this book, or in the form of footnotes. In addition to this, a select list of useful works has been appended to this section of the volume.

Relatively little exists in European languages, covering Asian magic and its theory. Anthropological works, almost without exception, do not concern themselves with collating magical practices with the literature of the subject. Of those which are extant, hardly one such work is available to the general public. Much useful work has been done, but it is nearly all buried in periodical literature and the proceedings of learned societies. Some ultra-scholarly works are far too heavy going for most people, and attempt to cover too much ground. Facts are often collected and piled upon one another until almost anything could be "proved".

SUFISM

The following are the most important works on Sufism, and are available in their complete form only in Arabic or

Persian. This list covers the major classical works by the Sufi saints:

Sheikh Abu-Hamid Mohd. AL-GHAZZALI (*c.* 1056–1111)	1. Ihya Ulum ed-Din 2. Al-Munqidh min ad-Dalal 3. Ibtida el-Hidaya 4. Kimiyya es-Saadat
Ibn el-Arabi: (1164-1240)	Risail
Mullah Nur-ed-Din Abd-er-Rahman JAMI (1414–1492)	1. Nafahat el Uns 2. Lawaih 3. Salman O Abdal 4. Yusuf O Zulaikha 5. Baharistan
Sheikh Farid-ed-Din ATTAR (1140–1234)	1. Tadkhirat el-Awliya 2. Mantiq ut-Tuyur
Maulana Jalal-ed-Din RUMI (1207–1273)	1. Mathnavi-i-Maanavi 2. Diwan-i-Mawlana-Rum
Abu el-Muwahih ash-Shadhili	Qawanin Hikam el-Ishraq
Sheikh Masiihuddin SAADI, of Shiraz (1184–1291)	1. Gulistan 2. Bostan 3. Risa'il
Sheikh Mohd. SHABISTARI (13th–14th century)	Gulshan-i-Raz
Khwaja Shams-ed-Din HAFIZ, of Shiraz (1300–1388)	Diwan

The following books published in European languages contain valuable material about Sufism and the Fakirs:

Shah, Sirdar I. Ali. *Islamic Sufism* (London, 1938)
Asín Palacios, M. *Mistico murciano Abenarabi* (Madrid, 1925)
Smith, M. *Early Mysticism in the Near and Middle East* (London, 1931)
Massignon, L. *Technique de la Mystique Musulmane* (Paris, 1928)

JEWISH MAGIC

Gaster, M. (tr.) *Sword of Moses* (London, 1896)
Weiner, W. *Sippurim eine Sammlung jüdischer Volkssagen, Mythen, Legenden* (USF, Prague, 1848)
Van Dale. *De Origine ac Progressu Idolitatraae* (Amstel, 1696)
Davies, T. W. *Magic and Divination among the Hebrews* (London, 1898)

ASSYRIA AND BABYLONIA

Thompson, R. C. *Devils and Evil Spirits of Babylonia* (London, 1903)
Thompson, R. C. *Reports of the Magicians and Astrologers of Nineveh and Babylon* (London, 1900)
King, L. W. *Babylonian Magic and Sorcery* (London, 1896)
Fossey, C. *La Magie Assyrienne* (Paris, 1902)
Laurent, A. *La Magie et la Divination chez les Chaldéo-Assyriens* (Paris, 1894)

Lenormant, F. *Science Occulte: Magie Chez les Chaldéens* (Paris, 1874)

INDIA

Henry, V. *La Magie dans l'Inde Antique* (Paris, 1904)
Hatch, W. J. *Land Pirates of India* (London, 1928)
Marques-Rivière, J. *L'Inde Secrete et sa Magie* (Paris, 1937)
Carrington, H. *Hindu Magic* (London, 1909)
Barbe, P. "Indian Death-Spell", in *Journ. Asiatic Soc. Bengal*, XV, 1848, 351 ff.
Shah, S. *Occultism* (London, 1952)
Raghunathji, K. (tr.) *Manirama, the Book of Fate* (Bombay, 1886)
Jacolliot, L. *Occ. Sci. in India* (1884)
Nana-Prakásam Pillai. *Personal Magnetism and Occultism* (Madras, 1911)
Bosc, E. *Addha-Nari, ou l'Occultisme dans l'Inde* (Paris, 1893)

CHINA

Shen Chung-tao. *Symbols of the Yi-King* (Shanghai, 1934)
Cibot, P. "Magie des Chinois", in *Mémoires Concernant les Chinois* (Weimar, 1802)
De Groot, J. J. M. *Religious System of China* (Leyden, 1892)
Legge, J. *The Yi-King* (Vol. XVI of Sacred Books of the East, ed. Prof. Max Muller) (Oxford, 1882)
de Harlez, C. *Les Croyances religieuses des premiers Chinois* (Brussels (Acad. des Sciences), 1887)
Bouinais, A., and Paulus, A. *Le Culte des Morts dans le Céleste Empire* (Paris, Musée Guimet, 1893)

EGYPT

Crum, W. E. *La Magie Copte* (Paris, 1922)
Budge, A. Wallis. *Egyptian Magic* (London, 1899)
Groff, P. *Études sur la Sorcellerie: Mémoires Présentés á l'Institut Égyptien* (Cairo, 1897)
Knight, A. E. *Amentet: Account of the Gods, Amulets and Scarabs of the Ancient Egyptians* (London, 1915)
Petrie, W. M. F. *Egyptian Festivals and Nile Shrines* (Brit. School of Arch. in Egypt, STUDIES , 1911)
Wiedemann, A. *Magie und Zauberie im alten Ägypten* (1905)
Lexa, F. *La Magie dans l'Egypte antique de l'ancien Empire jusqu'à l'epoque copte* (Paris, 3 vols, 1925)

IRAN

Donaldson, B. A. *The Wild Rue* (London, 1938)
Abdullah b. Muh., b. Husain. *Khawas-i-Ayat* (Copenhagen, 1920)
Benveniste, E. *Les Mages dans l'ancien Iran* (Paris (Etudes iraniennes, xv), 1938)
Williams-Jackson, A. V. *Die Iranische Religion* (Strasbourg, 1901)

TIBET

Bonvalot, G. *L'Asie Inconnu* (Paris, 1910)
Shah, A. *Four Years in Tibet* (Benares, 1906)
Neel, A. D. *Mystiques et Magiciens du Thibet* (Paris, 1929)
Schlagintweit, E. *Buddhism in Tibet* (London, 1881)
Waddell, L. A. *Buddhism of Tibet* (London, 1895)

Koppen, C. F. *Die lamaische Hierarchie und Kirche* (Berlin, 1859)
Rockhill, W. W. *Ethnology of Tibet* (Washington, 1895)

ARAB (NORTH AFRICA)

Ibn al-Wahshiyya. *Kitab Shauq el Mustakham* (Cairo, 1350)
Westermarck, E. *Ritual and Belief in Morocco* (London, 1926)
Hammer (ed.). *Ancient Alphabets* (1922)
Doutté, E. *Magie et Religion* (Alger, 1909)

JAPAN

Chikashige, Prof. M. *Alchemy and other Achievements of the Ancient Orient* (Tokyo, 1936)
Aston, W. G., in *Folklore*, Vol. XXIII (1912)
Hildburgh, W. L., in *Man*, Vol. LXVII (1915–17)
Aston, W. G. *Shinto* (London, 1907)
Lowell, P. *Occult Japan* (London, 1895)

ORIENTAL MAGIC IN GENERAL, AND COMPARATIVE STUDIES

Lenormant. *La Science Occulte en Asie* (Paris, 2 vols, 1874–75)
Thimmy, R. *La Magie aux Colonies* (Paris, 1935)
Tchéraz, M. *Armenian Magic.* Trans. (IX Oriental Cong, ii, 826)
Budge, F. W. *Lives of Mabá Seyôn and gabra Krestos*

Gimlette, J. D. *Malay Poisons and Charm Cures* (1915)
Skeat, W. W. *Malay Magic* (London, 1900)
Marinas, Albert. "Quelques problèmes de méthode dans l'étude de la magie" (*Extrait de Bulletin de la Société Royale d'Anthropologie et de la Préhistoire*) (Merxplas, 1933)
Sayce, A. H. *The Religions of Ancient Egypt and Babylonia* (Edinburgh, 1902)
Gollancz, H. *Book of Protection* (Frowde, 1912)
Davies, M. *Magic, Divination and Demonology among the Hebrews and their Neighbours* (London, 1898)
Thompson, R. C. *Semitic Magic* (Vol. 3, Luzac's Oriental Religions Series) (London, 1908)
Daiches, S. *Babylonian Oil Magic in the Talmud and later Jewish Literature* (London, 1913)
Cooke, J. T. *Inquiry into Psychic and Nervous Forces* (Dublin, 1905)

Notes

1 Lenormant, C.: "Chaldean Magic" (*Sri. Occ. en Asie*). Eng. ed., London, 1877, p. 380.

2 Maqlu ("Burning") Tablets, in: Tallquist, K. *Die Assyr. Beschwörungsserie "Maqlu"*. Leipzig, 1895.

3 "We have compared the data of the system of these books to the ante-Iranian past and Median Magism and the Finnish mythology, and so have been able to prove the existence of an independent family of religions which must be called Turanian, religions having no other worship but magic, and proceeding from the old fund of demonological naturalism" – Lenormant, op. cit., loc. cit.

4 Schütte, G., ap: *Scot. Geogr. Mag.*, XXXVI, 4, pp. 244 ff.

5 Stewart Blacker, Col. L. V.: unpublished thesis on Aryan origins, consulted by the author, 1953.

6 Lea, H. C.: *Hist, of the Inquisit. in the Middle Ages*, 3 vols., 1887–88.

7 "Key of Solomon" (*Les Clavicules*), anon. Paris, 1817.

8 Winkler, M.: *Die Gesetze Hammurabis*. Leipzig, 1902, p. 10.

9 MSS. (unpublished), courtesy of Mme M. M. Abdullah.

10 The last "adept" to leave his testamentary magical book was Francis Barrett: *The Magus*. London, 1801.

11 *Hekau* (Words of Power) form Chap. 24 of the *Book of the Dead*, tr. and ed. Wallis Budge (Sir E. A. T.), London, 1895 and 1902. Cf. *Talmud*: ZERAIM, Berakhoth, 19a, 56a.

12 *Catholic Encyclopaedia*, Vol. XV, pp. 674 ff. (1907–12).
13 I.e. investigations carried on since the study of magic ceased to be conducted mainly in Europe by the Church.
14 In the *Talmud* and elsewhere. Cf. SAN., 106B, SOTAH, 47B.
15 *Jewish Encyclopaedia*, s.v. *Magic*. New York, 1901–06.
16 Book of Enoch (Apocrypha), tr. and ed. Odenburg, H., Cambridge, 1928. See also idem., ed. Charles. Oxford, 1912.
17 One rabbi, in the first century AD, actually caught eighty witches practising magic at Ashkelon, and hanged them all in one day.
18 *Book of Enoch*, ix, 7.
19 Ménard, L.: *Hermes Trismégiste*. Paris, 1866.
20 *The Zohar*, tr. as *Le Livre de la Splendeur*, by J. de Pauly. Paris, 1906–11.
21 *The Book of Sacred Magic of Abramelin the Mage*, tr. and ed. MacGregor Mathers, S. L. London, 1898.
22 Cf. Sefer Raziel: British Museum MSS. No. Sloane 3826; and Bloch: *History of the Development of the Kabala*. Treves, 1894.
23 Anon.: *Les Véritables Clavicules (Grimorium Verum)*. Memphis (?Rome), "1517".
24 Exodus vii, 12.
25 Thompson, C. J. S.: *Semitic Magic*. London, 1908, passim. Maury: *La Magie el l'Astrologie*, Paris, 1860. Lane: *Manners and Customs*, 2 vols, London, 1836.
26 Nostradame, Michel de: *Les Vrayes Centuries de M. M. Nostradamus*. Rouen, 1649.
27 Barrett, F.: *The Magus*, or *Celestial Intellegencer.* London, 1801.
28 Qur'an: Sura 27, verse 15.
29 Ibid., 27: 22.
30 Fleck, F.: "*Wissenschaftl*", *Reise,* II, 3. 1882.

31 Sifra de-Ashmedai, frequently quoted in the *Zohar* (q.v.) as "The Book of Asmodeus, given to King Solomon" (III, 194b and 77a), "The Magic Book of Asmodeus" (III, 43a), and under similar titles, e.g. ibid., II, 128a, III, 19a.

32 Crawley, E.: *Oath, Curse and Blessing*. London, 1934.

33 The library, containing thousands of books, was unearthed at Kuyunjik, the site of Nineveh.

34 Tablets of Assur-bani-Pal, in Smith, S.A.: *Die Keilschrifttexte Asurbanipals*. 1887.

35 Lenormant: *La Magie Chez les Chaldéens*. Paris, 1874, pp. 254–5.

36 Ibid.

37 Ibid.

38 Kalevala of the Finns, I, 12.

39 Most of the god-spirits have dual natures, being known as male by one name, female by another.

40 These unexplained numbers are thought to be connected with cabbalism.

41 Qur'an: Chap. 26, verses 43–6.

42 In 1863 a Mr S. Sharp brought a statue of this magician to the British Museum. It was identified in 1903.

43 In the Egyptian, as in the Accadian and Chaldean magico-religious systems, the idea of sin and punishment in a future life was not well developed. Magic was divided socially rather than spiritually. Legitimate magic was a part of religion; illicit magic was a crime, and punishable by death through obligatory suicide.

44 Maspero, G.: *Hist. Ane. des Peuples de l'Orient*. Paris, 1875, p. 39.

45 Elliot Smith (see Ref. 47, below), studying this question as an anatomist, concurs with other authorities that there was a continual ethnic drift from inner Africa to ancient Egypt.

Further evidence of the wider spreading of purely African ideas is found in this extract from the works of another Egyptologist (Ref. No. 48, below): "... towards the end of the Palaeolithic Age, it is possible that similar ethnical waves invaded all Northern Africa. Favoured by climatic conditions other than the present, they laid the basis of a proto-Ethiopian substratum reaching from the Red Sea to the Atlantic in all those countries where they have left their rough stone implements along the great water-courses now dried up".

46 The Pyramid of Cheops was built *circa* 3733 BC.

47 Elliot Smith, C.: *Anc. Egyptians and their Influence upon the Civilisation of Europe*. London, 1911, p. 213.

48 Giuffrida-Ruggeri, Prof. V., in Man. 1915, No. 32.

49 Capart, C.: *Lessons in Egyptian Art*, pp. 300 et seq.

50 "Porphyry, apud Euseb", *Praep. Evang.*, V, 7.

51 Cf. "Rite of Lucifuge", *Veritable Clavicule du Roy Salomon.*

52 Chabas, F. J.: *La Papyrus Magique Harris*. Paris, 1860.

53 Brit. Mus. Papyrus No. 10, 474. Presumably "UU" stands for "very unlucky" here.

54 Chabas, F. J.: *La Calendrier*, 24 ff.; where this day is marked "L", as in *Papyrus Sallier*, IV.

55 In the countries of the Arabised and Semitic Middle East, magic is considered to be *destroyed* by water, especially running water.

56 Akbar Khan: *Tasawwuf-i-Azim*. Persian MS., seventeenth century.

57 These are said to be the original mines of King Solomon, worked by the *jinn* (genies), whose magical powers still linger there. I examined some of these workings – and recalled the words of the Qur'an: "And to Solomon we taught the use of blowing winds... and we subjected to him some of the evil ones, who dived for him, and

did other things besides." (Qur'an: The Prophets, xxi, 81–2.)

58 Interesting pioneer work has been done in this subject by R. Pettazoni, in a little-known work dealing with African rituals in Sardinia (*La Religione Primitiva in Sardegna*, 1912).

59 The word is incorrectly used, of course, to describe itinerant jugglers in India. A similar vulgarisation is that of the word "magician" in English – where it is generally used to denote a juggler or illusionist.

60 Mystics and miracle-workers of this type were known in Arabia even before Muhammad. Most Sufis hold that the cult dates from Adam himself, and is actually the only true "secret tradition" of high occultism.

61 Akbar Khan, op. cit.

62 Sheikh Shahabuddin Suharawardi: *Awarif el-Maarif* and: *Ghayath el-Lughat*.

63 Vide infra, Chap. 8, s.v. Sihr.

64 Farid-ud-Din Attar: *Tadkhirat el-Awliya*.

65 Typical dhikrs are "La Hawla wa la Quwwata Illa-Billah" (No Power and No Justice except in Allah); "Astighfirullah" (I seek Refuge in Allah); "Allah-o-Akbar" (Allah is Greater than all Else).

66 The life of Ibn Sina ("Avicenna") is one of the main magical works of the period still extant.

67 I came across an interesting instance of the extent of the diffusion of Arabic magical formulae or Dhikrs in Argentina. I saw in Buenos Aires a small locket upon which was the following phrase, as printed:

OJALA
OJAL
OJA
OJ
O

This is clearly a version of the "abracadabra-motif", as it was described to me as a charm worn by a girl desiring a husband. When the Arabs were in Spain, as is well known, this word *ojalá* (from Ar. *Inshallah*, "may Allah will it") passed into the Spanish. It is still much used; e.g. "Ojalá that such-and-such may happen". I had not, however, heard of it in Spain as a charm or spell. Most Spaniards and Latin Americans are ignorant of the philology of ojalá.

68 Anon.: "Tilism wa'l Quwwa" ("Talismans and Power"), undated MS. in the Turkish Library, Nicosia.

69 The swastika is, of course, generally taken to be a solar symbol.

70 Qur'an, Sura 113.

71 Vide, s.v. *Arabian Magic*, Shah, *Occultism*, Rider, 1950, one such process in detail.

72 Kenyon, Sir F. G.: *Palaeography of Greek Papyrus*, 123. London, 1889.

73 Zimmern, H.: The Surpu Series (Alte Orient, 1905–06).

74 Atharva-Veda: Sacred Books of the East Series, Vol. XLII. Ed. Muller, tr. Bloomfield. London, 1892.

75 Shah, *Golden East*. London, 1931. 185 f.

76 Atharva-Veda, op. cit. XIX, Spell 25.

77 Rhine, Prof. J. B.: *Reach of the Mind*. London, 1951.

78 Louis de Wohl: *Stars of War and Peace*. Rider, 1952, p. 232.

79 E.g. Bennett, S. K.: *Astrology*. California, 1945. Chap. 14, pp. 127 ff.

80 Bulfinch, *Age of Chivalry*, Pt. I, Chap. III, p. 50; *Alfonson de Spina: Fortalitum Fidei*, 1458, pp. 281 ff.; and Father P. Sinistrari: *Demonality*, paras. 29 et seq.

81 Bulfinch, *Age of Chivalry*, Pt. I, Chap. III, p. 50; *Alfonson de Spina: Fortalitum Fidei*, 1458, pp. 281 ff.; and Father P. Sinistrari: *Demonality*, paras. 29 et seq.

82 *Social Life of the Chinese*, II, 308.
83 Shen: *Sien Ch'wen,* Chap. 9.
84 Doolittle, Rev. J.: *China Mail*, 1860, and Yule: *Marco Polo*, I, 290 ff.
85 Li Siun: The Chi i Ki: "On Strange Matters Collected and Written Down" – T'ang Dynasty.
86 Khu i Shwoh: *Discourses upon the Dissipation of Doubt.*
87 *Mung Khi Pih Tian*, Chap. 21, II, 5 ff. Quoted in De Groot, J. J. M.: *Religious System of China*. Leyden, 1892.
88 Eitel: *Notes and Queries on China and Japan*, II, 20. Quoted in De Groot, J. J. M.: *Religious System of China.* Leyden, 1892.
89 Bushell, S. W.: *Trans. R. Asiatic Soc.* 1880, 441.
90 *Book of Overthrowing Apep*, 24: 19. *Book of the Dead*, LXIV; Naville: *Destruction des Hommes*, *Trans. Soc. Bibl. Arch.*, iv, 16: 79.
91 Unpublished MS. of Mme M. M. Abdullah, by courtesy of the Author.
92 De Becker, J. E.: *Nightless City*, 1905, p. 44.
93 Ibid., p. 145.
94 De Visser, M. W.: *Trans. Asiatic Soc. of Japan*, Vol. XXXVII, p. 18.
95 Aston, W. G.: in *Folklore*, Vol. XXIII, p. 191.

A Request

If you enjoyed this book, please review it on Amazon and Goodreads.

Reviews are an author's best friend.

To stay in touch with news on forthcoming editions of Idries Shah works, please sign up for the mailing list:

http://bit.ly/ISFlist

And to follow him on social media, please go to any of the following links:

https://twitter.com/idriesshah

https://www.facebook.com/IdriesShah

http://www.youtube.com/idriesshah999

http://www.pinterest.com/idriesshah/

http://bit.ly/ISgoodreads

http://idriesshah.tumblr.com

http://idriesshahfoundation.org

Lightning Source UK Ltd.
Milton Keynes UK
UKOW04f1409200116

266736UK00002B/24/P

9 781784 790424